D0582653

EDITORS
    Jan Brand
    José Teunissen
    in co-operation with Catelijne de Muijnck

AUTHORS
    Els de Baan
    Nanda van den Berg
    Judith Donath & Christine M. Liu
    Martine Elzingre
    Agnes Gomes-Koizumi
    Georgette Koning
    Gilles Lipovetsky
    Luca Marchetti
    Arjen Mulder
    Birgit Richard
    Karin Schacknat
    Anneke Smelik
    José Teunissen
    Marjan Unger
    Virginie Viallon
    Minke Vos

FASHION & ACCESSORIES

TERRA

ArtEZ Press

IN SEARCH OF THE ESSENCE

ICONS

STYLES

CONTENT

Why are accessories so important in the fashion world today? Ever since Prada launched the *Pocone backpack* in 1987 and Tom Ford transformed the classical 'Gucci' bag label into a luxury fashion brand it's been impossible to imagine the collections of the major fashion houses without accessories and accessory campaigns. This live topic constitutes the basic theme of this book, where the focus is on the specific meaning of the accessory in the context of fashion. What significance do accessories have in relation to fashion? How do accessories reflect the culture of our time? And in what ways do they represent or illustrate a cultural shift in the perception of fashion? This book will also sketch out a number of developments in the history of the fashion accessory and its typologies, and will show that themes and design principles from schools such as Surrealism, Modernism, the carnivalesque and Postmodernism keep recurring in accessory design.

The ArtEZ Modelectoraat regards fashion today as a mirror of the times in which important social and cultural developments are being articulated. Twice a year, the Modelectoraat chooses a theme from the current fashion scene and places it in a theoretical and social context, thereby providing insight into the underlying layers of meaning. In 2004 the Modelectoraat published *The Ideal Woman*, which dealt with the changing position of the woman as role model in the fashion world. *Global Fashion/Local Tradition*, issued in 2005, discussed the impact that today's globalisation has on fashion. A book on the relationship between Fashion and Art is being prepared for 2009. With *The Power of Fashion*, a book that appeared in 2006, the Modelectoraat put on the market a new fashion handbook that looks back on fashion history from a contemporary point of view and by way of disciplines such as sociology, semiotics, philosophy and anthropology.

The ArtEZ Modelectoraat and the ArtEZ Press hope that this publication will stimulate reflection on fashion as a theoretical discipline among students as well as among those members of the general public who are interested in design.

Jan Brand
Head of the ArtEZ Press and dAcapo-ArtEZ,
Publishing House and General Studies
Department of the ArtEZ Institute of the Arts

José Teunissen
Professor of Fashion Design
ArtEZ Institute of the Arts

IN SEARCH OF THE ESSENCE
IN SEARCH OF THE ESSENCE
IN SEARCH OF THE ESSENCE
IN SEARCH OF THE ESSENCE
IN SEARCH OF THE ESSENCE
IN SEARCH OF THE ESSENCE
IN SEARCH OF THE ESSENCE
IN SEARCH OF THE ESSENCE
IN SEARCH OF THE ESSENCE
IN SEARCH OF THE ESSENCE
IN SEARCH OF THE ESSENCE
IN SEARCH OF THE ESSENCE
IN SEARCH OF THE ESSENCE
IN SEARCH OF THE ESSENCE
IN SEARCH OF THE ESSENCE
IN SEARCH OF THE ESSENCE
IN SEARCH OF THE ESSENCE
IN SEARCH OF THE ESSENCE
IN SEARCH OF THE ESSENCE
IN SEARCH OF THE ESSENCE
IN SEARCH OF THE ESSENCE
IN SEARCH OF THE ESSENCE
IN SEARCH OF THE ESSENCE
IN SEARCH OF THE ESSENCE
IN SEARCH OF THE ESSENCE
IN SEARCH OF THE ESSENCE
IN SEARCH OF THE ESSENCE
IN SEARCH OF THE ESSENCE
IN SEARCH OF THE ESSENCE

WHY ACCESSORIES ARE IN FASHION

José Teunissen

01.

As though a fairy had touched them with her magic wand and managed to stop them in time for good. This is the impression made by Viktor & Rolf's winter 2006/2007 collection. Viktor & Rolf had plunged items and details of clothing into a silver bath so they looked solidified. It is the custom in the Netherlands to plate baby shoes in silver as a souvenir of infancy. In a similar way, Viktor & Rolf were attempting to endow their fashion collection with eternal life. They hence represented one of the nicest paradoxes of fashion: fashion is by definition ephemeral and just as fleeting as a darling baby foot, and can thus never be held onto over time.

But the silver-plated details – the cuffs, frills, bodices and bows in the garments – foregrounded a second theme. The silver bath had made the details so solid and heavy that they seemed to become detached from the clothes: the cuffs looked like bracelets, the frills became a necklace and the bows a brooch. Parts of garments grew into autonomous accessories. Viktor & Rolf thus visualised an extremely topical theme within contemporary fashion: fashion is no longer focussed on clothes but on accessories.

INTRODUCTION

Anyone leafing through today's fashion magazines or looking at the billboards in the street could come to the same conclusion. All the advertisements of the major fashion houses are currently centred on accessories. Prada, for instance, is now showing in one of its campaigns a model who is not even dressed but is surrounded by all sorts of bags and shoes and wearing a head covering. Other important couture houses like Dior, Yves Saint Laurent, Chanel and Balenciaga are also now concentrating on promoting their latest bag, shoes, perfume or make-up rather than their new collections.

Last October the influential fashion journalist Suzy Menkes noted in the *International Herald Tribune* that what she remembered most after visiting the prêt-à-porter shows in Paris were the extreme shoes and bracelets and bags by Chanel and Lacroix and not the clothes. 'Does this mean that accessories have become more important in fashion than the clothes themselves?' Menkes wondered.[1]

The answer is affirmative. On the one hand we see the fashion houses using slick marketing and an overdose of ads and billboards to focus attention on their accessories, and on the other hand

02.

01, 02.
Viktor & Rolf, autumn/winter 2006-
2007 collection show, details

WHY ACCESSORIES ARE IN FASHION

03.

PRADA

04.

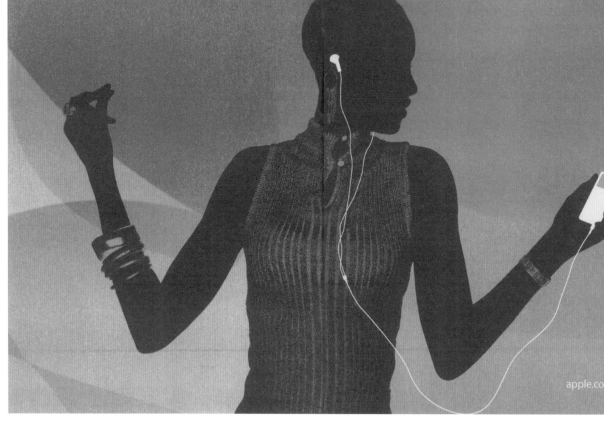

 iPod

apple.com/fr

JOSÉ TEUNISSEN

accessories are so conspicuous with most fashion labels at the moment that the accompanying clothes literally pale before them.

In this essay I will be looking into why and when accessories started to play such a determining role in contemporary fashion. What exactly is the role of the accessory in fashion and how has this changed in recent times?

THE ROLE OF THE ACCESSORY

Accessories have always been closely connected with what is in fashion at a particular time. Some accessories disappear completely from the picture with the advent of new times and customs. Right now, for example, masks, fans and hats scarcely play a role in fashion or on the street and it looks like men's ties have also had their day.

On the other hand, new times also bring with them new accessories. The best example of this is the mobile phone which is available today in all colours, forms and price ranges. The Millionaires Fair travelling through Europe at the moment is presenting the first mobile phone inlaid with real diamonds. In the meantime, almost everyone is in the habit of exchanging their mobile once a year for an even more ingenious appliance that can take photographs, contains an MP3 player or can function as an organiser. Then there are all the different types of mobile phone holders and bits and pieces that can be attached to the phone like dangly earrings. This makes the mobile phone one of the most important accessories at the moment – even Prada is making covers for them. In the same way, i-Pods are playing an essential role in fashion; just the campaign in which the white earpiece glides from the ear along the neck like a conspicuous piece of jewellery subtly illustrates how this appliance is a fashionable addition to your daily outfit. Ingenious technological appliances are one of the indispensable elements in today's outfits. In a few years time we can expect an explosion of laptops in the form of fashionable handbags or elegant men's briefcases. The possibility of giving your bag a new appearance every day, as Judith Donath and Christine Liu describe in 'Urbanhermes' (p. 98), will eventually be completely normal.

ACCESSORIES AND THE SPIRIT OF THE TIMES

Just as they are today, accessories were also earlier an expression of the spirit of the times. Chic ladies used their fans in the eighteenth century to keep themselves cool during a sultry evening at the opera, but the same fan was also an essential attribute in seducing and impressing men. What mattered was how you looked up from behind the fan, how quickly and agitatedly you were able to wave it. They were all codes in love-play. The most important role of the accessory is not its practical function, but the key part it plays in the so-called performance of fashion. The dictionary talks about 'something that serves as a supplement but is not functional.' Masks, wigs and fans made an essential contribution to the culture of masquerade in the eighteenth century. In the fashion in this period – and, analogous to this, in life – it was not a question of who one is but of how one 'comes across' in public.[2] The extreme wigs, the white-powdered faces, the conspicuous beauty spots and the fans all contributed to the

05.

03.
Prada, advertising campaign, 2006
04.
Apple, advertising campaign for i-Pod, 2006
05.
Coiffure à la Belle Poule, 1778
06.
Daniël Maclise, *Alfred d'Orsay*, ca. 1830

06.

masquerade where 'under the shiny, varnished layer of good manners, nobody sought the secret soul of the true personality'.[3]

It was only with the penetration of Enlightenment ideas and democracy in the nineteenth century that one went in search of the soul and personality. These ideas led to a major cultural revolution, which is also reflected in fashion.[4] It was during this period that men started to abandon their colourful and showy clothing and opted instead for a sober black suit so as to underline the fact that they were involved with serious, social matters rather than a vain display of power, as had been the case with the aristocracy. In this new context, accessories were suddenly important attributes in expressing a 'serious' and 'well-bred' personality. Now that appearances were seen as mirroring the soul, at the same time as clothing was almost uniform, it was principally accessories that were able to express this 'personality': in the case of the man it was a question of how he knotted his scarf, the way in which he doffed his hat in greeting or how he paraded along the street with his cane. It is precisely his accessories that say something about the uniqueness of his person when he is sauntering anonymously in the street and yet manage to direct attention to himself through small details.

The bit of excess and luxury that the sober and serious man was still able to permit himself in this period lay in the accessories, but these were also meant to serve a 'practical' function. A man in the nineteenth century was suddenly no longer able to wear jewellery, but a practical pocket-watch or a pin to keep his scarf or tie in place was still permitted. Luxury and frippery were mainly expressed through practical and functional accessories like a walking stick, gloves or a hat, the important thing being that it should be of the very best quality. We know that Beau Brummel, for example, had the parts of his gloves made by different craftsmen so as to finally obtain that one perfect pair of gloves. Although in menswear in particular more and more could be manufactured industrially, quality and craftsmanship remained important criteria for the value of the accessory. Surprisingly enough, two centuries later these criteria still apply to formal, classic men's fashion: the attractiveness of the accessory is determined by 'heritage', that is, the image of classical craftsmanship evinced by a fashion label.

This radical swing to new accessories with a new function came much later for women. The reason for this is that, with the rise of the bourgeoisie in the nineteenth century, women continued to lead their lives largely indoors. Her moments of fashion occurred when she paid an afternoon visit for tea or attended a dinner or the opera in the evening. The nineteenth-century woman retained her colourful, richly decorated clothing, which allowed her to continue to show off, and the accessories she wore matched this. The parasols, the little bags for her needlework and the silk shoes and boots were not yet aimed at practical outdoor life, as they were for men. It was not until the mid-nineteenth century that this changed, when it became customary for women to travel more and to go shopping and strolling in the then brand-new department stores. Women's fashions and the accompanying accessories gradually became more practical. Women started to wear practical laced boots outdoors, which were comfortable because they now had a left and a right insole. Umbrellas emerged in 1870 that could be hooked onto a belt next to a chatelaine bag, which also fitted onto the belt and can be seen as a predecessor of a handbag.[5]

But in this period the visual distinction and the difference in function between accessories and clothing was not yet so sharp in women's wear as it was in men's. Both accessories and clothes were excessively decorated. This only changed when mobility and the emancipation of women really got going at the beginning of the twentieth century.

COCO CHANEL AND THE TOTAL LOOK AVANT LA LETTRE

The most important motor behind the radical change in women's wear and the function of the accessory was Coco Chanel. In 1913 she introduced onto the market cardigans and ensembles made of comfortable tricot that until then had only been used in menswear. In this way she made women's wear at once much simpler and more comfortable. A second revolution took place in 1924 when she introduced the famous black dress. From then on, women no longer had to change clothes seven times a day, but now had, like the man, a single outfit in which they could appear on all occasions. Chanel did not so much introduce into fashion a different aesthetic or a different feminine image as base her designs on a new ethics. 'I design for a new society. Until now, clothes were designed for an inactive woman. I design for the active woman. A woman who feels at ease in her dress.'[6]

Unlike her male predecessors Charles Frederick Worth and Paul Poiret, she designed for an independent woman who needed to walk, work and move in her clothes. Chanel's designs are practical and comfortable down to the smallest details. Pockets are large enough to stick one's hands in and buttons do not just serve as decoration, a jacket can also be worn open or closed. The ultimate translation of her philosophy came a little later when Chanel introduced the famous woman's suit, which had extra space in the back so that women could really move their arms and a chain in the seam to make the jacket heavier so that it hung well and didn't wrinkle.[7] In terms of proportions, uniformity and the line of the cut, this suit looked just as practical, sober and simple as the men's suit. What was revolutionary was that Chanel succeeded in shifting the luxury and excess, which up until then had not disappeared from women's wear, to the margins of clothing by incorporating luxury, colour and excess in the accompanying accessories and luxurious fabrics. Chanel's suit is as sober and graphically contoured as the men's suit, but as the fabric of her suits is made of exquisite, colourful weaves it retains a luxurious appearance. Chanel's garments may therefore have been sober and functional, but the choice of fabrics and particularly the accessories enabled women to continue to indulge in their need for luxury and excess. Chanel had already achieved a lot of success with her introduction of imitation jewellery in 1924. She loved the long pearl necklaces, rubies and large, broad bracelets that she had made from imitation stones. In this way it was suddenly possible to completely match jewellery and clothes with each other in terms of taste and colour. The advent of imitation jewels resulted in a radical change. The German philosopher Georg Simmel was the first to point out that imitation jewels add something to individuality, whereas the classic family jewels of before tended much more to confirm the status of the wearer. The result, in his view, was that fashion was more and more about the creation of personality than about the confirmation of status.[8] A concomitant advantage was that it meant that jewellery could now be worn by a much wider group of women – those who had no family jewels (p. 178).

Chanel was the first to discover the full strength of the accessory as a luxury item, a determinant factor in the sober and uniform 'style' of the modern woman. It made the Chanel style so recognisable and clear that it could be varied endlessly. On taking over the reins as designer for Chanel in 1983, Karl Lagerfeld summarised Chanel's style

07.
Coco Chanel, 1937
08.
Karl Lagerfeld, drawing with patrimony of Coco Chanel, 1991

09.

10.

09.
Collection of Chanel accessories
that form the 'total look'
10.
Christian Dior, *Bar* collection, 1947

in a single drawing in which all of Chanel's regular icons appear – the camellia, the jewellery, the cut of the jacket. For Lagerfeld this was the spiritual patrimony of Chanel, the basis for all his designs for the house. Chanel's 'visually recognisable style' was ahead of its times. In the 1930s, 40s and 50s she had already succeeded in creating a total look which other fashion houses would only start developing in the 1980s with the rise of marketing, when communication and a label's recognisability became vitally important.

THE ACCESSORY AS AN EXPRESSION OF COMFORT AND INNOVATION

Yet it was not just the feeling of luxury that Chanel brought to the fore in her accessories. The 2.55 handbag she introduced in 1955 was practical and austerely designed. The beige shoe (1957) with a black toe, which made the feet look smaller, also grew into a model that still exists today. Just as in her clothing designs, Chanel regarded innovative elements in her accessories as important since they were a symbol of modernity and contributed to comfort – something that had previously never been important in women's fashion when it was exclusively a matter of embellishing outward appearances or creating an overwhelming effect. The special thing about Chanel was that she introduced for the first time a form of luxury aimed at women's subjective pleasures: the feeling of comfort or a nice refinement which women themselves could enjoy.

'Chanel is an example of a new style of female corporal pleasure – women designers try to express a subjective, tactile delight in wearing clothes. (...) These suits suggested the kind of erotic self-possession that has no aggression in it, but rather an element of constant low-keyed personal bodily delight, a quiet feline sensuality that is no barrier to active work and thought.'[9]

WHAT IS LUXURY?

This brings us to the question as to what luxury actually entails. Since antiquity, according to the philosopher Gilles Lipovetsky, luxury has been the dream that embellishes life's decor. Luxury stands the test of time, amazes us, makes us happy and can be compared to a divine or aesthetic experience (p. 28). Luxury has to do with the human need for *jouissance* (defined by Roland Barthes as 'sensual pleasure'). It enables us to enjoy, to experience emotional and physical pleasure as a necessary counterbalance to the logic and rational thought that permeates our culture and which we

JOSÉ TEUNISSEN

take pleasure in in a different way.[10]

Until the nineteenth century, luxury products were made exclusively from the most beautiful and most expensive materials. Luxury was therefore scarce and reserved only for the small elite of the aristocracy. The rise of new industrial techniques made it possible to produce imitations of luxury products much more cheaply and on a much wider scale. They were then put on sale in the brand-new department stores where the shopping public was seduced into purchasing things.[11] Products no longer had to be ordered specially, but were offered on the shelves at low fixed prices. This is the time when advertising and marketing made their entry and attempted to seduce the public.

Industrial manufacturing also brought with it new criteria for characterising 'luxury'. Semi-luxurious products can be divided into two categories: on the one hand there are 'kitsch' products, cheap copies of luxurious originals but of an inferior quality. Such products contributed to the initial democratisation of luxury, which now became attainable for the better-off bourgeoisie. On the other hand, the spirit of the times also led to a more avant-garde approach to design, which became known as modernism, a trend whose embrace of industrialisation and technology was emphasised with new designs that broke radically with the past and did away with all classical meanings and references. The use of new materials and a search for a new, abstract language of forms meant that products exuded a sense of modernity and progress. Luxury was linked within modernism to new concepts such as 'soberness', 'pure form', 'technological progress' and 'ingenious comfort'. Modernism acquired its first form in the sober men's suit.[12] But it was not until the beginning of the twentieth century that this filtered through to accessories (p. 196). Luxury could now be form, light, space, comfort and intimacy, and this was translated into, among other things, imitation jewellery, modern handbags and new chemical-based perfumes such as Chanel N°5. More and more 'modern' products thus came within reach of a larger public. Yet it was not until the 1980s that these accessories and perfumes from chic fashion houses would become mass-produced articles.

ACCESSORIES AND THE WAVE OF DEMOCRATISATION IN THE 1960S

Until the 1960s a woman's outfit was only complete if the right hat, a bag and shoes and a pair of gloves were worn with it. The total look created by Chanel was different from the one set down by Christian Dior, for example, but the basic accessories were the same with all designers. A woman could not appear 'smartly dressed' in public without these accessories. But when Paris lost its absolute authority over fashion to youth culture and the street in the 1960s, the result was that fashion drastically 'rejuvenated' itself and became much more 'informal'. The hat, the handbag, the court shoes and gloves suddenly became fussy, formal and too 'ladylike', and they disappeared from the fashion scene. Boutiques and flourishing second-hand shops brought inexpensive clothes and accessories within reach of youth and, secondly, of the masses who followed this fashion in clothing and accessories via the clothing industry that imitated things on a large scale. Young people were buying shoulder bags and boxes at army surplus stores or Indian slippers at the market. Luxury thus temporarily took shape in an attitude of anti-luxury: people opted for functional or ethnic products and tried in this way to escape for a while from the imperative laws of fashion and accessories.

LUXURY IN THE POSTMODERN ERA

With the revaluation of design in the early 1980s came a return of the influence of Parisian fashion houses and the need for luxury products. A young generation of designers arose – including Thierry Mugler and Jean Paul Gaultier – who brought in contemporary prêt-à-porter. Their 'design' collections were much more affordable than the classic haute couture and they deliberately appealed to a wide public. Jean Paul Gaultier quickly grew into a hero after clothing Madonna on her Blond Ambition tour. From then on, all fashion houses did everything they could to establish contact with youth culture and the masses by means of sophisticated ads in all sorts of magazines as well as via billboard campaigns extending as far as bus shelters in small villages. Most of the designers themselves now became media icons, with the country houses and private lives of notable designers like Gianni Versace or Jean Paul Gaultier receiving widespread press attention. By launching new perfumes every two years, developing make-up lines every season and coming up with their own brand of sunglasses, the fashion houses ensured that almost everyone could purchase a brand product.[13]

It was during this period that the focus came to lie for the first time not on the accessory (as a semiproduct), as had been the development since the nineteenth century. What was now being sold was primarily a vision and a lifestyle. It was now a question of the label's identity and the lifestyle it evinced. This meant that communicating the label became of vital importance. A product's value was no longer determined by its monetary value or its uniqueness, but first of all by its image[14] (p. 48 and 60).

The product thus started to function as a sign, as a philosophy or a lifestyle. The brand's logo became the password for entering the world of dreamed-of values, as Patricia Calefato points out.[15]

Since the 1960s we have started to dress much more informally and status has become less important. Nowadays people can dress them-selves differently at different moments – some-times formally, other times informally. The thing that is most striking is that fashion itself has hardly changed in the last fifteen years. There are no longer any absolute skirt lengths or fashion-able colours. In this context, in which suddenly 'everything is possible' in fashion and one can go through life 'dressed down' or 'informally', acces-sories acquire another, more important role. Since the 1980s they have been explicitly designed, and it may happen that one season the Balenciaga Laureat is the 'it bag' and the next season the must-have bag is Dior's Saddle Bag (p. 133). Consumers may well wear an ordinary pair of jeans and a cashmere sweater, but they will want to show off with extremely luxurious and expen-sive accessories. That too has become conspicu-ous. The price of shoes and bags has risen con-siderably in the last fifteen years. Shops are increasing their range of branded shoes and bags and this is because consumers are all too keen to buy a particular brand of bag or shoes. But what is the origin of this revaluation of accessories?

PRADA AND THE REVALUATION OF THE BAG

The current fad for designer bags was born when Miuccia Prada came to boost the family firm after studying political science. In 1985 she launched a handbag and two years later a rucksack, both of which were made of Pocone, a very durable type of nylon used in space travel. At that time Prada already had a 50-year reputation as a classic brand of luggage. That image changed at a stroke, since Pocone gave the bag a technological look. The very combination of a top-quality classic label and a new technology was what made the Pocone bag legendary. Prada, which shortly afterwards brought out clothing collections as well, thus became in the early 1990s the first

classic luxury brand of bags that was completely up to date and even grew into a prominent fashion label. It was both revolutionary and technologi-cally advanced, but at the same time it relied on its reputation as a luxury make of the very best quality.

In 1990 the Italian luggage brand Gucci under-went a radical metamorphosis with the appoint-ment of Tom Ford as its new designer. Ford's strength was that he managed to rejuvenate the Gucci label by translating stylistic elements from the 1970s into modern clothes and accessories. The story goes that he kept a close eye on his girlfriends from Texas who were buying hip clothes from second-hand shops and translated their clothing habits into a line of garments and accessories that turned Gucci into an appealing, sexy and fashionable label in the early 1990s. Here, too, an important component of the new Gucci image was an ingenious line of bags with which Gucci had already built up a reputation in the 1950s.

Both Gucci and Prada thus reveal how a tradi-tional luxury fashion house that in the 1960s and 70s had appeared to be forever stuffy and petri-fied and doomed to extinction could construct a new image based on 'rejuvenation' and 'innova-tion' and thus reconnect with the new times. The reason for their success was that in the 1990s people started to realise that with the threatened demise of traditional luggage and haute couture labels something important was in danger of dis-appearing: a craftsmanship, tradition and quality that modern accessories and clothes no longer possessed. This concern for craftsmanship and the desire to cultivate one's own heritage (which goes with this) ensured that interest in 'old' brands and qualitatively better products increased enormously. Luxury thus gained a new interpretation in the 1990s. Henceforth the 'new' was valued in the context of existing traditions and the heritage of craftsmanship. According to Lipovetsky, this is ultimately based on our desire in postmodern times to reconcile the ephemeral quality of fashion with the timelessness of his-tory.[16]

YOUNG, DYNAMIC AND SHOCKING: DIOR, LOUIS VUITTON AND GUCCI

In 1998 another classic luggage brand managed to transform its somewhat dull image into an extremely fashionable label. Marc Jacobs was invited to re-establish the Louis Vuitton brand on the map of fashion and in a short time he suc-

11.
Yves Saint Laurent, advertising campaign, 2006

WHY ACCESSORIES ARE IN FASHION

12.

13.

14.

15.

WWW.DIOR.COM
TEL 800 929.DIOR

ceeded in making the Vuitton bag a hit. Among other things, he managed to make a connection with youth and street culture by asking the graffiti artist Stephen Sprouse to spray the Louis Vuitton logo onto a bag, thus integrating the brutality and language of the street into the brand.

One of the ways that today's classic couture and luxury houses differ from the 1950s is that they have become more open to influences from the street. On the one hand they retain their tradition and the quality of their brand, but on the other hand they realise that they can only survive if they 'rejuvenate' their brand or make it more 'brutal', and thus endow their brand with the qualities that, since the 1960s, have become an important part of fashion. Tom Ford added that aspect to Gucci mainly through campaigns focussed on eroticism (p. 48).

In 1996 the fashion designer John Galliano was initially hired by LVMH as a designer for Givenchy, but after six months he was allowed to move on to the renowned house of Dior. For the first few years Galliano came up with a mixture of different periods from costume history, combined with all manner of ethnic styles collected on his worldwide travels. Galliano managed to impress large audiences with his mega-shows, but Dior was also smart enough to start selling affordable versions of this spectacular haute couture. Dior further succeeded in connecting with teenagers through its lines of make-up, perfume, spectacles and T-shirts. Galliano cheerfully mixed street influences with ethnic styles and the history of the house of Dior. It was in this context that he also designed The Saddle Bag which grew into an icon, even though it actually has nothing to do with the history of the house of Dior. But Galliano decided on a form that refers to high-quality vintage bags (one of which is the saddle bag) and then managed to translate this into a recognisable Dior bag by attaching to it a sort of stirrup with the letter D hanging from it. At the same time this letter D refers to the Diana bag that Gianfranco Ferré designed in 1995 for Dior and which was famously carried by Princess Diana. This bag was – and is – recognisable from the letters D, I, O and R hanging from the handle like charms. Galliano is thus not simply referring to the history and style of Dior with this bag; he is presenting Dior as a patchwork that not only corresponds to the need for heritage but also reveals an interesting visual game and at the same time bears a number of Dior hallmarks. In this respect, Dior has the least fixed style of all the classic fashion houses. For those in the know, Dior is recognisable by a few details, but it keeps renewing itself in the designs themselves and in its products. There is a world of difference between Dior and a label like Chanel, which always plays with the same elements within the same established lines, thus always evoking a recognisable image that is subtly adapted to the latest fashion trends.

CULTIVATING HERITAGE: HERMÈS AND GERARD DAREL

The luxury brand that has remained even closer to its classic image than Chanel is undoubtedly Hermès. In 1956 Grace Kelly appeared on the cover of Life with a Hermès bag held in front of her stomach to conceal her pregnancy. It made the model, which had already existed for more than twenty years, world famous. It became the first 'it bag', long before the bag mania broke out in the 1990s. Today, in order to get one's hands on a genuine Kelly bag, one has to subscribe to a waiting list. After six months one gets to choose the type of leather and the colour and the bag is then made. Depending on the type of leather, the bag costs between 7,000 and 25,000 Euros. The latter is made from the skin of crocodiles reared in a special pool. What makes the bag special is that it is the only bag which is assembled by a single craftsman who works on it for seventeen hours. The bag is then given a number and, should there be any faults, it is then returned to the same craftsman. In this way Hermès continues to produce the ultimate artisanal product. The newer variant, the Birkin bag (1981), named after the actress Jane Birkin, looks exactly the same except that it is a bit bigger and thus more practical. In the case of Hermès, then, innovation means elaborating on time-honoured traditions rather than rejuvenating, as is also evident from the Hermès shawls that throughout the years continue to embroider on the same themes. When Martin Margiela was the chief designer for Hermès he too mainly embroidered on these old values. Even Jean Paul Gaultier, who has been designing for Hermès since 2003, mainly creates a sophisticated classic brand with wool, cashmere and a great deal of supple leather with a bit of equestrian symbolism here and there like caps and whips.

In conclusion we can say that strategies like rejuvenation or being shocking, as practised by Marc Jacobs and John Galliano for Louis Vuitton and Dior respectively, are not the only methods to make a fashion house attractive. Focussing attention on classic heritage and ultimate craftsmanship can also make a brand very attractive these

12.
Thierry Mugler, jackets, left and right, autumn/winter 1988 collection, and middle, spring/summer 1990 collection
13.
Stephen Sprouse for Louis Vuitton, graffiti bags, 2001
14.
Dior, advertising campaign with *Lady Dior*, 2006
15.
Dior, advertising campaign with *Gaucho Bag*, 2006
16.
Chanel, advertising campaign, 2006
17.
Grace Kelly with the *Kelly bag* named after her, Hermès, 1956

18.

19.

20.

18.
Gerard Darel, advertising campaign
with Charlotte Gainsbourg, 2006
19.
Viktor & Rolf, advertising campaign
for Flowerbomb, 2005
20.
Celux Store, Louis Vuitton building,
Tokyo

days. This applies particularly when the product is scarce and exclusive and difficult to get hold of. For if everything is available to the masses, as has been the case since the 1980s, then exclusiveness also becomes attractive again.

Even fake heritage has been a feature during the last ten years, enabling one fashion label to become enormously popular. Until 1996, Gerard Darel was a barely known French prêt-à-porter label with little prestige. Everything changed when Mrs Darel bought a Jackie Kennedy necklace at an auction and decided to imitate it so as to sell it with the collection. Stephanie Seymour (a Kennedy look-alike) was hired as a model and so little by little Jackie Kennedy was deployed as the label's stylistic icon. It is thus possible to build an extremely successful and chic fashion brand (with heritage) around a cultivated, borrowed history. In the film *The Devil Wears Prada*, Meryl Streep very prominently wears a Gerard Darel necklace. The shoe brand Tod's is also an example of a similar brand that carries the touch of a classic luxury house even though the firm is less than 30 years old.[17]

CONCLUSION

Since the democratisation of the 1960s, luxury has in principle come within everyone's reach, with the result that the value of luxury suddenly acquires a new interpretation. The advent of industrialisation in the nineteenth century had already produced the semi-luxury product that democratised luxury to a certain extent, but nevertheless one of the most important values of luxury was still that people were able to use it to display their status. When luxury became attainable for all in the 1980s, displaying one's status was suddenly no longer a motive for buying luxury products. Consumers now purchased luxury products for narcissistic reasons – to admire themselves and to play with their own identity (p. 28). It was a matter of promoting one's own image. On the other hand, luxury is also more about the experience of a product, something that Chanel already understood in the 1950s when she designed shoes and bags that were primarily comfortable and ingenious. But it also means that the experience and image of the luxury product has become much more important than the (semi-)product itself, as testified to by many advertising campaigns. In other words, the consumer is now susceptible to purchasing empty air.

As a major counterpart to the democratisation of the luxury product, a contrary reaction has emerged since the mid-1990s: very expensive products that exude exclusivity and craftsmanship because they contain a history (heritage) that is almost in danger of disappearing. It is precisely such exclusive, scarce products that we will want to enjoy more in the near future. For after having been immersed for a time in the excess of luxury presented by fashion houses, we are now ready for the exclusive, authentic, original product.

The fact that we have been exposed for years to an excess of luxury products has had a second effect. Consumers have become so glutted that from now on they would prefer to deal more frugally with luxury and to choose just the one very exclusive and almost unattainable thing in the hope that they can enjoy it longer and in a different way, since it is exclusive and of the highest quality, and because gaining possession of it is a whole adventure in itself. Such luxury articles are not promoted in advertising campaigns; you have to search for them. A good example of this is Louis Vuitton's exclusive Celux Store in Tokyo. To gain admittance you first have to pay 2,000 dollars to become a member. Once inside the club/store you can use a laptop to view the very latest designs which will shortly be arriving in the store in a limited edition. As this example illustrates, the luxury of the future will no longer be a question of something extra that is available in large quantities, but of intensity and restriction. Ultimately, it is only partly a question of the high quality of the product. The experience, the story, the search and the hunt to acquire it are what largely provide the satisfaction that these luxury products bring.

Notes
1. Suzy Menkes, 'Baubles, Bangles and bags: Who cares about the clothes?' *International Herald Tribune*, 6 October 2006.
2. Richard Sennett, *The Fall of Public Man* (New York: Knopf, 1974), p. 65.
3. Philippe Perrot, *Le Travail des Apparences* (Paris: Seuil, 1984).
4. Gilles Lipovetsky, *The Empire of Fashion: Dressing Modern Democracy* (Princeton: Princeton University Press, 2002).
5. Marian Conrads, *Handboek kostuum accessoires* (Baarn: Tirion, 1991), p. 40.
6. J.M Floch, *Identités visuelles* (Paris: P.U.F., 1995), p. 112.
7. Coco Chanel closed her fashion house before the Second World War, but decided in 1954, at the age of 71, to start again because she detested the New Look launched by Christian Dior in 1947. She felt that it was a fashion that took women back to the nineteenth century. It was one of the reasons why she decided to reopen her house.
8. Georg Simmel, 'Ëxkurs uber der Schmuck', in: *Soziologie* (Berlin: Dunker & Humblot, 1908), pp. 278-281. Accessible at www.socio.ch.sim.
9. Anne Hollander, *Sex and Suits* (Wilts: Claridge Press, 1994), pp. 132-133.
10. Roland Barthes, *Mythologieën* (Amsterdam: Arbeiderspers, 1975).
11. Philippe Perrot, *Fashioning the Bourgeoisie* (Princeton: Princeton University Press, 1994), pp. 58-60.
12. See note 9.
13. Guillaume Erner, *Verslaafd aan mode* (Amsterdam: AP, 2006), p. 70.
14. Ibid., p. 78
15. Patricia Calefato, 'Fashion as Sign System', in: Jan Brand and José Teunissen, *The Power of Fashion* (Arnhem: Terra|Lannoo/ArtEZ Press, 2006), p. 144.
16. Gilles Lipovetsky, *Le Bonheur Paradoxal* (Paris: Gallimard, 2006), p. 43.
17. See note 13, pp. 80-81.

LUXURY AND THE SIXTH SENSE

Gilles Lipovetsky

01. Matthew Barney, *Cremaster 5: Bocáss el*, 1997

Since the classical works on luxury by Veblen, Mauss, Bataille and Elias, it has become usual to interpret luxury as a phenomenon structured by status-enhancing competition, antagonism and social rivalry. Mauss stressed that the purpose of the potlatch[1] ceremony was to establish hierarchies of rank and honour. Veblen and Elias emphasised the importance of conflict for rank and prestige. Competition for social recognition and the desire to gain an advantage over others lies at the heart of extravagance. And at the root of that phenomenon lies agonistic challenge and warring consciences.

Luxury behaviour cannot be separated from symbolic confrontations between people, nor can it be reduced to that alone. Consequently it has always been associated in part with other goals and beliefs, including those related to death, to the sacred and the hereafter. 'Luxury man' was first and foremost *homo religiosus* who produced socially established responses to questions of death or survival. Throughout the world, confrontation with others was matched by confrontation with the supernatural and the fear of death. On a long view, luxury was invented as much to satisfy a relationship with time as with men; it was as much a war against temporal limitations as a battle for social standing.

That was also true of festivals in the past, where wealth was a way to offset the degeneration of the universe, to prepare its renewal and to resuscitate Time. Festive expenditure was marked by time because, in primitive symbolism, excessive consumption was used to bring primordial time up to date and repeat the passage of chaos to cosmos. This ensured a new cycle of life, a rejuvenation and recreation of the world. Sacrifices and precious offerings to the gods were always accompanied by prayers for fertility and longevity. It was necessary to be generous to the gods in order to ensure long life and one's due rewards in the afterlife. Rich funerary gifts were intended to appease the dead. During the Middle Ages and the Classical Period, the rich made generous provisions in their wills to the Church to ensure their afterlife. Even when an appetite for worldly honours took precedence, a relationship between time and eternity could be found in the construction of public works. The rich erected statues, steles and epigraphs so that their names would be engraved on human memory for all eternity. Luxury was as much a way of ensuring the cycle of reincarnation – a kind of magical combat between the enduring and the perishable – as a symbolic inter-human struggle. Extravagant behaviour was

motivated less by the negation of things and the submission of nature by which man affirms his subjectivity[2] than by an appropriation of supranatural forces to bring about rebirth, a process of harnessing powers to fend off the finality of mortal existence.

Of course this type of behaviour and mentality has ceased to exist. Since the middle of the eighteenth century, donations to the Church in exchange for eternal life have all but disappeared and nobody is buried with gold and jewellery. Festivals no longer symbolise a regeneration of the cosmos and we no longer build 'eternal mansions'. The temporal nature of luxury in contemporary society is henceforth the social and individual *present*; innovation prevails over permanence, personal pleasure in the here-and-now over traditional attitudes and values. The use of magic to conquer eternity has been replaced by the *consumption* of immortal works from the past, of cultural tourism that functions as a new form of mass entertainment to 'fill in the time'.

The strategy of the major fashion houses also reflects this switch from temporal logic to the present. For centuries luxury was used according to the standards of the past. After the nineteenth century, through the innovations in haute couture, there was a change in favour of the imperatives of the present-future. That is the prevalent trend in the luxury business, as reflected in the new requirements for high return on investment. We know that luxury brands are used to reconcile contradictory demands: they must perpetuate tradition and yet innovate, be faithful to their heritage and yet be resolutely modern. Nevertheless, the emphasis is increasingly on the need for dynamic brand management and the priority is renewal and creativity to prevent brand atrophy. Brands must be given a chance to conquer new domains and acquire new market shares. Many consultants in the luxury business speak of the irreversible decline of former strategies that are based on the 'the rent earned from tradition'. The dominant theory is that if luxury is not to be fossilised it must cease to repeat past formulas; instead it must revisit them, develop them and bring them up to date. Today creative policies and images are the backbone of the business and the precondition for brand development. In other words, luxury must assimilate the principles of the 'form-fashion', namely change, seduction, communication and the diversification of supply.[3] In luxury's composite mix of tradition and innovation, of backward looking logic and here-and-now logic, the creative aspect is becoming increasingly pivotal, for that is where the future of luxury lies. Today it is neither tradition nor fashion but a hybrid of both, a restructuring of a time of tradition and one of fashion, a reinvention and reinterpretation of the past using the fashion-logic of the present.

If postmodern luxury has been reorganised around the temporal axis of the present, it nevertheless maintains its association with the durable and the timeless. A luxury enterprise is not just a place of creation but also of memory, firstly because it perpetuates traditional techniques and craftsmanship, and secondly because of the way it presents and promotes itself and develops its own history. The cult of the founding designers, the glorification of the spirit of the brand and its faithfulness to a style or a code of recognition, the celebration of significant events, everything that goes into the construction of a luxury brand is inseparable from the symbolic management of its origins and the work of constructing a *myth*. Luxury brands are built on references to the myths and legends of their past. Luxury goods, even cars, come into their own only once they have become legends, when they succeed in transforming themselves from perishable consumer goods into timeless myths.

Thus the management of luxury consists of far more than the promotion of rare and expensive objects; it is an orchestration of time. On the one hand, brand innovation and creation glamorise the brand and rejuvenate its image. This calls up the short timeframe, that of fashion. On the other hand there is the need to let time do its work, to perpetuate a memory and create a halo of intemporality, which is the image of the brand's 'eternity'.[4] Here, the strategies are the capitalisation and sedimentation of time. Sometimes topical, marked by the fast and fickle timeframe of fashion; sometimes immobile, marked by the classic and the long timeframe of memory, a luxury brand cannot be constructed without this paradoxical effort that marshals opposing temporal demands.

Because of contemporary luxury's relationship with continuity and timelessness, there are analogies to be made with mythical thought through the ages. This is perfectly legitimate since both refer to fundamental events of the past that need to be ceremoniously brought up to date. In both cases 'heroes' are honoured, along with creativity and what Mircea Eliade called the 'prestige of beginnings', an ever up-to-date eternity, an 'eternal present' that is venerated and from which the order of things originates.[5] Thus one of the underlying principles that consecrates modern luxury – illustrious origins – is the same principle that fed the systems of primitive beliefs. Viewed in this light, luxury appears as something that perpetuates a kind of mythical thought at the very heart of deconsecrated merchant cultures.

Since luxury is closely connected to ritual and ceremony, its 'sacred' aspect is even to be found in consumer practices. We offer the most lavish gifts on holidays and symbolic anniversaries. We usually consume the most expensive products according to a ceremonial code of conduct. Tasting a great wine has its rituals, the connoisseur tilts his glass to examine the wine's colour, he gently turns the liquid around in the glass and inhales its bouquet. It is considered a sacrilege to swig a great wine or to drink it from a plastic cup. Since the nineteenth century the best restaurants have become a kind of temple in which a ritual is played out, with the chef in the role of high priest and master of ceremonies.[6] Even in an informal period such as ours that discards rites and most conventional behaviour, luxury usage remains charged with ceremony. Therein lies the charm of luxury: its ability to resuscitate an aura of formal tradition and what remains 'sacred' in our society, to provide a note of ceremony to the universe of things, and restore ritual to a disillusioned world of mediatised mass-consumption. But there is one difference. This reactivation of ritual has been recycled by way of a hedonistic and emotional logic. The way of life that accompanies luxury is no longer a class convention. Rather it is a setting in which to enjoy the pleasure of the senses, a formal game for the purpose of bestowing a sensual quality on the relationships to things.

As an emblem of beauty, of good taste and refinement, luxury is often linked to the pleasures of the senses. We have previously shown that there is far more to it than this, for luxury cannot be disassociated from another sense, a non-materialistic one that is so much a part of human nature it may be considered a sixth sense: the one that relates to time. We cannot reduce costly consumption to a mere desire for pleasure and social status. The time factor is, and always has been, a part of it. The major luxury brands aim to supply continuity and goods that never go out of fashion. Even where demand is concerned, albeit less obviously, desire and pleasure are connected to time and eternity. There is a new desire for timelessness, for long-lasting, enduring goods that contrast with the temporary and disposable – perhaps to compensate or counterbalance a con-

GILLES LIPOVETSKY

sumer society in the throes of constant renewal and the accelerated obsolescence of goods. Today's taste for roots and 'eternity' arises from the ever-growing spiral of the transitory. A gnawing 'spiritual' need, albeit an ambiguous one, always underlies our relationship with luxury – a need to get away from the flimsiness of the ephemeral and to touch terra firma, to find a place in which the present becomes charged with a system of reference.

In that respect, luxury is similar to love, with its denial of constant change ('everything flows, nothing stands still') and its desire for eternity. Even the pleasure of 'splurging' is connected to eternity when it generates a present so intense that it becomes unforgettable. It may be that luxury passions – or at least some of them – are not so much expressions of the urge to destroy as the conjuration of destruction: luxury that is more compatible with Eros than with Thanatos, more on the side of being than becoming, more on the side of memory than forgetting. Perhaps something metaphysical will always haunt our desire to imitate the gods in our enjoyment of the rarest and most beautiful of things.

Notes
1. A potlatch is a ceremonial gathering among certain North American Indian tribes. Its purpose was to establish or reinforce the status of the host. It involved the consumption or squandering of great quantities of food. The guests were also often given gifts or money.
2. See Claude Lefort, *The Political Forms of Modern Society* (Cambridge: Polity Press, 1986).
3. See the second part of my book, *The Empire of Fashion: Dressing Modern Democracy* (Princeton: Princeton University Press, 2002).
4. See Bernard Arnault, 'The Perfect Paradox of Star Brands', *Harvard Business Review* 79 (October 2001).
5. Mircea Eliade, *Myth and Reality* (Long Grove, Illinois: Waveland Press, 1998).
6. See Jean-Paul Aron, *Le mangeur du XIXè siècle* (Paris: Robert Laffont, 1973).

MODERN AND POSTMODERN LUXURY

Gilles Lipovetsky

Until the mid-nineteenth century, luxury was based on a model that was both aristocratic and artisanal. While artists had acquired fame and glory after the Renaissance, most artisans had no prestige and remained in the background. The customer ruled, and the craftspeople worked in the shadows. Their work was worth far less than the materials they used and was carried out 'on demand' for the aristocracy and the well-heeled bourgeoisie. In those pre-democratic times, luxury was characterised by the creation of unique items, the predominance of customer demand and the lowly and anonymous status of the artisan.

LUXURY AND MODERNITY

But everything changed in the modern era, and the sudden emergence of haute couture perfectly illustrates the new rationale. Charles Frederick Worth laid down the foundations of haute couture in the second half of the nineteenth century when he established a luxury goods industry devoted to creating made-to-measure and frequently renewed models for individual customers[1]. This represented a clear break with the past. The designer was liberated because models were no longer made to order in obedience to customers' dictates. Instead the designer was free to impose his own tastes and designs on the customers, who became passive consumers. In the modern era of luxury, the couturier was liberated from his previous subordination to the customer and asserted his new authority by being a leader of fashion. The golden age of the demiurge-couturier was born. It was to last for one hundred years. Previously an obscure artisan, the couturier was suddenly recognised as a sublime artist, a creator of worldwide renown. This honouring, this democratic recognition of the great couturiers, was an extension of the eighteenth-century trend of considering the great hairdressers and 'fashion merchants' as artists, thereby giving them a claim to fame. After the middle of the nineteenth century whole sections of the luxury universe would be linked to a particular name, either that of an exceptional individual or a prestigious firm. Some of those names, in fashion as elsewhere, have lasted right up to recent times.[2] Luxury thus became personalised; it now bore the name of a couturier or a fashion house and was no longer linked to a patron or place. It was no longer the richness of the materials used but the aura of the name and fame of a great house, the prestige of a trademark and the magic of a brand. And competition for that prestige took place not only among the upper classes but also among the producers of luxury goods themselves.

With haute couture, luxury became a 'creation industry' for the first time. The major fashion houses continued to function on a craft basis; clothes were hand-made to measure, quality prevailed over quantity, and the know-how of the couturiers was crucial. Nevertheless the modern concept of series production came into being,[3] and although the production runs were short they still represented several hundred, or even several thousand, copies of a given model. Haute couture launched the 'limited edition' even before the new industrial manufacturing techniques that appeared after 1880 enabled standardised goods to be churned out in vast quantities. A few numbers give an idea of luxury's new industrial dimension: in 1873 Worth employed 1,200 people; in 1935 Chanel employed 4,000; and by 1956 Dior had a staff of 1,200. In the mid-1930s Chanel was producing 28,000 items per year and in 1953 the Parisian haute couture industry as a whole produced 90,000.[4]

Added to this were sales to overseas buyers, particularly from the United States, who bought several copies of each model in a variety of sizes. In 1925 haute couture sales accounted for 15 percent of global French exports and ranked second in foreign trade. After 1929 higher import duties led to increased sales of cloth and patterns to foreign manufacturers, who were granted rights to reproduce certain series in their respective countries. Until 1960 these sales represented about 20 percent of total haute couture sales, proof that the luxury goods market had become industrialised. In short, luxury's entry into the modern era was marked by a compromise between craft and industry; it became both a work of art and a production model.

LUXURY AND SEMI-LUXURY

While haute couture embodied the union of arts and crafts with industry, advances in mechanisation during the same period led to the appearance of cheaper 'semi-luxury' or 'pseudo-luxury' goods aimed at the middle classes. The modern era is contemporaneous with the rift between the authentic, exclusive and priceless, on the one hand, and the shoddy imitation, standardised and democratised goods on the other. A wave of reproductions flooded the stores during this period – jewellery, toilet requisites, knick-knacks, statues, carpets, furniture, glassware, wallpaper and so forth – all for the benefit of a broader clientele. The materials they were made of were far less lavish but nevertheless imitated the prestigious originals.[5] The first stage in the democratisation of luxury was not the acquisition of ruin-ously expensive goods by a broader section of the social spectrum but the dissemination of copies and ersatz, of neo-antiques and goods that made up for their lack of personality by their superflu-ity: overloaded ornaments, a proliferation of dec-oration and expressive overstatement. These goods were displayed under the auspices of kitsch as the bourgeois way of life.

The department store is a large-scale example of this new democratic semi-luxury. The stores were founded in the second half of the nineteenth cen-tury and were based on new commercial concepts that targeted the middle-class consumer: prices that were both low and fixed, no entrance fee, a broad range of goods, and advertising. By bring-ing down prices, the department stores suc-ceeded in 'democratising luxury', or to be precise, in transforming certain types of goods previously reserved for the wealthy elite into everyday con-sumer products and promoting the purchase of goods that were not strictly necessary. More than that, department stores were conceived as extra-ordinary showpieces, palaces of light and colour filled with sparking wonders. Their ornamental facades with their cupolas, statues and gilded domes, transformed the department stores into a merchandise extravaganza, 'fairy-tale palaces'.[6] The profusion of goods, window displays and sumptuous arrangements, the concerts, oriental carpets and drapes, did their utmost to sublimate the utilitarian purpose of trade, to transcend its materialistic dimension by appearing in the guise of a dazzling show of festivity, excess and pomp. In addition, attractive prices, sales, special offers and promotions created an enchanted universe and enhanced perceptions of gift and extrava-gance. The department store was a mercantile power dispensing spectacle and beauty, abun-dance and wealth. The former agonistic trading spectacle was transformed into an unparalleled and unchallenged merchant universe. Ceremonial and reciprocal exchange gave way to the irresist-ible urge to shop and obtain bargains. The era of sacred time and festive rituals gave way to an era of non-stop, accumulative consumption. Nothing remained of the magic of rites and sacred words; now there were only prices and goods, the new lure of happiness for the middle classes. In demo-cratic times, luxury became synonymous with 'cheap', excess with financial calculations, waste with the indispensable, and exaltation with the daily excitement and entertainment of shopping. The noble cult of extravagant expenditure gave way to status and comfort, to the private happi-ness of men and women.

But there is more to this than semi-luxury kitsch, for a new unobtrusive aesthetic developed simul-taneously. While ornamental knick-knacks were piling up, a revolution of modern understatement was taking place. Throughout history, because luxury was at the service of celestial, royal and aristocratic grandeur, it was inseparable from the extravagant visible signs of that grandeur, its ostentatious theatricality. But all that changed in the democratic era. In societies where 'the other' is recognised as equal, there is a tendency to reduce any brazen signs of difference or power. It started with black-coloured clothing for men in the nineteenth century, and then, rather late in the day, with the revolution in women's clothing that occurred in the 1920s and which completed the democratic process of eliminating anything that 'overwhelmed' the other, or that could hinder mutual recognition. True elegance had to be dis-creet and euphemised, what Balzac called 'the luxury of simplicity'.

The rejection of pompous decoration in architec-ture and artefacts that began in the early twenti-eth century was the result of a number of avant-garde trends. The modernist spirit rose up against kitsch, the ornamental tradition, the aesthetic of the superfluous, and replaced it with abstract rig-our, a figurative paring-down to the angular and geometric. Luxury remained distinctive but was removed from the symbolic confrontations of the upper classes. Modernist aesthetics in home fur-nishings and artefacts gave rise to new designs in the plastic arts, new use of space and time, a new relationship with the world and with others, with cleanliness and light, with comfort and intimacy. Even luxury embraced democratic ideals: the new aspirations of modern man to material well-being and to freedom; a rejection of the past and the traditions that inevitably accompany the decline of an aristocratic universe.

LUXURY MARKETING

What is the situation today? Judging by the past couple of decades, we appear to be entering a new age of luxury. It is luxury's postmodern, or hyper-modern moment, both globalised and financialised. Up to now, luxury depended on fam-ily firms and independent founders or creators. These have since given way to the global giants, large corporate groups with massive sales that are publicly listed and founded on a huge portfo-lio of prestigious brands. There has been a change of scale in the economic and entrepre-neurial universe of luxury. Traditional competition for prestige has been replaced by 'luxury wars', by mergers and acquisitions, by consolidation and restructuring, in a struggle to build international industrial empires. Luxury has entered the world of mega-enterprises, globalisation, stock options and corporate strategies, which sound the death knell for the small independent houses as well as the sovereign artist-creators. It is true that the luxury sector is at one and the same time economical and uneconomical,[7] but it is obvious that the economic and financial side of this hybrid dominates and is imposing its laws on product development, the buying and selling of brands and stock market flotations, all in the name of double-digit profit margins. The sublime artistic age of luxury has given way to a hyper-realistic financial age, in which creation and the search for high profitability have become inseparable.

The previous luxury model had succeeded in combining industrial and craft logic. Even so, the craft aspect that began dominating with the reproduction of models was limited and made to order. The trend is now reversed and the industrial logic of series production has taken over. The result is the collapse of made-to-measure haute couture and the rise of perfumes and accessories, ready-to-wear and licensed manufacturing. Luxury no longer means the exclusive model as opposed to the production model, since special editions are only a marginal aspect of the business today. Hundreds of thousands of bottles of perfume are produced, and several thousand copies of ready-to-wear luxury clothing. This industrial logic applies even to top-of-the-range products. In 2001, BMW sold 900,000 cars and Audi 720,000. Mercedes launched the 'Vision GST', a people-carrier and high-end SUV rolled into one, and it intends to manufacture some 100,000 units per year. Issuing an item in vast numbers is no longer considered semi-luxury.

While the major fashion houses are launching an increasing number of easily accessible items such as perfumes and accessories, the large industrial consumer groups are becoming interested in the high-end segments. The phenomenon of 'going upmarket' is especially true in the automobile industry. Renault showed its hand when it launched the Avantime and the Vel Satis, and has transformed itself from being a 'creator of automobiles', as depicted in a former advertising slogan, to a manufacturer of 'cars for living'. According to Renault, the high end of the range represented 12 percent of sales in 2003 compared with 8 percent in 1999. Volkswagen also entered the premium-class segment with its Phaeton limousine, having previously acquired Audi, Bentley,

Bugatti and Lamborghini. Luxury remains an element of social distinction, but it also works increasingly well as a management tool for large popular brands, since the prestige of the luxury range has a trickle-down effect on the other models, too. Now that the performance and reliability of cars is becoming standard, the attraction of a given car is boosted by a trademark's high-end segment, which epitomises the company's know-how. A growing number of luxury models now generate margins and enhance the manufacturers' reputations. But if the major mass-market car-makers are investing in the luxury segment, the prestigious trademarks will need to set their sights even higher. Mercedes, which already has a luxury Class S model, recently brought out a 'mega-limousine', the six-meter-long Maybach which carries a €300,000 price tag. The democratic and industrial supremacy of series production in no way constitutes the decline of ruinous excess or a levelling of luxury.

In its pioneering days, haute couture was headed by an artist-creator who imposed his taste on a rich clientele. That era is over, and the ready-to-wear collections of the major fashion houses are far less capricious and considerably more attentive to the tastes of their customers, whether overtly expressed or otherwise. The diktats of the designers and the great stylistic revolutions are over – or at least they no longer have any visible impact. Tom Ford has replaced Yves Saint Laurent. After a one-hundred-year cycle of artistic luxury in which supply was dominated by supply-driven studios, we have entered the era of luxury marketing centred on demand and market logic.

With the rapid increase in demand[8] and growing competition, the luxury universe is beginning to imitate the behaviour of the mass-market brands. It is marked by hugely expensive product launches and publicity, transgressive or shock advertising campaigns, a vast increase in new product launches,[9] shorter shelf-lives, a slew of promotional offers for perfumes and cosmetics, and the demand for short-term financial performance.[10] True, these new strategies may not last forever, particularly since they could have a negative result in the long term. But they do show that luxury industries have entered the marketing era with a bang.

EMOTIONAL LUXURY

What might be called the new age of luxury is not just the visible transformation of supply, but also the metamorphosis of demand, its aspirations and motivations, the relations of individuals with social standards and with each other as well as with consumption and scarcity. Individualising, emotionalising and democratising are the processes that are reorganising the contemporary culture of luxury.

It must be admitted that, at first glance, there appears to be more of a social and historical continuity in the consumption of luxury than any break with the past. There is no doubt that the traditional social function of luxury consumption is perpetuated in the uppermost social strata, among the monarchs, princes, industrial and financial magnates. Exhibitions of wealth, wasteful expenditure, displays of largesse or patronage continue to exist and, in many ways, to function as required social standards. Even at the next level down, the consumption of the new millionaires, city traders and golden boys is still part of the Veblen phenomenon. Since the 1980s the new financial elite has unabashedly displayed its taste for luxury goods and symbols of social status. In the United States, more so than in Europe, the rich flaunt their wealth as a symbol of worth and personal success; it is the apotheosis of an economic and social project.[11] In any case, on both sides of the Atlantic, former ideals of Puritan frugality have been thrown overboard along with political protest, while luxury goods and prestigious brands have been rehabilitated. They are back in fashion and are far less controversial.[12] The contemporary era may have pushed back the dictates of fashion, but brands and rare objects flourish. The latest developments in our democratic and market culture have not succeeded in overcoming snobbery, a desire to appear rich and stand out from the crowd or to seek social status by means of ostentatious signs of wealth.

Is there nothing new then, in the relationship people have with each other or with costly consumption? The reality is more complex. Veblen makes one important remark that makes sense of the current changes. 'The wealth or power must be put in evidence', he says, 'for esteem is awarded only on evidence. And not only does the evidence of wealth serve to impress one's importance on others and to keep their sense of one's importance alive and alert, but it is of scarcely less use in building up and preserving one's self-complacency.'[13] A passion for luxury is not exclusively fed by a desire to be admired, to arouse envy, or be recognised by others. It is also fed by a desire to admire oneself and bask in one's elitist image. It is this narcissistic dimension that now dominates. The importance of the judgement of

others may have decreased in contemporary neo-narcissism, but there is no correlated reduction in the importance of self in relation to others. In a period of rampant individualism, there is a need to stand out from the crowd, to be different, to feel special. So elitist motivation remains but is founded less on honour and social ostentation than on a distancing from the other, the pleasure of differentiation achieved through the consumption of rare luxury and the resultant contrast with the mundane.[14] If one aspect of postmodern individualism leads to 'living for oneself', to being less susceptible to the opinions of others and gratifying one's private emotions, the other aspect encourages people to compare themselves with their peers, to feel they are living more intensely, to embrace their idiosyncrasies and build a positive image of themselves for themselves, to feel privileged and different from others. There is nothing new about elitist sentiment or needing to compare oneself favourably with others, but this is currently being redefined on the basis of that particular neo-individualistic logic that is more for self than for the esteem of others.

Even the traditional rationale of social distinction carries traces of individualism. The luxury universe no longer functions exclusively along the classic lines that oppose the rich and the less rich, the dominant and the dominated, and old money with nouveaux riches. For a whole category of luxury consumers such as celebrities and stars, luxury is not a matter of belonging to a group or showing off one's wealth. Rather it is a way of expressing a specific personality, of being original and revealing personal tastes free from conventional forms and trappings. Today luxury is devoted to promoting an image of an individual rather than of a class.

But the fundamental changes do not stop there. Since the dawn of history, lavish expenditure has gone hand in hand with restrictive social regulations, some sacred, some profane, but in all cases synonymous with strict limitations imposed on individual behaviour by the collective order. And that is where our societies are undergoing a profound change: they no longer function under social obligation but according to individual judgement. The socially imposed pomp and lifestyle of the upper classes has given way to free, non-conformist luxury, 'without obligation or sanction'. Thus expensive consumption emerges free of social dictates, translating the rise in individual aspirations and motivations. Luxury consumption – sometimes ruinous expenditure, some-

GILLES LIPOVETSKY

times bargain shopping – is in the process of being 'de-institutionalised' in the same way that family, sexuality, religion, fashion and politics are. Everywhere neo-individualistic culture is accompanied by the emancipation from former constraints of class membership and the corresponding erosion of the authority of collective standards. With the diversification of life-styles and the deterioration of the regulatory force of social institutions and group control, this so-called postmodern era is characterised by a deregulated, optional individualism.

This drive towards individual self-reliance has not spared consumption as a whole, especially the consumption of luxury, since the latter obeys a disunited, uncoordinated, variable logic. The category of people now called 'bobos', or bourgeois bohemians, is merely the latest illustration of the promotion of a post-conventional culture that is both odd and eclectic, sustained by the principle of freedom to do what one wants with oneself. The ideal or typical consumer of luxuries now has many facets. He or she may borrow models from different groups, mix different types of objects of different prices and styles. Mobility, hybridisation and the disparate have taken over from formal 'proper' luxury.

But the de-institutionalising and individualising of luxury has also led to the emergence of a more affective relationship with it, one that is more sensitive to luxury goods. Of course there is nothing new in this trend; it has been apparent at least since the Renaissance. But in that period, luxury was associated with constraints that were, to a greater or lesser extent, ceremonial and reflected the predominance of collective imposition on subjective taste. In this respect it is worth highlighting the change that is currently taking place. As neo-individualism progresses, new forms of extravagant consumption appear that have more to do with emotions and personal sensations than with any specific strategy to acquire social status. People do not use extravagant expenditure to conform to society but to acquire aesthetic or sensory moments. It is used not so much to display wealth as to enjoy a moment of voluptuous pleasure. Luxury is an invitation to travel and delight the senses; it is a private party, a feast of sensations. The quest for personal pleasure has overtaken the requirement of social display and recognition. The contemporary era has given rise to a new kind of luxury, an emotional one that is lived and analysed, and where intimate sensations have replaced social preening.

For many years luxury was synonymous with watches, décor, theatricality, an ostentatious show of wealth, generally manifested through artifice and finery: ostentation for the benefit of others. This is still the case, but new trends have appeared which show that honorific symbols have given way to instant gratification, health, the body and subjective well-being. Beauty creams now take first place in cosmetics sales, well ahead of make-up. Health is a growth industry in which thalasso therapy, beauty parlours and fitness centres abound. Cosmetic surgery is enjoying an unprecedented boom. All four-star hotels now have special areas devoted to working out, beautifying, relaxing, slimming or harmonising one's energies. Luxury spas are everywhere. Although the desire to be noticed remains important – as may be seen in the spiralling rise in beauty care – the shift remains significant, for the importance lies not in displaying one's fortune but in looking young and enhancing one's beauty. The importance of what others think no longer dominates luxury trends; these are now subservient to the quest for health and experiential learning, for sensorial and emotional well-being. Luxury, the theatre of appearances, is devoting itself to the private individual and to subjective sensations, thus becoming luxury for one's self.

THE RIGHT TO LUXURY

The current process of making luxury subjective is not restricted to consumer practices. It can be seen in the way luxury is defined and talked about. Discussions about luxury today are revealing, because everyone has their own definition or interpretation of what 'real' luxury is. It is the individual who now defines luxury. Consequently it may be identified with a whole range of concepts such as free time, the quality of life, love, inner harmony, responsibility, freedom, peace, humanitarian work, knowledge and nature.[15] The rise of individualism has led to a desire to reacquire, in an ideological and subjectivist way, an inaccessible realm defined according to material criteria. Thus, ideologically speaking, by celebrating a plethora of luxuries, à la carte, free from the impersonal criteria of cost, a last hierarchical bastion has fallen to democratic fantasy. It is as though the contemporary individual, with his aspirations to personal accomplishment, has become resistant to any restrictive definition of luxury that might prohibit his access to the realm of dreams, sensuous pleasure and absolute beauty. While rare and expensive products continually reintroduce objective barriers and social disparity, postmodern culture embraces perspec-

MODERN AND POSTMODERN LUXURY

tivism and subjectivism as an expression of dem-ocratic demands for happiness and luxury.

So luxury for whom? Not so long ago, consump-tion and lifestyles were regulated by the opposi-tion of the 'preference for luxury' of the rich with the 'preference for necessities' of the poor. The former enjoyed refinement and remained aloof from the simple pleasures of the senses, while the latter rejected anything superfluous or that had 'airs and graces'. In this way objective constraints were transformed into preferences, leading the working classes to consistently choose things that were practical, simple or necessary.[16] The idea that 'luxury is not for us' arose because ave-nues of possibility were closed off. What remains of that ethos today?

One of the main results of the individualist-con-sumer culture is that it has profoundly changed the relationship between people and 'things' and 'necessities'. At present there is enormous insist-ence on the quality of goods and of the environ-ment, on the protection of consumers and on information. There is a sharp increase in demand for top-of-the-range products. Observers of con-sumer behaviour agree that there is less interest in 'popular' goods that may smack of 'necessities', and greater interest in quality and 'special' prod-ucts. There is a widespread desire for healthy foods, and 'light' products have gained ground over 'heavy' ones. Similarly, travel and leisure, the ideal of well-being and appearance, are no longer the sole preserve of the elite. It is not so much that habits and tastes have become stand-ardised, but rather that our culture has become more fluid, marked by a social decompartmentali-sation of behaviour and a significant reduction in the class restrictions that were commonplace just a short while ago. Almost nobody in our society sets out to acquire only the 'bare necessities' in the course of their lives. With the rise in consum-erism, leisure and well-being, the 'superfluous' has acquired its democratic credentials and become a legitimate mass aspiration.

At the same time, preventative and corrective attitudes are gaining ground in the form of health, sports, dieting and cosmetic surgery. In every category of the population, people are fighting off signs of age and excess weight. Instead of tradi-tional attitudes of resignation and acceptance of 'fate' and social status, people are demanding indefinite progress in living standards, and the right to novelty and prestigious brands, to quality, beauty and leisure. The postmodern era is con-temporaneous with the removal of former class

taboos and of popular reservations about expen-sive consumption. Every young person now con-siders it normal to own 'trendy' brands. There are no class boundaries in the fascination with con-sumer brands and the 'gimme more'. The former 'forbidden fruit' aspect of luxury has given rise to 'Why can't I have luxury, too?'

This trend is not purely ideological; it occurred after the 1970s, with its rise in 'occasional' luxury products, the so-called 'intermediary' or 'acces-sible' luxury items worn by the middle and some-time the lower social classes. With the increase in the 'right' to certain insignia, the spread of pres-tigious gifts, impulse purchases and aesthetic crazes, the postmodern era has set the scene for a democratisation of desires and luxury pur-chases. Of course, ostentation, snobbery and flashiness still exist, but they should not hide the change that has occurred in motivation. The occasional 'binge' is less a case of class preten-sion than of giving oneself or a loved one a *present*. It lies in the realm of dreams or follies that allow people briefly to escape the banality of everyday life. It is less a matter of showing off than a desire to experience something new and enjoy a special moment. The occasional luxury consumer simply wants to present an *image* of having a superior lifestyle, to *play* at being rich. For a moment he or she will amuse themselves by changing roles and appearing in a different guise. Consumption has been transformed from a regu-latory event to something that is detached and playful, and bears no real or symbolic challenge. It is merely a tongue-in-cheek participation in a world, which, while not considered 'ours', is no longer totally alien either. Mimicry has dethroned *agon*.[17]

It should once against be stressed that distinc-tive passions remain. But what once lay at the heart of ruinous consumption is now merely one element in a motivational whole with multiple causes. Symbolic struggles have lost their former relevance. Just as in fashion women now wear only what they like and what 'suits' them, so a multitude of luxury goods are acquired as prom-ises of happiness, little oases of pleasure, beauty and well-being. Class pretension and distinction may persist, but they are no longer the corner-stone of luxury consumption, which is now moti-vated by subjectivity and affectivity. Most of the struggle for social recognition now takes place elsewhere.

The age of mass consumption and mass communi-cation has transformed people's relationship with luxury into something subjective and democratic. By propagating standards of personal happiness and by sanctioning new standards of well-being, pleasure and leisure, the media and markets have succeeded in undermining the ethics of resignation, self-sacrifice and thrift. At the same time psychologism and the cult of the body-beautiful have sanctified life in the present tense along with everything that contributes to personal expression and fulfilment – to the extent that personal well-being and self-interest have become legitimate aspirations for all and sundry. Everyone may now pursue the better and the more beautiful and may, in theory, take boundless pleasure in the here-and-now and the wonders of the world. Why should we not benefit from the best the world has to offer? Why deprive ourselves? The new democratic requirements for luxury have no roots in symbolic class conflict. Nor are they the result of a supposed escalation of desire, frustration and dissatisfaction that may take hold of people as they become more prosperous and social distinctions dwindle. These luxury needs merely put the finishing touches to consumerism; they are the crowning glory of private pleasure and the democratic right to happiness. People's relationship with luxury has been democratised by materialistic and psychological mass culture.

THE LUXURY CHALLENGE

Since time immemorial, extravagance has been linked in part with inter-personal challenges, one-upmanship and the agonistic competition between signs. During Tlingit and Kwakiutl potlatches, tribal chiefs would vie with each other in their generosity. Every Greek and Roman benefactor strove to outdo his predecessor in the splendour of his gifts to the people. Luxury was orchestrated by ruinous consumption to such an extent that, between the ninth and the eighteenth centuries, royalty in Europe regularly issued edicts to limit the squandering of precious materials and the blurring of social distinctions.

As we have seen, after the nineteenth century, a new, almost adverse phase emerged for the first time, which celebrated a 'democratic' luxury that was less domineering and less 'showy'. The post- or hyper-modern moment is an extension of this, not only because of its discreet aesthetic but also because it promotes a type of luxury that is more defensive than aggressive. In what is perceived as a threatening era, high security has proliferated. Luxury residences have round-the-clock security, private houses are fenced off and pro-

tected by guards, alarm systems and video surveillance.[18] The rapid increase in control and surveillance equipment – a true obsession with security and safety – goes hand in hand with the escalation of pomp and decorum. Long before Michael Jackson, the American millionaire Howard Hughes lived in terror of germs and viruses; he secluded himself from the outside world, communicating with it only through mediums. Today security is increasingly a major selling-point in luxury. Analysts confirm that the safety of people and possessions is a vital requirement for people buying luxury residences. The core of luxury is to have marble and exotic wood everywhere, as well as a swimming pool and garden – not to mention the major asset, which is security. Luxury consists of a safe, hidden in a cupboard in an apartment monitored by video cameras that are connected to a guard room, which in turn is connected to the Monaco police, one of the world's most efficient. Agonistic luxury has given way to paranoid luxury.

The car industry is another good example of the combination of luxury and security. Since Mercedes launched the 'Class S' in 1965 – nicknamed the 'mobile safe' – all the company's advertising campaigns have focused on optimum security. The safety theme is present in the sales pitch for every luxury car. It may be 'passive' safety, to reduce or eliminate injuries in the event of an accident (reinforced passenger compartments, front, side and curtain airbags), or 'active' safety designed to prevent the driver from having an accident in the first place (braking systems, acceleration, electronic guidance). Added to this are the locking devices to prevent anyone from opening the door from the outside, laminated glass side windows and anti-intrusion systems. One car parts manufacturer now sells an electronic fingerprinting system that prevents unauthorised persons from opening car doors or starting the engine. At a time when security is on everyone's mind, the luxury of protection takes precedence over ostentatious signs of wealth and symbolic challenges. To possess the highest possible degree of security is more important than one-upmanship.

But however much the trend for security is emphasised, it does not mean that luxury has been ridden of its former connections with challenge and prestige. A whole range of extravagant behaviours – acquisition of Old Masters, auctions, patronage – continue to perpetuate the tradition of agonistic, aristocratic-type competition. Moreover there has been an increase in astro-

04. John Galliano, spring/summer 2006 collection show

GILLES LIPOVETSKY

nomic expenditure on gratuitous but challenging and competitive activities, of which motor racing is a prime example – a race to obtain fame and image. Take the massive budget of a Formula 1 racing stable, which usually exceeds €100 million per year, or four times that amount in the case of Ferrari. Of course this expenditure is not lost, for it provides exposure and consumer recognition to the brands and sponsors of these spectacles-cum-exploits based on challenge, competition and risk.

Sponsors today are less likely to finance artistic events than spectacular and high-risk sports. Since the 1980s, there has been a stunning rise in the financing of dangerous and gratuitous exploits such as the sponsorship of solo races, rallies, long-distance races across deserts, expeditions to the North Pole, or paragliding from the top of Mount Everest. It is quite legitimate to call these 'luxury exploits', and not just because most of them are extremely expensive and require sponsorship, but also because they are a spectacle for no good purpose other than to beat a record, or to be the first to do it; to defy time, space, age and the human body. Luxury's connection to one-upmanship and excess remains intact, the only difference being that it now gives rise to practices that are more hyper-realistic and emotional than symbolic. 'Extreme' activities have followed on from the *agon* of extravagant signs, accompanied by exhaustion, hunger, thirst, accidents and risk.[19] The theatricality of wealth is no longer important, now that we have the subjective thrills of adventure and victory, the intensity of heightened sensations achieved by extreme experiences in which risk and death play a role.

No one can define the emotional luxury of the future. But Denis Tito, history's first space tourist, spent more than €22 million for one week aboard the international space station. Today luxury is no longer inter-human but extra-terrestrial. It is a search for a sidereal journey and unknown sensations. The principle of challenge remains, not a challenge to other people but rather to gravity, to space, to perception, to our time on earth. The purpose is no longer to amaze others but to amaze oneself by being torn away from Planet Earth, by seeing the splendour of the cosmos and the 'eternal silence of infinite space'.

Advertising campaigns for luxury brands are also taking this aspect of challenge on board by exploiting transgression. Parades of fetishists on Dior or Givenchy catwalks, sexual images for Gucci, hints of orgies for Versace, and lesbianism,

masturbation and androgyny for others. A recent Dior poster flaunted the word 'Addict'. It seems that 'porn chic' is already passé; luxury long ago exchanged its respectable image for one of provocation, taboo-breaking and sensationalism.

But this is a playful challenge without risk or stakes, since the sexual order of our liberal societies has rid itself of moral criteria. Brands may be provocative because sex no longer has the power to upset. Symbols of wealth have ceased to drive advertising campaigns, so signs of 'daring' are used instead to revamp the image of the fashion houses. The challenge no longer has any status-enhancing purpose in itself; it serves as a communicational face-lift. Now that fashion is no longer the scene for major stylistic change, now that clothing no longer has ceremonial meaning and is not motivated by competition for prestige, luxury is obliged to recreate and reinvent spectacles of excess, to design a new 'debauchery' of signs. One-upmanship has been removed from supply and demand but it has re-emerged in marketing messages. Ostentatious extravagance is no longer a sign of superiority. To cause a stir one must display a provocatively different kind of 'freedom'. When fashion distances itself from avant-garde breaches with the past and agonistic rivalries, challenge remains as a sham and media show.

Notes

1. For more on this, see Diana De Marly, *Worth, Father of Haute Couture* (London: Elm Tree Books, 1980), or by the same author *The History of Haute Couture, 1850-1950* (London: Batsford, 1980). Also G. Lipovetsky, *The Empire of Fashion* (Princeton: Princeton University Press, 2002).

2. Daum was founded in 1875, Lalique in 1910, Boucheron in 1858, S.T. Dupont in 1872, Hermès in 1837, Louis Vuitton in 1854, Guerlain in 1828 and Jeanne Lanvin in 1889. Boucheron set up his establishment in Place Vendôme, Paris, in 1893, and Cartier in 1899.

3. Haute couture's partnership with industry also gave rise to its connections with perfumes. From the early twentieth century, fashion houses would manufacture fragrances – or lend their names to them – starting with Poiret's 'Fruit Défendu' in 1914 (for Rosine), and Chanel's 'N°5' in 1921.

4. See Didier Grumbach, *Histoires de la Mode* (Paris: Seuil, 1993).

5. See Philippe Perrot, *Le Luxe. Une richesse entre faste et confort, XVIIIe-XIXe siècle* (Paris: Seuil, 1995).

6. See Michael B. Miller, *Au Bon Marché, 1869-1920* (Paris: Armand Colin, 1987). For American department stores see William Leach, *Land of Desire* (New York: Vintage Books, 1993).

7. See Elyette Roux and Jean-Marie Floch, 'Gérer l'ingérable: la contradiction interne de toute maison de luxe', *Décisions Marketing* 9 (Paris, September-December 1996).

8. According to a research report by investment bank Merrill Lynch, 7.2 million people in the world have savings of over one million dollars. Currently 57,000 people have assets worth 30 million dollars.

9. The phenomenon is no longer restricted to fashion and perfumes: BMW expects to launch 20 new products over the next six years.

10. See Elyette Roux, 'Le luxe entre prestige et le marché de masse', *Décisions Marketing* 1 (Paris, January-April, 1994).

11. See Bruno Rémaury, 'Luxe et identité culturelle américaine', *Revue française du marketing* 187 (Paris, 2002).

12. See Danielle Allérès, *Luxe... Stratégies-Marketing* (Paris: Economica, 1997).

13. See Thorstein Veblen, *Theory of the Leisure Class* (1899), reprinted by Penguin Books, London, 1994.

14. From an aristocratic perspective, Nietzsche in *Beyond Good and Evil* mentions being 'pleasantly conscious of being different'.

15. See for example Saphia Richou and Michel Lombard *Le luxe dans tous ses états* (Paris: Economica, 1999).

16. See Pierre Bourdieu, *The Distinction: A Social Critique of the Judgement of Taste* (London: Routledge, 1986).

17. For more on this, see Roger Caillois, *Man, Play and Games* (Champaign: University of Illinois Press, 2001).

18. Robert Reich reports that private security is one of the fastest growing markets in the United States. In 1990 private security agents accounted for 2.6 percent of the total workforce, twice as much as in 1970. See *L'économie mondialisée* (Paris: Dunod, 1993).

19. See David Le Breton, *Passions du risque* (Paris: Métailié, 1991).

GILLES LIPOVETSKY

05.
Michelle Olley in the show of
Alexander McQueen, spring/summer
2001 collection
06.
Jean Louis Scherrer, haute couture
fitting rooms, Paris, 2003

VICTIM OF BANALITY

Luca Marchetti

01.

During a discussion with students about the semiotic construction of a valuable object, I explained how the layout of a designer boutique on the Place Vendôme in Paris played on the codes of the adjacent jewellery shops – so much so that the clothes in the boutique's window were displayed like precious objects. The question most frequently asked by my students was, 'How can ready-to-wear clothing sell for the same price as precious jewels?'

That is a relevant question since it raises basic issues about the understanding of contemporary luxury. The value of these objects does not only derive from the materials they are made of or the way they are made, but from a special relationship between those factors and the cultural significance of the context in which they are produced and received. This is a definition of value-added that could, interestingly enough, apply to a work of art. Indeed, it might be said that certain kinds of industrial goods have taken on – at least partly – an artistic sensibility traditionally reserved for fine art.[1] This transformation has affected the market but is also part of a broader process of social change. During the past centuries, power passed from the nobility, which traditionally handed down their assets through the generations, to more dynamic groups in which wealth was more mobile and values were constantly renewed. This expanding category of the population was constantly seeking new aesthetic points of reference in order to position themselves on a constantly moving social scale. And the 'creator' was in an ideal position to supply these markers.[2] Therefore the quantitative increase of this new social elite (the modern industrial bourgeoisie)

coincided historically with the birth of haute couture and modern design.[3] Under these circumstances, industrial products became the main conduit of artistic worth in everyday life.

A similar process also affected the art world at the beginning of the last century. On the one hand artists[4] were exploring ways to take commonplace objects into the art gallery, and on the other, new 'creators'[5] were doing their utmost to take artistic value out of the museums and galleries and into everyday life. Of the two, the latter trend has probably remained more in line with contemporary sensibilities. It seems more relevant today to force art beyond the constraints of gallery shows rather than to straitjacket popular creativity inside museums. That is probably connected with the postmodern aesthetic sympathy for the peripheral, the centrifugal.

This centrifugal energy, pushing outwards from within, is not unrelated to the developments in the media. First came the widespread popularity of the transistor radio in the 1950s, which allowed urban youth to listen to whatever they wanted. This led them to express their stylistic differences and break away once and for all from the existing sartorial uniformity between generations.[6] Then a decade later, the spread of television led us to believe, with greater or lesser gullibility, that images moving over that luminous surface could reveal things that were distant or hidden 'in the centre'.[7] But then along came electronic media, and that surface-based rationale gave way to the rationale of relationships. The fragmentation of identity-bearing media was compounded and made more pervasive by digital technologies, leading Lev Manovich to use the expression 'augmented space' to describe a communication context in which information is omnipresent and can be retrieved at all times by a variety of means.[8] According to Manovich, one symbolic example of augmented space is the Prada Epicentre in New York,[9] which develops the brand's identity in a relational and interactive way. In fact the retail outlets of the major brands such as Louis Vuitton or Prada[10] are an ideal observatory for measuring how the communication of identity has been transformed in the world of luxury goods. The change is visible precisely at the level of relational strategies. It extends from the display window – viewed as windows onto the inside or into the label, at a personal scale – to the entire architectural system viewed as an urban statement. Once again, we are moving from the centre to the periphery.

02.

01, 02
Interior, Prada Epicentre, New York

GIVENCHY

04.

FENDI

05.

03.
Givenchy, advertising campaign,
2006
04.
Fendi, advertising campaign, 2006
05.
Helmut Lang, handcuffs, autumn/
winter 2004 collection for men

In the fashion landscape, accessories are an accurate witness to this movement. Aside from their role as linguistic signifiers, whereby they are presented as something liminal, their very nature as objects means that they are satellites of the clothing universe. Because of its proximity to the body, clothing is perceived as a personal prosthesis, a second protective skin on which we inscribe our identifying signs. Conversely, an accessory has all the characteristics of the independent body. Like an electron in an atomic structure, the accessory is connected to the individual but may easily be separated from it. It is an object of exchange that is put down, lent, given or lost. It is more a materialisation of our relationship with the environment than an augmentation of the body, as clothes can be.

We are certainly not used to casting a critical eye on accessories. The recent studies of fashion – and they are rare – are mostly about clothing. And yet the fashion accessory is gaining ground, both commercially and in its representational value. The huge increase in accessories – which often come in a variety of styles so as to offset increasingly sober and standardised ready-to-wear fashions – has given them a symbolic value that once belonged only to clothes. The oversized bags that were seen in last year's collections, for instance, from Givenchy to Dolce & Gabbana, are obvious signs of this transfer of power. They may have a small impact on the market, but they are very important in terms of specialised communication and the products of the imagination that result from it. Quite apart from the sheer quantity of accessories, an expressive vocabulary has now grown up around them. The accessory's appearance is now less about function and more about narrative. It has already been compared with the adjective or adverb in the language of fashion;[11] now it aims to tell stories in the same way that clothes do. The Hermès Kelly bag, designed in the early 1930s, emphasised the handles, the closure and the bag's function as a container. This is communicated through a literal use of the codes that make the family of objects identifiable. On the other hand, Dior's Gaucho bag plays with the legibility (and illegibility) of the product by means of plastic, figurative play that shies away from the category's usual codes but borrows codes from other worlds, such as saddle-making. It also blurs the relationship between the elements that structure the object – by the use of a metal key, for instance, that has no functional use whatsoever, thereby creating a *trompe l'œil* effect between the bag's various strata. These 'rhetorical' artifices may verge on the conceptual, as is the case of Helmut Lang's handcuff bracelet in his 2004 winter collection, or the partnership between bag makers and contemporary artists, such as Vuitton-Murakami or Longchamp-Tracey Emin.

Using Donald Norman's triad for describing the experience of design, it is possible to understand recent developments in accessories as a gentle shift from the behavioural level to the visceral-reflexive level,[12] which means a greater degree of the expressive and a superior degree of abstraction. The accessory's new semantic potential and its propensity to circulate easily within a community of individuals place it among the 'intermediary worlds' that Gérard Chazal calls 'cultural interfaces',[13] that is to say, those elements through which the very components of culture are transmitted and exchanged. In this respect, the specific nature of the fashion accessory arises from its affiliation with luxury, a so-called 'aspirational' sector that crystallises hopes or ambitions for obtaining personal or social gratification. Since we define the impact of an artefact in a given society on the basis of its presence, possession, display and consumption,[14] the accessory may be seen as a vector for values that command special attention. In fact Paolo Inghilleri, a specialist in primitive and industrial material cultures, claims that objects not only transmit symbolic representations related to their appearance but also 'emit information: they induce actions and behaviour that can terrorise or upset, nurse or unite people, or make people in a community change their minds and their feelings'.[15] When an artefact 'makes' us do something because of its appearance and design, it is referred to as 'factitive' by semioticians specialised in objects.[16] This occurs, for instance when a bag induces an unusual movement in order to hang it on one's shoulders, or a pair of shoes makes the wearer walk in a special way, or quite simply when a commonplace accessory obliges us to make a cognitive detour in order to understand the way it works.[17]

Since the accessory is both sign and body, the same accumulation of learning experiences may be extended to the perceptive and proprioceptive. An accessory's identity depends on many things, including its weight, textures or temperature, as well as on the direct interaction it may have with the body it touches, constrains or deforms. On the subject of the relationship between the accessory and the body, the epistemologist Eleonora Fiorani once wrote that 'the accessories speak of the body on the body: they enrich the narrative that each of us makes about ourselves and have a fun-

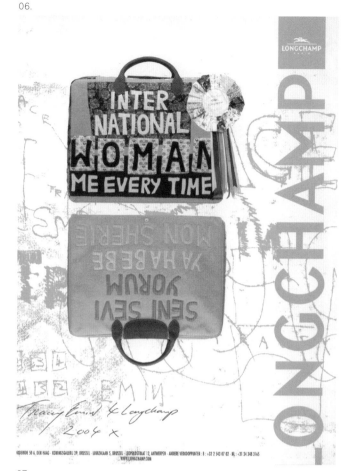

06.
Longchamp, advertising campaign for bags made by Tracey Emin, 2004
07.
Annemarie Herckes, miniature versions of Dior and Fendi bags for mobile phones, design for Celux Store, Tokyo

damental role in the aesthetics and ethics of sartorial appearance'.[18] But we can well imagine that the accessory may also speak *to* the body on the body, thereby going well beyond the aesthetic dimension and entering the broader field of aesthesia, or the aptitude of perceiving sensation. The object's sensuality is aroused by the same activators that arouse the sensuality of the body itself: the organic contours of a bag, the silky feel of a fur belt, the bewitching scent of leather boots warmed by a pair of legs – this is de-moralised sensuality since it has been displaced from the body to the object and is therefore free of physical taboos. The act of stroking, touching, pressing or slipping on, as practiced on the inanimate skin of the accessory, is a simulacrum of what one might do to the living skin of a person, thus blurring the frontiers between object and body. This syncretic dimension between the animate and inanimate is defined by sensation[19] and is particularly relevant when materials such as leather, latex or silicone become involved in this confusion.

Today the fashion accessory is developing into a singular artefact, a vector of both identity and perception. On the one hand it is the cultural interface between 'self' and the rest of the world, a conduit for values, knowledge and habits. On the other hand it is a frontier zone between bodily proprioception and the exteroception of what lies beyond. As often as not it feeds what Paolo Inghilleri defines as a 'terminal materialism', the sole purpose of which is the ownership of goods, as opposed to 'instrumental materialism', which is endowed with meaning and leads to the achievement of both individual and social goals.[20] Apparently, the only thing missing between these two perspectives is a positive social utopia, a more integrated and organic vision of 'common living', as well as a deeper knowledge of everyday objects that all too often succumb to their own banality.

Notes
1. Flaviano Celaschi, Alba Cappellieri, Alessandra Vasile, Lusso Versus Design: Italian style, beni culturali e luxury system (Milan: Franco Angeli, 2004).
2. Ibid.
3. Charles Frederick Worth was strongly influenced by the production logic of the series that was being developed in areas such as industrial design. A good example was the work of the furniture manufacturer Gebruder Thonet.
4. Marcel Duchamp's work is a good example of this process.
5. A term that I use in the broad sense, in relation to all sectors of the applied arts.
6. Domenico Baldini, MTV: 'Il nuovo mondo della televisione' (Rome: Castelvecchi, 2000).
7. Joshua Meyrowitz, No Sense of Place (New York: Oxford University Press, 1985).
8. Lev Manovich, The Language of New Media (Cambridge, MA: The MIT Press, 2002).
9. Lev Manovich, The Poetics of Augmented Space: Learning from Prada (May 2002) at www.manovich.net.
10. I have in mind the Louis Vuitton store on the Champs Elysées in Paris, or the Prada store in Tokyo's Aoyama district.
11. Alison Lurie, The Language of Clothes (New York: Random House, 1983).
12. According to Donald Norman the visceral is the level of appearance and its tangible characteristics, the behavioural is the level of use and function, and lastly the reflective is the level of connectivity to our pre-existing experience. See Emotional Design (New York: Basic Books, 2004).
13. Gérard, Chazal, Interfaces: Enquête sur les mondes intermediaries (Seyssel: Champ Vallon, 2002).
14. Paolo Inghilleri, La 'Buona Vita' (Milan: Guerini e Associati, 2003).
15. Ibid., p. 19 (translation).
16. A.-J. Greimas and J. Courtès theorised on factivity in Sémiotique: Dictionnaire raisonné de la théorie du langage (Paris: Hachette, 1979) and then applied it to objects by Michela Deni in Oggetti in Azione (Milan: Franco Angeli, 2002).
17. The single-strap backpack is a good example of an accessory that induces a creative movement, while Vivienne Westwood, who has frequently stressed this aspect in her designs, has shown the point of an unnatural walk with her platform shoes. Jérôme Olivet's creations on the other hand, are a brilliant example of accessories requiring a specific cognitive process in order to be understood.
18. Elenora Fiorani, Moda Corpo Immaginario (Milan: Edizioni Poli Design, 2006; translation), p. 27.
19. The aesthetic of 'smelling things' lies at the heart of Mario Perniola's philosophy, see Il sexappeal dell'inorganico (Milan: Einaudi, 2004).
20. Ibid.

08.
Christophe Coppens, hat, design for a fashion production in *De Morgen Magazine*, 2003
09.
Naomi Filmer, *Chocolate Mask*, design for *Another Magazine*, October 2001
10.
Jean Paul Gaultier, perfume bottles, 1993

10.

THE MAGIC OF THE IMAGE

Karin Schacknat

01. Hermès, advertising campaign with carré, 2006

HERMÈS
PARIS

ALL ABOARD HERMÈS

"La vie du fleuve" silk twill scarf.
Dress in feather lambskin.
"Kelly2" watch. Bracelet
in white gold and diamonds.
Lambskin gloves.

Buying luxury goods comes from a sense of poverty, not from a sense of wealth. So actually we should feel sympathy towards people who are decked out from head to foot in Chanel.
Alain de Botton

Most inhabitants of the industrialised world are supplied with enough clothes. Buying something new thus seldom stems from dire necessity; rather, people succumb to the particular temptations of products that promise an interesting surplus value above their utility. Going beyond practical or visual needs, such surplus values are connected with a deep-seated lack of status, youth, sex, love or self-esteem. In the wondrous world of styling and advertising nothing is irrational or too crazy for the sake of the product's magic. An appreciable part of this magic is based on the producer's image.

A good image is the mother of all sales arguments, certainly in the fashion segment with the steepest price tags. What is the secret of this? Following this, I shall endeavour to explain the concept in more detail and to sketch the images of a number of famous fashion houses. My selection is in a certain sense arbitrary, but all the names included have a strong image, which is why they are subject to misuse by being faked. I have arranged the labels concerned according to certain similarities between them, even though they may be dissimilar. What I hope to show, among other things, is that an image is always open to change, as is the position of the designer, which varies from creative motor to signboard. Accessories play a crucial role in the way an image functions and in a fashion label's success. For consumers they are often cult objects that bear a surplus value. When Rochas was recently forced to close down, the press ascribed it in part to the lack of a good range of accessories.

IMAGE

The word 'image' is used here to mean a stereotyped image of something or someone, which is then cherished by certain sections of the public. The notion is related to 'imaginary' and 'imagination'. Its degree of reality is variable and is always reduced to simple, immediately comprehensible entities. An image is therefore not an actual identity but rather the illusion of one. In the fashion world and other commercial sectors, the image of a brand is apparently at least as important as the quality of the products. It is based on goal-oriented, communicative elements such as the location and staging of shows, styling, press releases,

advertising campaigns, websites, symbols and logo, coupled with the name of the brand or label and the design scheme. These factors together contribute to the formation of a coherent and easily recognisable image that evokes associations meant to stimulate the purchase of the product.

The structure of an image is like a tissue of different components, with certain designers, photographers or models each having an image of their own that in turn consists of separate building blocks. This involves not only those who are paid by the fashion house for their help in constructing the image; unforeseen factors also contribute to determining the image, such as celebrities photographed with a particular make of dress or handbag that they have chosen on their own initiative. This works best in the case of fashion-conscious stars from the film, soaps or pop music circuits. In a certain sense, the way fashion houses construct their image is similar to that of classic Hollywood film stars, whose status likewise relied on numerous specialists working together; in both cases the efforts resulted in the creation of 'icons' and their cultural worship.

The image is always a concept, a careful construction which, however, remains implicit as such. But the strongest, most magical images within film and fashion are often based on the genius of a real person such as Greta Garbo or Vivienne Westwood.

An image is connected with the factor of time. A talented young designer initially has no image at all; it takes years before it begins to ripen. And then a close eye has to be kept on its quality. Certain components become irrevocably obsolete in the long run. A concept like 'luxury' or 'elegance', for example, cannot be interpreted the same way today as it was five decades ago. In the 1990s a surprising number of venerable fashion houses that had dozed off over the course of time suddenly became hip again after bringing in a young designer to modernise their image.

The unique character of an image is always under threat since many designers, photographers and models are currently working for several labels at the same time. Advertising campaigns are all placed one after the other in the same glossy magazines, which all look identical because of the input that the advertisers have on the magazines' contents. This is why disturbing or critical comments are never to be found in such magazines. The world of houses like Chanel is not supposed to display any scratches. A certain levelling out is inevitable; what remains is mainly the common denominator of 'luxury' or 'status'.

PARISIAN HAUTE COUTURE

During the 1950s the image of fashion was largely determined by Parisian couturiers, of whom Chanel and Dior were undoubtedly the best known worldwide. In the same way that Picasso is synonymous in popular parlance with 'modern art', both Chanel and Dior are identified with 'Parisian elegance'. So much for their general similarities; a closer look chiefly reveals their differences.

Gabrielle 'Coco' Chanel (1883-1971) became celebrated as an avant-garde designer in the 1920s because she combined elegance with practical, wearable comfort and freedom of movement for the modern, emancipated woman. The quintessence of her vision is represented by the multifunctional *petite robe noire* and the two-piece tweed or bouclé suit. Accessories were made in the same spirit, such as shoulder bags with a long strap or the famous two-tone beige goatskin shoes with a black point.

Coco Chanel grew up in a poor environment, but she possessed a lively spirit and a lot of charisma. Perhaps it was this European version of the American myth of newspaper boy becoming millionaire that contributed to her great popularity in the United States.

Christian Dior (1905-1957) was a modest, introverted person. As a designer, however, he is still regarded as the last great dictator, an image that actually owes more to the slavish behaviour of the followers of fashion in the 1950s, who unquestioningly obeyed every one of the maestro's new lines.

His first collection – the *New Look* in 1947 – was grafted onto a traditional female silhouette. Dior became instantly famous. And the image of Paris as the world's capital of fashion rose again after the sombre war years like a phoenix from the ashes.

Dior launched a new line every season, each time enriched by a series of accessories that in his view were indispensable for a perfect total image. He played the conventional role of 'arbiter of elegance', the expert in matters of good taste for the international *haute bourgeoisie*.

In their time Dior and Chanel both represented a particular type of elegance whose basis reaches way back into history. Dior's creations reveal a conventional but artificial image of femininity that required corset-like devices, as with the aristocrats in olden times. Lacing-up idealised the body's natural proportions, thereby subjecting nature to culture. Corsets are uncomfortable and demand discipline. And this is precisely the way the elite was able to distinguish itself from the lower classes, for whom neither the body nor emotions were governed by discipline.

Dior supplied more luxury than comfort, in contrast to Chanel who combined luxury with comfort and was more oriented towards the way women functioned in contemporary reality, which naturally included a greater degree of mobility. The

02.

03.

04.

CHANEL

02.
Chanel, illustration of the little black dress, 1926
03.
Chanel, advertising campaign, 2003
04.
Chanel, advertising campaign with Kate Moss, 2004
05.
Christian Dior, spring/summer 1951 collection
06.
John Galliano for Dior, spring/summer 2005 collection
07.
Kate Moss with Gaucho Bag by Dior, autumn/winter 2006/2007 collection

discipline of the Chanel woman was more likely to be found on a mental or intellectual level than in constrictive garments. Chanel offered women the opportunity to be just as modern and unorthodox as herself. In a certain sense, we can see similarities with the humanistic spirit of antiquity, when man counted as the measure of all things and the body was not trapped but looked elegant in a relaxed, self-assured way.

Today the classic Chanel suit has long ceased to stand for modernity; on the contrary, it makes us think of the wrinkled wives of heads of state and other elderly representatives of the well-to-do class. Since 1983, innovations have been in the hands of Karl Lagerfeld who, out of respect for Chanel, never loses sight of the continuity of the image. His perennial themes are simplicity and elegance, each time with new versions of recognisable ingredients such as elements from men's wear, two-tone shoes, fancy jewels, padded handbags, chain belts and the camellia. The biannual shows are never spectacular.

What were – and continue to be – desirable are the perfumes. With the launch of Chanel N°5 in 1921 all the rules were broken, as it was the first perfume to rely heavily on a compound of the brand-new synthetic aldehyde together with the then popular sultry, Oriental fragrances. The simple, taut lines of the bottle were as unusual as the cool naming (at the time 'laboratory test no. 5' appealed the most to Chanel). The avant-garde austerity acquired a saucy turn when Marilyn Monroe later made the immortal remark that she never wore anything in bed except a few drops of Chanel N°5. In the sixties, Andy Warhol made silk

screens of the bottle, thus sealing its status as a Western cultural icon.

The combination of luxuriousness and austerity emerges in advertisements, particularly in the sans serif lettering and the logo of two facing C's, as well as in the use of a lot of black and white and empty space on the page. The shops, too, are minimally furnished and offer more than enough freedom of movement. 'Chanel' is more a style than a fashion trend.

Dior's image is less coherent. The label has been taken over by the Louis Vuitton Moët Hennessy conglomerate, whose chairman, Bernard Arnault, shuffles designers around like chess pieces among the moribund fashion companies bought up by LVMH in order to make them profitable again. John Galliano, for instance, was brought in first for Givenchy and then for Dior. John Galliano, repeatedly named British Designer of the Year, brings with him a highly extroverted image of his own, giving rise to a somewhat diffuse climate within the house of Dior. The autumn/winter 2006 show, for example, was staged as a rock concert, featuring a lot of gothic chic. Galliano, decked out in his inevitable black bandanna, black jacket and razor-sharp moustache, was called 'the rock designer of our time' on the internet, pursued by hysterical 'groupie editors'.

Galliano's design style is more extravagant and more excessive than the house of Dior's original aura. But his creations can't be imitated by off-the-peg pirates as easily as that; they're too exclusive. And that suits the Dior image to a T.

05.

06.

07.

In modernising the image, the logo's typeface and the initials CD have remained the same. The logo is prominent on handbags and other accessories. The British photographer Nick Knight, who has also worked for Yohji Yamamoto, made various advertising campaigns for the ready-to-wear collections. In the autumn/winter 2006 campaign we saw Kate Moss brandishing the latest edition of the famous asymmetrical Dior gaucho saddlebag – elevated by the press to a so-called 'it bag' – at different locations in Paris. The French capital has always been an important component of Dior's image.

LUXURIOUS LEATHER

Certain celebrated old brands originally manufactured high-quality leather goods. The production of accessories preceded that of garments. These accessories once served the leisure activities of the elite, such as horseback riding. Saddles and other goods were supplied by specialised companies like Hermès, established in France in 1837. Around 1900 travelling became an elegant pastime – on the Orient Express for example, or by ocean steamer or even by car. A demand arose for functional and handsome trunks and bags.

By that time Emile-Maurice Hermès was offering luxurious travel items, as was Louis Vuitton (established in 1854). The intertwined letters LV were introduced as the firm's monogram in 1896. The value of a recognisable emblem was already understood at the time.

Most likely the sinking of the ocean liner *Titanic* in 1912 meant that all manner of expensive pieces of luggage by Vuitton, Hermès and perhaps also by Gucci (established in Florence in 1906) were carried into the depths. There was nothing by Prada since this Milanese firm was only created in 1913. Prada also made first-class trunks, bags and shoes, including the famous walrus skin suitcase which, because of its weight, fell into disuse as air travel became more common.

These manufacturers' clientele corresponded more or less with that of the couture houses, and interest declined as the spirit of the times changed after the Second World War. Here, too, the image had to be refreshed by deploying avant-garde designers.

Although Hermès had also been producing haute couture and ready-to-wear garments since the 1920s, the house became best known for its bags

08.

09.

KARIN SCHACKNAT

and its square silk scarves with complex if hardly innovative prints, often featuring equestrian elements - a reference to the company's long tradition, which is also expressed in the names of its classic perfumes: *Amazone* and *Calèche*.

The Hermès image is traditionally rather conventional and its products are particularly expensive. A typical example is the so-called 'Kelly' bag, the handbag with which Grace Kelly, the former film star and later Princess of Monaco, appeared on the cover of *Life* in 1956. A variation of this lady-like classic became popular in 1984 as the 'Birkin' bag, since the model was specially adapted to the wishes of the actress Jane Birkin. Nowadays this bag travels through the media on the arm of fashion-conscious celebrities, going stylishly with a fur coat and nonchalantly with jeans. The Birkin featured in an instalment of *Sex & the City*, Kate Moss was photographed with it and Gwyneth Paltrow has one in the 2001 film *The Royal Tenenbaums*. The image of the name Hermès has thus been kept up to date. Customers are not deterred by often having to wait for a new, handmade model, nor by the price.

In 1998 Martin Margiela was taken on as designer in order to update the image. He is rather modest, however; a revitalisation required more spectacular effects. Since 2003 Jean Paul Gaultier has taken over the helm. His first collection for Hermès was immediately greeted with enthusiasm by the press. The show was presented in a military riding school, with the public seated on bales of hay.

Gaultier makes repeated reference to elements from the legacy associated with equestrian sports, with a lot of daring and flair. The suits and whips he designed for Madonna's Confessions Tour in 2006 were likewise inspired by horseback riding outfits. Suddenly, Hermès style equestrian scenes have become exciting and fashionable, including Gaultier's latest version of the Birkin bag.

In the past Gucci, too, was mainly known for his leather accessories, such as the classic Gucci loafers from 1932 or the Jackie O handbag from 1961 with a clasp in the form of a metal bit. Some of the newer models are also equipped with a bit and/or stirrup as part of the construction; this motif is also incorporated in printed scarves. The initials GG and (sometimes) green/red/green

10.

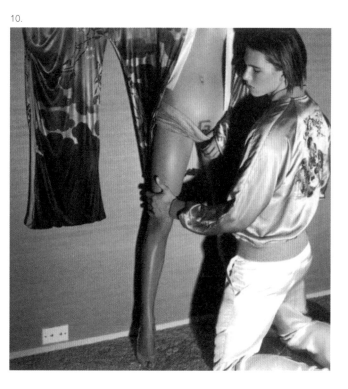

11.

08.
Hermès, spring/summer 2006 collection
09.
Hermès, autumn/winter 2005/2006 collection

10.
Gucci, advertising campaign with shaved pubic hair, 2003
11.
Gucci, advertising campaign, 2004

stripes serve as the company's logo. The initials generally figure blatantly, for example, on the sides of sunglasses, as well as being incorporated in patterns.

When the company teetered on the edge of bankruptcy at the end of the 1980s, the successful American designer Tom Ford was brought in. As art director from 1994 until 2004 he pulled Gucci out of its malaise. Ford designed all the collections and accessories and supervised the development of the perfume lines *Envy* and *Rush* as well as the advertising campaigns. For the latter he hired Mario Testino whose publicity has placed him among the posh realists' of fashion. His photographs now enjoy the status of works of art. The work of Terry Richardson, who worked for Gucci later, is more or less comparable.

In interviews, Ford is fond of stressing his commercial taste. His goal at the beginning was to turn Gucci into a sort of modern European Ralph Lauren, a complete lifestyle in which glamour, luxury and sex would call the tune. This turned out to be a golden formula, representing the antithesis of nineties minimalism with a strong emphasis on the sex component.

Gucci evolved from a company producing luxurious leather goods into a status brand for right-wing senior citizens and Japanese tourists, and finally into a symbol of hedonism associated here and there with 'football wives'. The question remains, however, as to how many successive revisions an image can undergo without becoming muddled. After Ford two more successors have taken over the firm's leadership. Since 2006 this

has been Frida Giannini, who was previously responsible for accessories. A certain change of course seems inevitable.

Gucci scarves, glasses and handbags are desirable things. The 7 August 2006 edition of *De Telegraaf Reiskrant* mentions a female passenger on a Cathay Pacific flight who refused to store her Gucci bag under the seat or in the overhead lockers. The police were called and the plane had to remain on the ground until the Gucci fan was removed, bag and all. Such a report not only confirms the image but also creates it.

On the official Louis Vuitton website you can read what the name is meant to stand for: quality, innovation, elegance and perfection. The visitor is then treated to a description of eleven different types of handbags and luggage items, all of them classics whose details are repeatedly brought up to date. All the types are referred to on the website as 'icons', which, together with the attractive stories, adds value to the image in the sense of qualifying visual elements within their cultural context. In 2006, the company asked nine artists to reinterpret the icons, a move that also turned the LV bags into cultural treasures.

In 1987 Louis Vuitton merged with the champagne producer Moët et Chandon, and was later joined by the cognac producer Hennessy. This alliance, abbreviated as LVMH, formed a holding company that now comprises more than 50 international luxury brands. The LVMH group advertises itself as 'patron of the arts and social solidarity', which apparently means that it is involved in art, supports young talent and devotes itself to

12.

13.

12.
Takashi Murakami for Louis Vuitton, pendants, 2003
13.
Louis Vuitton, shoe, 2006 collection
14.
Prada, advertising campaign, 2005
15.
Prada, advertising campaign, 2005
16.
Prada, advertising campaign, 2006

humanitarian goals. It is working hard on an artistically and ethically correct image.

The American designer Marc Jacobs has been artistic director of Louis Vuitton since 1997. His collections are fashionable, simple and luxurious. In collaboration with the Japanese artist Takashi Murakami he has designed pendants, for example, in the form of cartoon figures, executed in white gold and precious stones.

Yet Louis Vuitton's main emphasis is on its bags. There are a lot of fakes around, probably because the monogram initials LV are not difficult to copy and their presence can draw attention away from faulty details. Someone once sent Louis Vuitton the cover of a British magazine featuring Victoria Beckham with a Vuitton bag that was patently fake, upon which the company immediately sent her one of its bags with the comment that they thought 'she should have a real one'.

Such a gesture says something about the company and about the advertising value of celebrities in connection with a particular product (but it also says something about Victoria Beckham).

Prada, too, ran into financial problems, but it didn't solve them by bringing in a celebrated designer. The company was taken over in 1978 by Miuccia Prada, the granddaughter of its founder. She had studied political sciences and was a communist as well as a feminist. To begin with, she expanded the range in the 1980s with a series of simple handbags and black nylon rucksacks. These became a great success, in contrast to her first ready-to-wear collection (1989/90) which

was vilified by the press as too severe, too finicky and too plain. Yet the avant-garde appeared susceptible to Prada's anti-glamour, and there emerged a characteristic style and image of a new elegance without the ballast of traditional female role patterns and without postmodern jokes. As with Chanel, the ideal woman is independent and endowed with brains.

The Prada image has evolved from plain modesty to sophisticated simplicity, understatement and luxuriousness, with sometimes a touch of vintage. Garments, shoes and handbags are as attractive as they are useful, more contemporary than hyper-trendy. In advertisements and campaigns (by Glen Luchford, among others), the house style often features pale colours and models without make-up. The fact that the Dutch architect Rem Koolhaas has designed spectacular Prada stores all over the world lends an extra cachet to the image. In these palaces, the activity of 'fashion shopping' shifts from something unedifying and commercial to something with an aura of cultural importance, since the stores are also venues for art exhibitions and theatre and film performances.

The press regularly devote attention to the clothing and accessories of celebrities. Prada, it seems, is very popular among all manner of deities – and even with the devil. *The Devil Wears Prada,* written by Lauren Weisberger as a parody of *Vogue* and its American editor Anna 'Nuclear' Wintour, became a bestseller, while the film version directed by David Frankel (2006) received ample publicity. All of which has done a lot for Prada's reputation and image. Prada became synonymous with fashion in its ultimate, most

14.

15.

16.

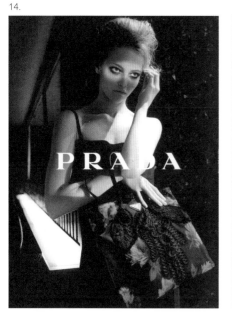

fabulous aspects. The title alone is invaluable, for who knows better than the devil what is intensely desirable? That touch of wickedness alone is enough to immediately inflame greed. The 'devil' in the film, played by Meryl Streep, is a powerful fashion divinity, superhumanly arrogant and demanding. Only the very best meets her standards, including Prada. Anna Wintour herself turned up at the première – wearing Prada, of course.

ENGLISH IDIOSYNCRASY

The general image of England is not associated with the sort of elegance on which France seems to have a patent, nor is there an equivalent of the famous Italian leather goods. The main thing that typifies Englishness is its own tradition, including the values, standards and sports of the upper class – and the often interesting reactions to these. Classical/class-conscious and bizarre/burlesque are two sides of the same English coin, as are the two fashion labels Burberry and Vivienne Westwood, which in many respects are each other's opposites while both represent something genuinely English. In both cases, the focus is on clothing rather than on accessories presented as cult objects.

Burberry started out in 1856 as a shop for outdoor clothing in Basingstoke and developed the waterproof fabric called gabardine, but mainly it became known for inventing the trenchcoat, originally worn by soldiers during the First World War. This practical, sporty and elegant coat became a universally loved classic. Nevertheless, at the end of the 1990s the time seemed ripe for Burberry to modernise its image. Under the direction of the American chief executive Rose Marie Bravo the age of the average Burberry customer was lowered by 30 years. She introduced Burberry Prorsum (from the Latin for 'forward') and hired the celebrity photographer Mario Testino for advertising campaigns that featured Kate Moss.

Kate Moss herself has a strong fashion image, posing for various advertising campaigns and fashion spreads. In 2005, the British magazine *Glamour* voted her the world's best dressed woman, and in 2006 she was acclaimed best dressed person of the year by *Vanity Fair*. The fact that she is also English goes well with Burberry's image, where Englishness is translated into three different lines: conservative, sporty (associated with the English landed aristocracy) and a hip London line. These three lines have prospered under the leadership of Christopher Bailey, Burberry's artistic director since 2001 and the person responsible for making the Burberry image fashionable. In his view, the Burberry woman par excellence is personified not only by Kate Moss but also by the model Stella Tennant.

To celebrate its 150th anniversary in 2006, the Burberry Icons Collection was launched. Typical, traditional designs were updated, including the trenchcoat, a quilted jacket and the Manor handbag.

Burberry's trademark Nova check is printed not only on all its clothes but also on accessories, including its collars and raincoats for dogs. The unrestrained imitation of this check has now resulted in over-saturation, and the association with pure luxury is beginning to wear out.

17.

18.

19.

'Intellectual, stubborn, witty, subversive, sexual, plucky' was how Vivienne Westwood was described in an article in *i-D* on the occasion of her label's 35th anniversary. The retrospective exhibition means that in the meantime Westwood's subversiveness has achieved museum status. Her collections are often inspired by English history and the monarchy – the Anglomania collections in particular – as well as by opposition to it. Conventional symbols are used in unorthodox ways. Not surprisingly, the house image is typified by the emblem of the orb, the symbol of royal power, encircled mockingly by a ring of satellites.

The Westwood image never needed modernising. Westwood herself is still fully active as a designer. Her concept of a femininity that is both voluptuous and aggressive remains topical. Other changes, however, have taken place. The 'mother of punk', who was part of the seventies London scene around the Sex Pistols and Siouxsie And The Banshees, now presents high-priced collections. In top place is her Gold Label, a biennial demi-couture collection which is finished off by hand in England. The less expensive Red Label ready-to-wear line is intended 'for the inquisitive yet reckless young woman'.

Westwood, however, is the least commercial label. There are no sacred cows. The text on her Cockroach T-shirt mocks the rivalry among fashion labels for the attention of consumers, comparing them with cockroaches: 'Consumers are like roaches – you spray them and spray them and they get immune after a while'.

Subversion remains the main theme, even though the initially raw form of rebellion has been transformed into sophisticated, postmodern forms of subversion whereby diverse stylistic elements are taken out of their context and merged together with the bonus of a dose of humour – an English equivalent of Jean Paul Gaultier. But, more so than in Gaultier's case, Westwood's subversion is connected with her own person. She likes breaking the prevailing rules concerning feminine beauty and decency – having herself photographed, for example, as a nude odalisque with white-powdered face enhancing her wrinkles, or a close-up of her face on the cover of the catalogue with slovenly make-up and a grimace that reveals her crowned front teeth. On being presented to Queen Elizabeth, Westwood appeared in an extravagant outfit. The press were confounded.

The Westwood image is recalcitrant, ambiguous, eccentric and not rooted in a long tradition like Chanel, Gucci or Burberry – at least not yet. Various accessories, licences and cosmetics have enhanced its reputation internationally. No 'icons', however, have emerged from her work, except perhaps the pirate boots with the twisted print from the early 1980s.

THE KEY ROLE OF ACCESSORIES

Certain components are apparently as indispensable for a top-rate fashion image as garlic in a pasta, which is why they are deployed by several brands at the same time so that their images overlap each other. Kate Moss, advertisements in *Vogue*, film stars and football wives with an attribute by house X, and so on. In recent years, elite brands appear to be seeking an alliance with

17.
Burberry, advertising campaign, 2003
18.
Stella Tennant on the catwalk for the Burberry Prorsum label
19.
Burberry, bag, 2006 collection
20.
Vivienne Westwood, photo for *i-D magazine*, 1999
21.
Vivienne Westwood, 2005 collection

20.

21.

visual art so as to culturally upgrade the significance of their wares.

For ordinary mortals, a dress by house X is usually not an option because it is very expensive and only looks beautiful in size 36. With accessories the situation is different. As far as cost is concerned, shoes, belts, glasses and sunglasses, jewellery and handbags are much more accessible. The size is hardly a problem and they can easily be combined with various components of the wardrobe, which means they last longer than that one eye-catching dress. Accessories are the democratic playgrounds of the most elite fashion images. A Prada handbag is more than a place for storing lipstick and change purse; as a tangible link to fashion's Shangri-La it is also a cult object, a fetish.

In addition, every look or style within a fashion image stands or falls - or varies - according to the choice of accessories. A traditional golden rule has it that a fantastic dress is botched by inferior shoes; conversely, a mediocre piece of clothing is improved by beautiful shoes and a splendid handbag. This rule is acquiring a completely new impulse through postmodern developments in fashion, whereby innovation is based less on pioneering constructions than on original combinations of styles and components, hence enhancing the significance of accessories even more.
An accessory can fulfil a dual function as both a visual element and as a fetish that compactly summarises particular values inherent in the brand concerned and symbolically transfers them to those who possess it. This is why fashion houses like to flaunt their own 'icons'. Such icons

lend themselves pre-eminently to such a dual function. They have a recognisable appearance, one that confirms the image of the fashion house, which keeps them from being tinkered with too much. The constancy of their form relates a quality over which the ravages of time have no hold - see, for example, Hermès' bag of bags.

The profit from accessories is essential for the fashion houses' survival. In this sense, every Chanel necklace, Burberry scarf or Gucci bag you own makes you not only a participant in the respective universe but also its co-creator.

22.
Vivienne Westwood, advertising campaign *Anglomania* collection, 2005
23.
Vivienne Westwood as odalisque, *Wild Beauty* collection, autumn/ winter 2001/2002
24.
Louis Vuitton, advertising campaign, 2006

22.

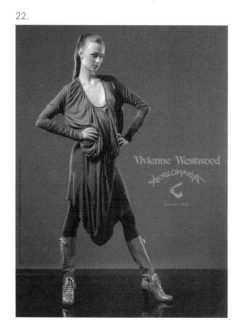

23.

LOUIS VUITTON

VICTIM OF BANALITY

THE SMELL OF FASHION

Virginie Viallon

01.

Perfume is worn in the same way as clothes. When Marilyn Monroe was asked what she wore to bed, she famously replied, 'Just a few drops of Chanel N°5'.

Many marketing and communications specialists have been surprised by the fame and longevity of Chanel N°5. What lies behind the success of that fragrance? Since Chanel was established in 1921, its fame has hinged on its ability to be both a fashion house and a provider of accessories (it launched a range of perfumes, jewellery, bags and shoes in the 1930s). The history of the brand, like that of the fragrance, is strongly connected to the personality and life – with its successes and set-backs – of Gabrielle (Coco) Chanel herself. To understand the reasons for N°5's long-lived success, we must briefly review its history and explain what sets it apart from the other perfumes of its time.

The choice of formula for Coco Chanel's N°5 was doubtless pure chance, but it was different in every way from all other fragrances. Its name was not just any number, but Gabrielle Chanel's lucky number. Choosing it was a bold move away from the romantic, sensual or exotic names used at the time. It immediately became associated with the personality of Coco Chanel, who always wore the fragrance and thus subtly advertised it and identified herself with the brand.

Its smell was also different from that of other perfumes. The creator of N°5 innovated to produce the first modern scent using aldehyde, a fragrance-enhancing chemical, as a base. Today Chanel continues to manufacture the perfume in the same way, depending on the constancy of its jasmine-based fragrance, a natural but expensive raw material that ensures the quality of the scent. Another original characteristic of N°5 is the square-shaped design of the bottle, an aesthetic object in itself that arouses admiration in the user and a desire to own it. It is surprisingly sober and unchanged since it was first conceived. It has even been on display in New York's Museum of Modern Art since 1959. Wertheimer, the company that has owned Chanel perfumes since 1924, attaches great importance to the quality of its products and ensures that the tradition is maintained. Is not Karl Lagerfeld's motto to 'make a better future by developing elements from the past'?

Another factor that also ensures the success of N°5 is the image of the women who wear it. Chanel fashion cannot be dissociated from the

02.

01.
Chanel, advertising campaign for Chanel N° 5 with Nicole Kidman, photographed by Baz Luhrmann, 2004-2006
02.
Marilyn Monroe and Chanel N° 5, 1955

Chanel woman. The image of an independent, resolutely modern woman made its mark as soon as it was created, and it remains inseparable from the brand's image today. Since the 1950s, numerous film stars from Marilyn Monroe to Catherine Deneuve, Carole Bouquet, Ines de la Fressange and most recently Nicole Kidman, have incarnated the fragrance. Over the years the brand has used famous stars to construct its image and that of its product. The movies have played an important part in creating the myth by using visual codes that reveal the body by means of attitudes and by casting it seductively. Each star has contributed to the perfume's image and perpetuated the myth of the elegant, refined woman with a strong personality. We shall see now what that star myth consists of today.

The success of N°5 can be explained by a combination of economic and symbolic aspects. Indeed, the perfume can no longer be considered as an accessory to the brand because it is the perfume that ensures a major part of the brand's success. There has been an inversion of products; haute couture is reserved for a small portion of the elite, but since the 1980s accessories have democratised the brand and its operations. If we analyse Chanel advertising campaigns over the past 20 years, we see that N°5 always comes first and the budget devoted to promoting it has continued to grow, reaching record levels in 2004. Brands have followed media developments and joined the race to fame.

The most recent campaign for N°5, held in 2004, is different from previous ones in that it is a 'film' rather than a mere commercial. Its movie-trailer style is visibly different, as was its huge budget – over $10m and a fee of $3.6m for the actress. Chanel's artistic director, Jacques Helleu, chose actress Nicole Kidman and Australian director Baz Luhrmann, who already has several major movies under his belt. This was not pure chance but a direct result of the success of the 2001 film *Moulin Rouge,* which starred Kidman. The making of Chanel's mini-film is comparable to that of a feature-length movie: 250 extras, six months' post-production and a symphony orchestra interpreting a piece by Debussy. The 'film' was distributed to the media in three formats ranging from two minutes for movie theatres in the US to between 60 and 30 seconds for TV. When the commercial came out, it was a media event. Information was leaked to the press in dribs and drabs and the actress was sworn to secrecy about the making of the film. The date and time of the com-

mercial's TV launch was even announced in the French press! Chanel's objective was to get back among the top five best-selling perfumes in the US. Only the future will tell if they succeeded. Since perfumes account for nearly half of total sales, one might well wonder whether the accessory hasn't become indispensable.

The perfume's symbolic aspect has been extensively developed by advertising to compensate for and embody its invisible nature. In the early days, advertising merely used the elements that contributed to N°5's originality, such as its name, the bottle, the brand and the star image. The perfume itself was seen as an object of seduction. It enhances the body and is a sign of refinement, and in this respect can be compared to a piece of jewellery. It gives pleasure to the woman wearing it as well as to those around her; it expresses a desire to please others. The olfactory aspect is, by definition, immaterial, so other senses must be called upon to make it exist, according to synesthetic principles. Wearing a perfume is compared to wearing a jewel, with the bottle being likened to a jewel case, thereby conveying its rare and precious nature. Moreover perfume becomes infused with life on contact with a woman's body. All its essences are revealed when it touches the

03.

04.

03.
Andy Warhol, *The Chanel classic bottle N° 5: The most treasured name in perfume,* 1985
04.
Chanel, advertising campaign for Chanel N° 5 with Nicole Kidman, photographed by Baz Luhrmann, 2004-2006
05.
Chanel, advertising campaign for Chanel N° 5 with Estella Warren, photographed by Jean Paul Goude, 2002

skin, and it incarnates the body's seductive powers. Thus there are two symbolic levels: the jewellery metaphor for wearing perfume, and the woman's body that will sublimate the perfume.

The myth of N°5 has been built up around film stars, but there has been a change in the representation of the perfume over time. Today, the product itself is no longer shown. Advertising uses a number of strategies to make up for its absence; the fragrance is evoked by appealing to two other senses: sight and hearing. Television advertising also uses narrative and the aesthetic aspect to tell stories. Perfume advertising relies on the visual enjoyment of the viewers, so the narrative is constructed in empathy with them and takes on board the audience's expectations and imagination. The object has been displaced to the person and universe of the star, which is a clear return to the era of the star system and its beauty icons.

The success of recent campaigns - directed by Luc Besson in 2000 and by Baz Luhrmann in 2004 - may be explained by the new vision these filmmakers brought to the product. Besson used the framework of a well-known story, Little Red Riding Hood, and a young Canadian model, Estella Warren. Both the theme and the photography, which are resolutely more dynamic as far as the body and postures are concerned, rejuvenated the product. The model is not a famous movie star, and the purpose is to seduce a new, younger public. The effect is compounded by the use of the colour red, breaking with Chanel's signature black-and-white motif.

In 'the film' with Nicole Kidman, the screenplay is a dual play on the life of the actress and is pure bourgeois Hollywood. The star is defined by the dialectic between the actress and the character she plays. The 'story' is about a famous dancer - a nod to the film Moulin Rouge as well as to the actress's own career - who disappears after being chased by paparazzi, meets a stranger and has an affair. After living a few moments of passion she returns to her life as a star. Luxury and beauty are the key elements. The star is the incarnation of the divine and appears to escape from the contingencies of time. Firstly, the heroine has one essential asset: a beautiful face and body that inspire admiration. Femininity is idealised in her face and body, enhanced by her blondness and immortalised by film. The body is glorified by dresses and jewellery against a supernatural backdrop of rooftops in the Australian capital Sydney. The extraordinary universe is also an

attribute; one might forget that this is an advertisement were it not for the ubiquitous Chanel logo. Several haute couture dresses by Karl Lagerfeld were created especially for this film, including the magnificent pink ostrich-feather outfit. Sound and image combine to create magic; the camera lingers over the dress fit for a princess. Another asset is the star herself and her personality. Her love affair highlights her purity of character and reveals her desire for freedom. She moves everyone she meets and she fascinates - by her professional life and by the way she hides her identity and her happiness. She dazzles the man she meets. Physical and moral beauty combine to create her personality. The background music by Debussy is pure romanticism, and yet the young man is not at the centre of her life, because this woman's destiny rises above her own feelings. In this respect she differs from many representations of women, such as the temptresses, used by other perfume makers. Here we have a woman who is faithful to the personality associated with the brand, the exceptional woman (with Coco Chanel as the model), whose individuality comes across more though her personality than through her body.

The star's final asset is social success. The last scene, with the star climbing the red-carpeted steps, evokes the Cannes film festival, the consecration of the movie star. She herself has become ubiquitous because, thanks to the media, she is seen simultaneously on every television set in the world. The actress wears a low-cut black evening dress with a diamond pendant in the shape of a number five. The perfume bottle may not be visible but it is subtly brought to mind by the Chanel pendant. It has now become part of the collective unconscious. Some researchers, including Remaury in 2004, see in the Chanel woman the mythical figure of the queen who combines talent and power, a woman who is independent but solitary in her success. The star's universe incites dreams and emotions in viewers, namely admiration for the life of the actress they idealise and identification with her social success and passionate love affair. The final image contains all the symbolic elements of the Chanel brand - haute couture, jewellery and perfume - and the star transcends the brand.

By hinting at an extraordinary universe, the scent arouses in women a desire to live that same moment and therefore to possess the perfume in order to live out that dream. The advertisement uses the eternal themes of beauty, love and social success to seduce the public. It is both the vehicle and the reflection of collective and stereo-typed values, presented at the end of the commercial as though they were a moral to the story: love ('her kiss'), moral beauty ('her smile') and femininity ('her perfume'). As Gilles Lipovetsky says in his book *La Troisième Femme*, 'The aesthetic importance of women continues to assert itself; the reign of beauty and appearance are part and parcel of contemporary cultural aspirations, and no longer only concern women's bodies now, but men's too'.

Chanel N°5 has succeeded in developing its image and that of the brand, in line with the social representations of its consumers, developments in the media and the democratisation of the brand. By using famous actresses, the perfume has become the emblem of the Chanel house for the public; it has been transformed from a mere accessory to a mythical object. For when we buy a luxury-brand product, do we not seek a kind of symbolic and social recognition? In buying a Chanel perfume we are recreating for ourselves that magic moment in the advertisement, enabling us to associate the star with the person wearing the perfume, if not the Chanel dress. But the real question is, are we buying a product? Surely we are buying an image of the brand, and through that a certain image of women.

References

Allérès, Danielle. *Luxe... Stratégies-Marketing*. Paris: Economica, 2003.

Barthes, Roland. *Système de la Mode*. Paris: Seuil, 1967.

Baudot, François. *Chanel*. Paris: Editions Assouline, 1996.

Laszlo, Pierre and Sylvie Rivière. *Les Sciences du Parfum*. Paris: PUF, 1997.

Lipovetsky, Gilles. *La Troisième Femme*. Paris: Gallimard, 1997.

Morin, Edgard. *Les Stars*. Paris: Seuil, 1972.

Remaury, Bruno. *Marques et Récits*. Paris: Institut Français de la Mode, 2004.

Vigarello, Georges. *Histoire de la Beauté*. Paris: Seuil, 2004.

THE LANGUAGE OF JEWELLERY

Marjan Unger

Jewellery consists of small objects, while the messages it can contain may be endlessly varied and often much greater than the jewellery itself. All human pleasure and pain has been represented by jewellery over the ages. Small is relative, of course, but jewellery is worn on the human body and its size is determined by the points on the body where it can be accommodated. It is always an added element; as soon as it covers the body we begin to speak of clothing, or of architecture if it serves as a shelter for the body.

A careful observer, however, can distil the same messages from architecture and clothing as from jewellery: display of power, pragmatism, enticement, the invocation of the supernatural, as well as the love of nature or of a particular person, grief, and the pure pursuit of beauty. What fascinates me is the concentration of all those messages in small objects like rings, necklaces, bracelets, belts and headwear. The limited size is an invitation to precision and excellence, to the heights of craftsmanship, but it also opens the way to impulsiveness, to ornaments that are worn for only a couple of hours. It's the masterly examples of the smith's trade, however, composed of long-lasting materials, that have stood the test of time and have imparted to jewellery the dubious aura of status symbol.

And indeed, in our capitalistic society it's quite common to measure the value of jewellery by the price that has to be paid for it. How expensive is an items of costume jewellery made of gleaming plastic and glass; what is an ornament made of rope and shells from Oceania worth; how much should be paid for gallery jewellery of blackened silver and hanging on a silk cord, made by a young designer; and what is the price of jewellery made of white gold and set with pearls and diamonds? The answers can be quite surprising, since the value of a piece of jewellery is not determined by the market value alone. In this text I would like to stimulate a better understanding of the language of jewellery.

PRIMEVAL TIMES AND PRIMEVAL IMPULSES

The most sensational news in recent years did not have to do with the newest rings set with coloured stones by Pomellato and Cartier, or a new youth culture. It was that the history of jewellery had been extended, and not by just a few years, either. In the spring of 2004, the first publications appeared concerning the discovery of 41 perforated shells near Bomblos Cave in South Africa that turned out to be 77,000 years old. Until then it

had been supposed that Homo sapiens, or modern man, who emerged in Africa 160,000 years ago, did not begin to ascribe symbolic value to non-functional objects until 40,000 years ago. That was the time to which the earliest rock drawings have been dated. Those 41 shells were found in small groups of varying numbers, and each group displayed a typical pattern of wear. Remains of ochre were also found in the shells, which led the scientists to believe that they had either been painted or worn against painted skin. There was no doubt that they had been worn as jewellery and that they had a symbolic value. With this discovery, the history of jewellery was increased by 37,000 years at a single stroke. Other finds show that in all probability modern man was already wearing ornaments before he left Africa and fanned out across Asia, finally ending up in Europe.

Shells are marvellous gifts from immense expanses of water, to which all sorts of values can be attributed. It is understandable that human beings would want to wear these solid natural forms as ornaments. And they didn't stop with shells. Beads and pendants found at various sites in northern Europe and the Mediterranean area and that date to the last Ice Age, ca. 38,000 to 28,000 years ago, were made of teeth, ivory, stone and antlers as well as shells. They could be divided into fifteen different sets of ornaments, which led to the conclusion that these were outstanding examples of symbols used for a particular identity.

From the perspective of the present day it is mainly important to know that the human need to decorate one's body is among the most basic of human impulses and that jewellery as 'non-functional objects' have possessed symbolic value since the earliest times. The term 'non-functional' is used by scientists to distinguish these objects from implements used for hunting, cultivating the land and preparing and preserving food. The makers, wearers and admirers of jewellery, however, have different ideas. They see decoration as a function. And they're right: there's an incredible amount of meaning hidden in body ornamentation.

So jewellery as a mark of identity may be as old as thinking man himself, but how old is the pursuit of beauty? When did jewellery become a means of emphasising physical attractiveness? The materials used in those earliest body ornaments suggest that a therapeutic value may have been attached to them and that they were seen as a means of warding off threatening natural phenomena. Since the earliest times, people have been confronted by the vulnerability and finitude of earthly existence; they transformed their hopes and fears into survival strategies, religion, lifestyles and community relations. Jewellery and other kinds of body ornamentation that have survived the test of time reveal a richly varied picture, but only a few pieces yield up their meaning unambiguously. And it makes your head spin when you think that of all those messages in the jewellery that have been lost over the centuries.

VOCABULARY AND GRAMMAR

If you regard all the jewellery that was ever made as a collection of statements, a vocabulary, is there also a grammar that imparts sense and coherence to this vocabulary and turns it into a language?

In specialist literature, jewellery is described, almost without exception, in terms of style history based on the pieces that have been preserved, ascribed to the great jewellers and enlivened with anecdotes about the illustrious persons who wore it. The ruthless struggle to obtain gold and diamonds does elicit a rather critical response from the profession, but hardly any attempt has been made to come up with a comprehensive theory. Quite the opposite has occurred with fashion, even though jewellery or ornamentation preceded all forms of clothing and fashion.

In 1930 John Carl Flügel published 'The Psychology of Clothes', the result of his research on the fundamental question why people wear clothes. He argued that the need to decorate one's own body was the most important motive, and that this was balanced by the notion of modesty. Protection was less important than the duality between decoration and modesty. Later researchers came up with the struggle for status and the need for decoration and protection, in which status was to be seen once again as bi-polar: as a way of distinguishing oneself from others and of affirming one's relationship to others. There could be no finer step towards a grammar for the language of jewellery.

Important building materials for forming a theory of clothing and fashion have also been trotted out from the fields of economics and the social sciences. In 1899, the American Thorstein Veblen published his 'Theory of the Leisure Class', in which he laid the foundations for a critical approach to consumerism. He analysed the process of fashion, the constant craving for innovation, as a manifestation of the money-based culture. There was a rich upper crust who were able to dress and decorate themselves with so much refinement that anyone could tell from a single glance that they never had to do a lick of work. And that by the time their social and financial inferiors had adapted the most important features of their clothing and decoration, the rich (with the help of their suppliers of clothing and ornaments) would already have been coming up with something else. Veblen's theory still holds true for the most part, and jewellery and other kinds of decoration can once again easily be included in that theory.

Anthropology has also provided important material for a better understanding of the ornamental additions to the human body. A number of cultural anthropologists have made good attempts to interpret the language of decoration. This has produced some splendid images, especially in the past 25 years with the books by Angela Fischer, which have been inspirational for many fashion and jewellery designers. It is clear that all the admirable and less admirable human character traits – such as providing love and care, cherishing hope, allaying fear, creating illusion and succumbing to enchantment, along with traits such as vanity, gluttony, envy and the desire to dominate others – have always resulted in wearable attributes, in decoration.

If we add the best of these studies to the history of jewellery as it has been written up until today, we find ourselves with the basis for a fine theory of jewellery. In my estimation, the most important impulse in this direction was the exhibition (and accompanying publication) entitled 'Sieraad Symbool Signaal' (Jewellery Symbol Signal) by Jan Walgrave of Antwerp, 1995. Walgrave showed unequivocally that the language of jewellery is uncommonly fascinating and versatile. Nevertheless, fashion and jewellery are still regarded as two different worlds that have very little in common and are sometimes even outright hostile to each other.

Yet all this suggests that fashion has always served as the best guide for a better understanding of the language of jewellery, and not only as far as theory formation is concerned. The full meaning of jewellery is not revealed unless it is worn, and there, too, clothing and fashion both provide helpful hints.

JEWELLERY AND FASHION

I'm equally fond of both subjects. Fashion for me symbolises the lust for life, the impulse to crawl out of your warm bed in the morning (I readily admit that fashion is something one can afford only if there's an equivalent to a warm bed at hand).

When I try to imagine fashion, I don't so much see skirts and pants or pretty dresses. Fashion for me is an abstraction. Fashion is light, it swirls in front of you and usually at such a height that you can't get close to it. Even if you're able to buy that pretty dress and you look good in it, the satisfaction is brief and possession of the dress becomes a seed of longing for something that you still *cannot* have. It is in fashion that the techniques of temptation have reached their ultimate perfection.

Jewellery has much more to do with possession, with memories of moments and certain people. Even the bracelet of daisies that can be braided anew every summer has to do with a memory of a sunny activity. A ring you receive from someone whom you really care about is something you wear regardless of the fashion of the moment. Jewellery, like vast compilations of messages, is heavy – figuratively and often literally. Jewellery, unlike fashion, cannot be an expression of its time, of the longing to create something that has never existed before. Despite all the meanings that designers and other creators invest in it, jewellery usually does not acquire significance for the wearer until the moment the ring is slipped on the finger or the necklace placed around the neck. In principle this makes jewellery much more able to resist the passing of time than fashion.

It is in this polarity that the uneasy relationship between jewellery and fashion lies, I believe. Valuable and stylish jewellery is worn on clothing that can best be described as conventional. Beautiful, fashionable suits that bear the signature of leading designers are combined with inconsequential little fake gold necklaces.

Yet excellent connections can be made between fashion and jewellery. Many's the time that jewellery has formed an integral part of a particular fashion statement by accenting an important aspect of that statement and by confirming the statement's features in terms of colour and style. Jewellery and other accessories are utilised to direct the eye to distinctive parts of the body, whether clothed or not. It's no accident that women wear most of their jewellery around the face, on the chest and on active parts of the body like hands and wrists, and that men often place valuable attributes on the chest and stomach, which is appropriate for macho behaviour. Take the watch chain that men of rank used to drape over their waistcoat, often across a portly belly, in which pulling out the watch was a reference to the lower part of that belly. Or take the 'devant de corsage' of the seventeenth and eighteenth centuries: a heavy, symmetrical ornament that needed a corseted torso to be fastened to, thereby drawing attention to the breasts beneath this armour. Jewellery has gone along with all the distortions of the body prescribed by the current fashion. In the 1920s it became fashionable to wear a coronet or headband low over the forehead as an integral part of the straight up-and-down if not distinctly flat fashion of those years. It was a trend which even a practical and somewhat older woman such as our Queen Wilhelmina, the highest-place lady in the Netherlands, was guilty of following.

The Netherlands is a strange country as far as the culture of jewellery is concerned. For centuries the Dutch were cursed with a resistance to dis-

02.
Wilhelmina and Hendrik, silver bridal couple, 1926

playing prosperity on the body. Then 'pillarisa-tion' – denominationalism along religious and po-litical lines – began to crumble and rising con-sumerism caused the resistance to ostentatious ornamentation to disappear. Decoration of the body was on the rise and the borders between the three most important poles in the contemporary jewellery market – author's jewellery, jeweller's jewellery and fashion jewellery or accessories – gradually became blurred. Yet this three-way di-vision does give us something to go on as we ex-plore this idea.

AUTHOR'S JEWELLERY

It's strange but true that the relationship between fashion and jewellery is especially troubled in the world of design. The egos of jewellery designers and fashion designers do not suffer each other gladly in the struggle for the consumer's attention and euros.

Among both the younger and the more well-established jewellery designers today we see a great variety of materials: a relatively large amount of textile, from old blankets to cheery strips of silk; rope; leather; all manner of little stones, from pebbles to glass; and various kinds of metals, including a lot of silver. Relatively new materials such as synthetics have a history in jewellery design that is almost as old as the syn-thetics themselves. Templates and mouldable ma-terials are used a great deal. Found objects are very much in demand. As for forms, allegiance is still paid to the basics; necklaces are favourites because you can let your imagination go wild, but rings, bracelets and earrings are still popular. Nothing really changes very much in the jewellery trade as far as basic forms and materials are con-cerned.

Jewellery designers usually work alone. They have to survive at a time when personal expres-sion has been elevated to the absolute norm and individualism is reigning supreme. Perhaps that's why jewellery designers don't easily pick up on widespread, contemporary developments and in-corporate them into their work. Individualism has become the prevailing standard, and its value is mainly determined by the meanings imposed on the work by the maker. It is impossible to enumer-ate all the meanings that have been expressed by means of this jewellery in the past twenty-five years or so. Symbolism arises from the use of nar-rative elements, from pure form, from the combi-nation of materials and from the inclusion of fa-miliar features that refer to another use and other

03.
Gijs Bakker, stovepipe necklace and bracelet, 1967
04.
Gem Kingdom, pendant worn by model, 1990
05.
Ted Noten, *Ageeth's Bruidsschat* (Ageeth's Dowry), 58 gold rings and string of pearls in acrylic resin, 1998

times. By placing meaning above material value, jewellery designers set themselves against the notion of jewellery as status symbol, as a combination of precious metals and stones, although most honest craftsmen in the trade will hasten to admit that highly exclusive status symbols are created with these small specimens of personal expression.

What I regard as a positive development within the whole design community at the moment is that young and not so young designers are again willing to relate their work to the world. They are responding in their work to all the exciting and sometimes threatening changes taking place in society, culture, politics, economics and science. I believe that the time of elevating extreme individualism and pure ego documents to the level of

products has peaked. The chance that this jewellery will link up with fashion in terms of design, either with the big designers or within the growing number of niches in the trade, is thereby increasing.

JEWELLER'S JEWELLERY

The jewellers' vocabulary is anchored in gold and precious stones, with diamonds as queen. The strict definition of a piece of jewellery is an expensive ornament made of precious metal in which one or more precious stones are incorporated. Jewellery is a much more general concept that in principle stands for a wide range of decorative additions to the human body, whether expensive or not. The notion of 'expensive' in connection with jewellery is also to be interpreted

05.

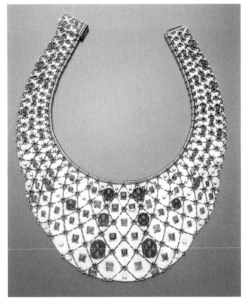

06.
Cartier, 18-carat gold necklace encrusted with jewels, 1945
07.
Duchess of Windsor wearing the gold necklace, 1940s
08.
Joseph Krantzinger, Marie-Antoinette, 1769

much more broadly than in relation to precious metals and precious stones. What is 'expensive' is determined by scarcity, which can differ depending on the place and time. For centuries, shells and glass beads were more expensive in Central Africa than the gold that was mined there.

It will not be surprising to learn that jewellers prefer to avoid the unsettling questions concerning precious metals and stone, nor do they have any problem with the jewel as the quintessential status symbol. This point of view is articulated and disseminated with the greatest conviction at places where differences in social standing are still very important and financial status is the measuring rod by which those differences are made known. The houses that are responsible for the most beautiful jewellery and that set the international tone are located in Paris, London, Rome, Hong Kong, Tokyo, New York and Los Angeles. Major houses like Cartier, Van Cleef and Arpels, Boucheron, Bulgari, Tiffany & Co., and people like Harry Winston, the 'King of the Stones', started out in one of these cities and established branches in the others. The crowning achievements of these houses have often provided the impulse for fashion jewellery of less precious composition.

The market value of jewellery is determined first of all by the market value of its stones and precious metal and only then by the design. In the case of the various colours of gold and of silver and platinum, the market value is determined by the weight and content of the metal. In the case of stones, the value is determined by the hardness, clarity, size and cut. Much expensive jewellery is destined for the scrap heap; the stones are tapped loose and placed in a new, more fashionable setting. The gold or platinum is melted down, a process that has been applied for centuries. What fascinates me is that every piece of jewellery made of precious metal that comes into your hands may contain gold once worn by Cleopatra, Hadrian, Marie-Antoinette or some other illustrious historical figure.

Jeweller's jewellery is regarded as an investment. As a result, conservatism is the norm in this part of the jewellers' trade and forms almost never change, especially when it comes to chains or what I call 'gold by the metre'. I have a soft spot in my heart for chains because even the smallest units, the links, are something from which a portrait of an age can be distilled. The result of that conservatism is that the visit to the jeweller once again becomes the norm for life's most important

rituals; that is where wedding rings are purchased, crosses for one's First Communion, a gold watch for an anniversary and a string of pearls or some other classical piece of jewellery for special moments such as a marriage proposal, the birth of a baby or sudden commercial gain. There's no need to search for a direct connection with fashion here.

There is a relationship between very expensive jewellery and fashion. The big jewellery houses of today are businesses that are directed in a way comparable to that of the most important fashion houses, certainly when it comes to public relations. Their clientele can afford the best in both worlds, and it goes without saying that jewellers attune their collections to developments in the most expensive fashion segment. Right now this is reflected in the use of many different colours of stones in a single ring of necklace. The discrepancy between the strongest examples of jeweller's work and fashion only arises with the passing of time. Expensive jewels are never cast aside. They're saved, while clothing that goes out of fashion disappears into the back of big walk-in closets or is otherwise disposed of. Jewellery with a sentimental value in particular is combined over and over again with new fashion and clothing.

The plus side of wearing precious metals is that despite all the inherent negative aspects the body tolerates it and it does not cause any reactions to the skin or airways. This is why the wearing of precious metals is connected to certain offices such as the papal ring, the crown of a secular ruler and the mayoral chain of office.

FASHION JEWELLERY, ETHNIC JEWELLERY AND ANTIQUES

The essential purpose of fashion jewellery is to serve fashion. Some of this jewellery is no more than a colour accent. Other fashion jewellery is more complex in design, and its glass stones and cheap metal alloys refer to precious jewels. Fashion jewellery therefore suffers from the prejudice that it is fake. This notion originated with prominent Paris fashion designers like Chanel and Elsa Schiaparelli, who in the 1920s came out with jewellery under their name that gave their clothing exactly the accent it needed. They used glass stones, fake pearls and sometimes new synthetic materials, although Chanel herself happily combined her real jewellery with what was called her 'costume jewellery'. The language of fashion jewellery takes on an uncommonly fascinating tone,

10.

09.
Collection of heart-shaped pendants, 1835-1855
10.
Papal ring of Pope Pius II (Aeneas Sylvius Piccolomini), 1458-1464
11.
Mobile telephone from Samsung with matching pendant by Rodrigo Otazu, 2006

11.

12.

13.

however, when you include the history of jewellery made from materials that are soft and natural, or from other materials that are usually accessible such as wood, porcelain, bone, ivory, tortoise shell, hair, textile fibres, leather, fur, flowers and non-precious stone. This quickly puts you in a grey area. Where does jewellery end and accessories and processed clothing begin? In a typical trend of the moment, gold on black, hardly any distinction can be made between make-up, embroidery with metal thread, sewn-on sequins and other ornaments and trinkets, whether of real gold or not.

It is probably under the influence of fashion, and implicitly of the current times, that two other categories of jewellery have come to receive so much attention: ethnic jewellery and antique pieces.

In the search for authenticity in a world rooted in illusion and overconsumption, many fashion designers from Paris, Milan or New York draw from local traditions. They seek inspiration in clothing that is stiff with ornamentation (whether it consists of jewellery or of other additions such as embroidery or beadwork is neither here nor there) that gives the impression of being part of a long tradition. The sympathetic opposite of this development is that designers from non-fashion circles the world over can also secure a place in the spotlights if they are able to come up with a suitable form for their own cultural roots. I'm inclined to think that the political tensions in the world, which are related to race and religious convictions, are resulting in a widespread game of ethnic accents in clothing, probably as a way of channelling feelings of anxiety and unrest.

Notions like 'natural' and 'homemade' play a central role in ethnic jewellery. Jewellery made of shells, beads and animal teeth, held together with coconut or banana fibres and braided with stones, feathers and brightly coloured balls of wool, are systematically called 'ethnic' in fashion circles, regardless of where they come from. Often they indeed are the products of cottage industries in Third World countries, an economic factor in those countries on which lives depend.

The thing that is attractive about this ethnic jewellery is a certain virility, or the reference to the magnificent colour display of male animals who want to make an impression on their often greyer females because they need the females to reproduce. Those who wear original pieces that were not made as souvenirs for the tourist trade may be unintentionally hanging more on their bodies than they intended to. Two terms are relevant in this connection: 'amulet' and 'talisman'. An amulet is in principle something to hold oil or balsam for warding off diseases and other evils. Pieces of text from the Koran or other holy sayings are also sometimes placed inside jewellery. A talisman is an object that brings luck and is therefore often worn on the body. In Western thought, the talisman and the amulet have been banned to the world of superstition, but at the moment they are bravely fighting back. Esotericism and astrology take for granted the therapeutic effects of precious stones, often coupled with the signs of the Zodiac. This interpretation may also serve as a warning: that there are certain stones which should never be worn by people born under a certain sign.

With the growing interest in religious as a means of imparting meaning to existence, the borders between religious faith, superstition and magic are shifting. Whatever one's point of view, it cannot be denied that the whole range of philosophical and ideological beliefs have a decisive role to play in a great many of the emotional values attributed to jewellery.

The current interest in antique jewellery fits right in with this need for authenticity, tradition and meaning. In fact, at the big auction houses, a piece of jewellery will bring in three to four times its scrap value if the previous owner bore an illustrious name and attracted public attention with the jewellery. In general, however, a fine antique piece gives the impression of being a family heirloom, suggesting that one has inherited it and apparently comes from a good family.

This brings me back to one of the intangible values of jewellery that is independent of its market value: the memory of the moment at which one received a certain piece of jewellery and of the person who gave it. This can make itself felt for generations. A mother who gives to her daughter the brooch that she herself received from her parents for her eighteenth birthday is giving a piece of jewellery of irreplaceable value. Only when the emotions no longer adhere to a piece of jewellery does the antique become part of the capitalistic market economy.

THE MORAL OF THIS STORY

Many of the meanings attributed to jewellery are essentially moral in nature, which is not always positive by any means. Over the course of history, owning an overabundance of jewellery has been

14.

15.

12.
Traditional hairstyle worn by Songhai women, Bandiagara Plateau, Mali
13.
Traditional clothing worn by the women of the Ait Hadiddu tribe, Berbers of the High Atlas Mountains

14.
Girl with loincloth from the Ndebele tribe, South Africa
15.
Akkà pa-ri, feather ornamentation of the Kaiapó Indians, central Brazil

regarded as proof of frivolity and dissolute living – and not only in the humanistic Netherlands, where this principle was more strictly applied than in other European countries. In the Bible, jewellery is regularly held up as an instrument of the devil. The great whore of Babylon is described in the Apocalypse as follows: 'The woman was arrayed in purple and scarlet, and bedecked with gold and jewels and pearls'. This aversion to jewellery was especially true for the public display of this worldly possession; in the same Bible the woman is urged to make herself beautiful and seductive for her husband in the intimate sphere of the marital relationship, jewellery and all. Veiled women in Islamic countries still live according to this custom, and outsiders will never know what splendour lies hidden beneath those veils.

Despite all morality, the fundamental impulse to decorate one's own body has never really been suppressed. The sexual symbolism in jewellery comes in many forms; just take the snake as an often-used motif. A great deal depends on the way in which jewellery is worn. The naked woman, adorned only in jewels, is the perfect image of sexual temptation. It is by wearing those small accents that the sense of nakedness is increased and the gaze is drawn to body parts that are deemed attractive. In the West that is usually the neck, the breasts and the hips. But among African tribes, bodily decoration sometimes focuses attention unambiguously on the buttocks (the backside?).

A good grammar is complex, and in analysing the messages hidden in jewellery we are also usually dealing with several meanings at once, whether they have to do with financial status, other forms of power, religion, superstition, profane love and sexuality or other family ties.

For connoisseurs of antique jewellery who are not only familiar with the pieces that have been preserved but who also know about other pieces and how they were worn through paintings and prints, the appearance of contemporary jewellery and fashion jewellery is often a feast of recognition. It's unbelievable how many forms come back, sometimes still bearing a trace of their original meaning, sometimes entirely stripped of that meaning: the shape of the heart, Cupid's bow and arrow, the death's head and other skulls, the faithful dog and other animals figures, all kinds of flowers, the egg, the moon and the stars and all the shapes that symbolise luck and higher powers such as the cross, the eye, the hand of Fatima and the humble four-leaf clover.

We wear jewellery to accent our own personalities, out of vanity, self-respect or convention. We also wear it as a signal for others. In this regard jewellery is a highly refined means of communication. The question that remains is: who understands the language of jewellery? I must resist being too optimistic here. As a minor cultural phenomenon, jewellery has always had to suffer from a high degree of dyslexia. It is undeniable, though, that the language – jewellery itself – has had an unbelievably long history and is extremely rich in form variations and meanings.

But there are indications of an inverse proportion when it comes to the theoretical basis for interpretation, although this impulse, too, is still in its very early stages. One thing is certain: fashion serves as a good guiding principle for establishing that basis. The good news, then, is that right now jewellery is very much in fashion and that the language of jewellery is being spoken without restraint.

ACKNOWLEDGEMENTS

This text was written on the basis of fieldwork carried out by researchers already mentioned in the text, such as Fischer, Flügel and Veblen.

I offer my deepest appreciation and thanks once again to Jan Walgrave, Belgian art historian and researcher. In 1995 in Antwerp he organised the exhibition 'Sieraad, Symbool, Signaal' (Jewellery, Symbol, Signal), and in the accompanying catalogue he signed on to one of the first and most successful efforts to create a broader framework for describing jewellery than the common style history.

I am grateful to Hendrik Spiering, who in recent years has published reports in the science section of the *NRC Handelsblad* on recent archaeological finds and the related conclusions that can be drawn:

'Oude kralen in Blombos-grot wijzen op symbolisch gedrag' (Old beads in Blombos Cave point to symbolic behaviour), *NRC Handelsblad*, Saturday 17 April 2004

'Variatie in sieraden wijst op stamverband Cro Magnonmensen' (Variation in jewellery points to tribal connection with Cro-Magnon man'), *NRC Handelsblad*, Saturday 28 May 2006

'Oudste kraaltjes duiken op, 130.000 jaar oud, uit Skuhl' (Oldest beads appear in Skuhl, 130,000 years old), *NRC Handelsblad*, Saturday 24 June 2006

I would also like to mention Graham Hughes, who was responsible for the spectacular exhibition 'Modern Jewelry' in 1961 in London and who has had some useful things to say in various publications on the market value of jewellery.

References
Fischer, Angela, *Africa Adorned*. New York: Harry N. Abrams, 1984.
Flügel, John Carl, *The Psychology of Clothes*. London: The Hogarth Press & The Institute of Psycho-Analysis, 1933.
Spiering, Hendrik, 'Oude kralen in Blombos' grot wijzen op symbolisch gedrag', *NRC Handelsblad*, 17-4-2004.
Spiering, Hendrik, 'Variatie in sieraden wijst op stamverband Cro Magnonmensen', *NRC Handelsblad*, 28-5-2006.
Spiering, Hendrik, 'Oudste kraaltjes duiken op, 130.000 jaar oud, uit Skuhl', *NRC Handelsblad*, 24-6-2006.
Veblen, Thorstein, *Theory of the Leisure Class*. London: Penguin Books, 1899.
Walgrave, Jan, et al., *Sieraad, symbool, signaal*. Antwerp: Provincie Bestuur van Antwerpen, 1995.

16.

17.

16.
Pomellato, advertising campaign 2006
17.
Rodrigo Otazu, advertising campaign 2006

FADING BORDERS
JEWELLERY AND ADORN-MENTS AND THEIR RELATION TO FASHION AND THE BODY

Martine Elzingre

01.
Fatima Lopez, autumn/winter
2002/2003 collection show

I should like to start by reviewing a few general but important characteristics of jewellery in contemporary Western fashion, as well as the scope of its creation and function. Jewellery is a blend of technique, imagination and applied fashion arts. It was described as 'the most intimate of the decorative arts' in the catalogue for a 2006 exhibition of nineteenth- and twentieth-century American jewellers in Paris. But our purpose here is not to discuss jewellery as such, but jewels and their relationship to luxury clothing, their seductive powers and their presence, as well as how we ourselves view them and the effects they produce.

I would like to consider that aspect in the creation of jewellery and clothing that gives them their brightness, glitter and shine, but without confusing the jewel-object with the materials from which it is made. From a broad anthropological perspective it should be remembered that decorative ornaments for humans are related to the sacred and the afterlife, while also existing for pleasure, seduction and power over others. They may be made of earth, stone or glass; they may be animal, vegetable or mineral; and in certain contexts, precious ornaments have been – and still are – a means for capturing superhuman strength and transmitting it to individuals, communities, the chiefs who represent it, to supernatural beings or to monarchs in ceremonies during their lifetimes or through funeral objects after their deaths.

If we view jewellery in the context of contemporary Western fashion, we must consider Roland Barthes's 1961 essay 'From Gemstones to Jewellery: The Language of Fashion'. According to Barthes, modern jewellery has become secularised by its use of materials such as wood, glass and plastic. It has broadened its scope and been democratised by its transformation into a mere product. Today it is almost nothing, just a piece of clothing. 'It is no longer a stunning, magical ornament for the enhancement of women...it has become a part of fashion: the detail'. The 'detached term has been created (a pocket, a flower, a scarf, a piece of jewellery). It is the detached term that holds the ultimate power of signification. That is the how far jewellery has travelled'. Barthes' semiological method admirably pinpointed and clarified the phenomenon of the 'detached term' which, it seems, may be extended to all segments of luxury clothing today.

Another specialist, a historian, discusses a different context that may be complementary to Roland Barthes's analysis. Chapter five[1] of

Philippe Perrot's book *Le Luxe: Une Richesse Entre Faste et Confort: XVIIIème, XIXème siècle* discusses the simulation of what was precious and unique in many luxury objects. That was the revolution of the modern era that occurred in the mid-nineteenth century. The industrial revolution appropriated the image and the facsimile of luxury. Industrial production imitated hand-crafted objects and art became industrialised. Perrot stresses the importance of design and its teaching at that time, and he also claims that kitsch is merely a way of imitating ancient works by fetishing and stylising them. At the end of the nineteenth century, the 'aesthetic of the practical gradually replaced parasitical ornamentation'. But the 'marriage of form and function does not compensate for symbolic deficiency any more than for expressive overstatement'.

So what do we observe today? Has fashion inherited something of the transformations of the past? These include the fact that, since the mid-nineteenth century, woman has taken on many aspects of men's pomp and seduction that men no longer use or flaunt, including jewellery.

Kitsch exists in fashion, but it is not only that. In the creation and production of ornaments in general, jewellery design implies a specific link between fine art and the applied arts. How does it do that? As Florence Müller has said, fashion really entered the 'flashy era' after the first decade of the twentieth century. Fashion became revolutionary and changes occurred one after another in the 1920s, 1950s and 1960s. There was Chanel in 1926. A chain and necklace of gold and precious stones worn with a casual suit, a pleated skirt, a sweater and a jacket in beige wool jersey.[2] That was the Chanel 'look'. 'Freedom and deportment' as semiologist Jean-Marie Floch put it so aptly.[3] We might include Chanel's black beret with gold embroidery in the shape of a large brooch. Then the 1920s and 1930s saw the advent of the costume jewellery designers.[4] Even before 1940, Jeanne Lanvin was embroidering enormous jewel-like shapes on her dresses, such as the 1937 model with the bow photographed by Sarah Moon. 'This was when haute couture became absolute art, the "total look" before its time. Clothing extended to accessories,' wrote Jérome Picon about Jeanne Lanvin.[5] In 1925, the year of the International Exhibition in Paris, 800 people were employed in Lanvin's workshops. Then, according to Tracy Tolkien, the 1950s became the Aladdin's Cave of costume jewellery. Post-1970, jewellery workshops disappeared with the advent of ready-to-wear. But now we see how

Alber Elbaz is embroidering gems and paste jewellery on his Lanvin prêt-à-porter collections. The reason lies in what happened in the new post-1980s fashion, which demanded loud, decorative jewellery such as big brooches pinned to the rigid lapels of so-called power suits, as Tracy Tolkien observes. But power suits are no longer in vogue. The relationship between the part and the whole has altered and been used for new attractions. The jewel has changed its location on the clothed body and bare skin, and has acquired a revived quality.

Two things happened between 1990 and 2000. Young designers introduced craft designs that they themselves had researched, in dyes, pleats, a mixture of novel textures and embroideries. A great deal of work went into the detail and sparkling new effects of the ready-to-wear and haute couture collections of designers such as Darja Richter, Fred Sathal, Hoshiki Hishinuma and Maurizio Galante. And yet the sub-cultures such as the Rockers, Punks, Goths and Rastas remained vibrant, with their explosions of colours or immersion into black or metal. Embroidery has also made a comeback in the past few years: gems or paste jewels are stitched onto clothes in the most unlikely places and dimensions, as on the black coat by Yohji Yamamoto.[6] Clothing and jewellery have emerged in new or renewed combinations. The same is true of accessories, such as the 2004 Dolce & Gabbana bag with its large jewel clasp, or the simple scarf-necklace in gold mesh and diamonds[7] by Boucheron, the jeweller. Instead of creating jewellery, couturiers invent, design and make clothes with their own built-in jewellery – rather than a single jewel – and that jewellery also plays on bare skin. This was especially noticeable in Georges Hobeika's haute couture collection, while in ready-to-wear, Fatima Lopez created a gold and diamond bikini for her 2001 spring-summer collection and Alexander McQueen made a swimsuit out of gems for summer 2006. Not forgetting the single armoured sleeve in the Dior collection.[8] Or the gilt of the bells embroidered in Viktor & Rolf's 2000-2001 collection, which enhanced the visual pleasure of the garments by the use of another sense: hearing.

ARE JEWELS OUR MICROCÓSM?

First there was the 1960s revolution with Paco Rabanne, who used the reflection of gems, metal and light and allowed them to transform themselves into clothes. He created a famous dress for Françoise Hardy and the diamond makers' exhibition in 1968[9] out of nine kilos of thin gold-plate and 300 carats of diamonds, as well as a dress made of Tyrol gems for Swarovski in 1970.[10]

We have seen jeweller-couturiers, architect-couturiers, jewellers-turned-couturiers and architect jewellery designers. Couturiers call themselves architect-couturiers, or designer-couturiers. So what do we learn from the works of two great artists such as Paco Rabanne and architect Frank Gehry? Perhaps that they consider jewels, like clothes, to be the result of an 'experimental gesture' – or what Paco Rabanne called 'a fashion gesture'. This has probably characterised the entire haute couture era from the early twentieth century to the present. As Rabanne put it, the couturier is there to accomplish 'the first, experimental, gesture of fashion that will inspire the eternal feminine principle in its constant aesthetic renewal'.[11] That may explain why Tiffany, the famous jeweller who has been making 'lightening' heavy jewellery since 1889, has asked Frank Gehry to design a jewellery collection. According to Gehry, who is fascinated by shiny metal, 'The idea is for it to become part of your clothes. It goes back to the idea of armour, although it's more feminine'.[12] With this jewellery the ceremonial code is still alive.

And so from jewels to *Biji's*.[13] In 2006 we saw a single brooch pinned to the waist of a pair of jeans. Could this be a new phase in the union of adornment, detail and intimacy? Or perhaps it represents a new pattern and method of seduction and communication.

02.
Fatima Lopez, spring/summer 2004 collection show
03.
Paco Rabanne, autumn/winter 1994/1995 collection show
04.
Darja Richter, invitation to 1998 collection show
05.
Fatima Lopez, gold jewelled bikini worn by the designer herself during the show, from the spring/summer 2001 collection

02.

03.

04.

05.

Notes

1. Philippe Perrot, *Le luxe: Une richesse entre faste et confort XVIII-XIXéme* (Paris: Seuil, 1995). Chapter 5, 'Luxes simulés, luxes empruntés', pp. 139, 152.
2. 'Inventive Clothes, 1909-1939', Chamber of Commerce and Industry, Kyoto, 1975. Record of the exhibitions held at the Metropolitan Museum of Art, New York, and the National Museum of Modern Art, Kyoto. Originally held from December 1973 to September 1974 in the Gallery of the Costume Institute of the Metropolitan Museum of Modern Art, New York. P. 131 Chanel 1926, spectator sports costume in wool jersey, p. 133 Chanel, Fall 1939, theatre suit detail from p. 132.
3. See Jean-Marie Floch, 'La liberté et le maintien. Esthétique et éthique du "Total Look de Chanel"', in: *Identités Visuelles* (Paris: PUF, 1995), pp.107-144.
4. See the exhibition catalogue, *Les Paruriers de la haute couture: Bijoux de mode* (Grand-Hornu, Belgium: Grand-Hornu Images, 2006).
5. See Jérome Picon in 'Histoire d'une couturière, Jeanne Lanvin', *Madame Figaro* 18065 (Paris, 7 September 2002): 92.
6. Black coat with strass. See 'Style 15, Mystère Karl' in 'Mode hiver 2005-2006', a free supplement to *Libération* 7594 (Paris, 8 October 2005).
7. See Flora Desprats, 'Fleurs de Peau', with photographs by Alexis Armanet, p. 153, *Jalouse Magazine* (Paris, October 2002).
8. Winter collection 2006/2007.
9. See Lydia Kamitsis, *Paco Rabanne: Le sens de la Recherche* (Paris: Lafon, 1996).
10. Ibid., p. 191.
11. Ibid.
12. See Carol Woolton, in 'Jewel Purpose', with photographs by Patrick Fraser, *Vogue UK* (June 2006).
13. A large button-shaped brooch in brilliants or other coloured stones, affixed to the waist button of a pair of jeans. See 'Dessine-moi un bouton', by Florence Aubenas, with photographs by Sophie Calle, in *Libération* (Paris, 15 November 2006).

References

Barillé, Elisabeth. *Jeanne Lanvin*. Paris: Assouline, 1997.
Barthes, Roland. *From Gemstones to Jewellery: The Language of Fashion*. Oxford: Berg Publishers (reprint), 2006.
Barthes, Roland. 'Le bleu est à la mode cette année et autres articles', *IFM* (Paris, 2001) and 'Des joyaux aux bijoux', *Jardin des Arts* 77 (Paris, 1961).
Kamitsis, Lydia. *Paco Rabanne (Fashion Memoir)*. London: Thames & Hudson, 1999.
Müller, Florence. The chapter entitled 'Mode' in *Les Années 1910* by Anne Bony. Vol. II. Paris: Editions du Regard, 1991.
Perrot, Philippe. *Le luxe: Une richesse entre faste et confort XVIII-XIXéme*. Paris: Seuil, 1995.
Tolkien, Tracy. *Vintage: The Art of Dressing Up*. London: Pavilion Books Limited, 2000.

06.
Seredin Vassiliev, spring/summer 2003 collection show
07.
Darja Richter, spring/summer 2001 collection show
08.
Fatima Lopez, autumn/winter 2002/2003 collection show

07.

08.

THE HANDBAG AS SYMBOL OF EMANCIPATION

Martine Elzingre

01. 02.
Vivienne Westwood, spring/summer
1995 collection show

It is quite a challenge to suggest a point of view for analysing the current situation regarding the handbag. To consider the object raises numerous socio-historical and aesthetic, semiological, economic and technical issues, not to mention psychological and psychoanalytical ones. As moving objects, handbags play a role in seduction and image-creation as part of the 'image-medium-body' triad analysed by Hans Belting. Today all aspects of the handbag are important: its production, its use and its representational value as it accompanies women's clothing in the public arena. In fact the term 'accessory' no longer truly applies, for the handbag itself now plays a major role – or almost, be it expensive, ordinary or priceless.

A few preliminary points are worth mentioning when introducing the bag. It started life very recently, at the end of the 1930s. It corresponded to a new situation at the time – since become commonplace – of active, mobile women moving about town on their own, away from their homes and families. Moreover, since the middle of the nineteenth century women have borne sartorial seduction on their own – seduction and, for the most part, representations of social power, wealth and heritage. In the 1920s bags were mostly small luxury evening bags or clutches. The bag itself was born out of a galaxy of clothing and finery, one in which the feminine and masculine poles attracted codes that were both affirmed and changing. Since the middle of the nineteenth century these elaborately-dressed codes of female seduction have borrowed signs of social and sexual power (those of men) and condensed them into full-dress regalia by means of collars and pleats, pockets, buttons, epaulettes, embroidery, long dresses, volume, and all the frills, not to mention archetypes such as the tight waist. These codes were torn apart between 1960-1990 by the haute couture avant-garde, people such as Cardin, Courrèges, Paco Rabanne, Ungaro and Yves Saint Laurent, and later by the Japanese ready-to-wear designers.

Even though the handbag has become an integral part of a woman's wardrobe, it cannot be qualified by being categorised as clothing – it is more an outgrowth, an offshoot. It is an object carried in the hand or on the shoulder; it relies on our anatomy but creates a body movement, postures, a presence, clichés, an image; it is one or several models of seduction. It defies sociological and aesthetic characteristics, which for some derive from fashion. But it does not dress the body. Consequently it does not have all the character, signs and paradigms of fashion, and those it does possess are displayed partially or by reference. We should like to consider the bag outside of its limited function of content, yet without forgetting its role as a secret place, 'a transitional object of interiority', according to François Dagognet,[1] a private burden and also something that thieves lust after. We will simply suggest a few lines of thought and observations and elaborate on these at a sociological level in the broad sense of the term, the one that touches both the most and the least tangible aspects but without excluding the vast wealth of its image. What we shall ask is this: is the handbag a model of society and socialisation, and if so, how? Can one examine a bag in the way that Frédéric Monneyron examined clothing, using the anthropological analyses of Gilbert Durand?[2] It being understood, of course, that the couturier's imagination corresponds to the imagination of the society in which – and for which – he or she is creating. What diurnal cycle designed it, what nocturnal cycle shaped it, defined the materials, colours and motifs used, or its weight? One example: Monneyron qualifies Paco Rabanne's creations in general as 'heroic' and schizomorphic. Admittedly handbags today, even more so than clothes (for the body is not contained in the bag), make little sense without the image they represent and the scene in which they appear alongside a person. But the absence of a bag may in some cases be as significant as its presence, or the clothing itself. That is certainly the case of the famous Yves Saint Laurent outfit – a 'heroic' designer, according to Monneyron. The photograph he refers to is of a woman in an Yves Saint Laurent safari jacket carrying a gun and a knife instead of a handbag – after all, she doesn't need one!

Following on from the heroic structure of fashion design in the 1960s, 70s and 80s we had mystical structures, a confusion of gender and a juxtaposition of opposites. For a current example I would suggest two Vuitton bags, panther and plastic and plastic and panther, seen in advertisements this year. Or the leather, snake and canvas bag by Prada. In both cases, the bags bring together materials of totally different values and qualities. Some of these categories can doubtless be linked to the 'structure of the imaginary', as far as bags are concerned. Nicole Parrot divides clothes into two categories 'stiff' and 'cool'. The bag is a symbol of a woman's individual mobility, the walker who crosses public urban space, the walker as a social model.

In 1976 Richard Lindner painted 'The Hunt'. Lindner painted 1960s fashions, whose 'miniskirts, outrageous sunglasses, bag and boots heighten the painter's attention and mock ambient materialism and excess'.[3] This comment brings to mind 'La Folle Epoque' by historian Jean-Paul Crespelle about the first outrageously made-up socialite models of the painter Kees Van Dongen. Yes, there is a fashion for bags bearing signs that resemble those of clothes. They are sporty and chic, exotic, youthfully adolescent, ornamental and fantastic, minimalist, with attention to detail in the variety of embroidery, lace, mirror-work, borrowings from subcultures (rock, punk and Goth, with their rivets, rubber, black leatherette and vinyl), the Rastas and other movements with a strong identity. And the bag has a representational role in body language, as a social model on the unique settings of the catwalks and the advertising images in the press and on the street. One might wonder what the limits are, the ultimate models or ideals that bag designers aim for. What does the handbag reveal about changing trends in communicating social codes, past society undergoing change, or even the future? The designers of expensive, stylish handbags have reverted to ceremonial in their use of precious materials and unusual manufacturing techniques: the use of stitching, fur, metals (clasps, handles, chains), silks, expensive embroidery and lace. Uniqueness and individuality are assured - or imitated - by engraving the owner's initials. The volume and size of the bag may also be a distinguishing feature, just like clothes. And in 1993 the corset - that archetype of seduction applied to women - was to be found...on the sides of a Dior handbag called 'Admit It' with crossed lace and small zippered pockets.

But the bag holds new associations, at least when represented in advertising, which show that it may well be a model of socialisation in the present period of instability and mixed references. Take, for instance, a sensual, indomitable woman who lives fast and furiously, who scarcely holds back her emotions or feelings, and communicates intimacy in a rather novel way. This woman's gestures and posture are vibrant, her expressions restrained and her presence hints at transience! This is particularly true with Dior. Over the past ten years, this vitality was clearly present in Dior's Saddle Bag, and in 2006 with the new Gaucho Bag, where the shape of the saddle evokes a masculine function as well as technical and physical control. It raises images of controlling vast areas of land and cattle on horseback. This is the bag for a firmly established social being and master of a universe. The bag has a double pocket,

each with a separate key. We cannot assert, as Diana Crane did, that 'Fashion today no longer projects cultural ideals and sexual appearance and behaviour, it targets certain groups and lifestyles with specific product types'. That remains to be seen, for some ideals, codes and cultural models of appearance and identity, as well as social groups, are currently being transformed or destroyed and new ones created. Why then cannot Diana Crane's two observations coexist in the dynamics of fashion? How can a designer deconstruct a handbag? Perhaps with a very specific creative gesture, one that aims at tension, or perhaps from the temptation to find seamless continuity with the body and its habitat. That blending might be comparable to the form-fitting dress, where body and apparel are fused at skin level, a single volume of flesh, so beautifully carried out by Paco Rabanne in the past.

There have been cases where bag and dress have merged. Two designers have shown this in recent collections: Yohji Yamamoto and Vivienne Westwood. The bags are sublimated by the dress; it is the body bathed in waves of shimmering water that matters. In both cases the bags are wrapped up in the dress and made from silk in cosmic shades of night, water or sky. They are steeped in poetry and part of a narrative.[4] Is the bag seeking a new setting for its presence and seduction, or perhaps even its effacement? For in this era of technology, cybernetics and robots, the moving body - clothed, seductive and social - becomes more of an art form, a state of recreation; and its image will suggest departure, travel, exceptional or ordinary stopovers in unknown poetic landscapes exalted by the bag, as in the clever photograph by Jean Larivière.[5] It is a picture of a woman with her Louis Vuitton bag being rowed across a river the colour of a pale dawn. She wears a red dress, the colour of the rowers' trousers. The three images we have mentioned show why the bag deserves an anthropological approach to identify the models of a changing society and the structures they contain. They are useful images that must be put into perspective so that we may perceive the new paradigms and their specific quality that could be resumed in a single process, which, according to Belting,[6] is to utter the euphemism of the transience of the human body.

Notes
1. See the François Dagognet interview with Farid Chenoune, 'Eloge d'un méta-objet: Le cas du sac', in: Farid Chenoune (ed.), *Le cas du Sac: L'Histoire d'une utopie portative* (Paris: Le Passage, 2004) pp. 56-61.
2 See Gilbert Durand, *Les structures anthropologiques de l'imaginaire* (Paris: Dunod, 1984; first edition Paris: Bordas, 1960).
3. See pages 147 and 151 of the catalogue of the Richard Lindner, 'Adults Only' exhibition held in Paris from 15 February-12 June 2005, published by the Musée de la Vie Romantique, Paris Musées Editions, Paris, 2005.
4. See Yohji Yamamoto's Spring/ Summer 2001 Prêt-à-porter collection and Vivienne Westwood's Spring/Summer 2006 collection, page 3, note 4.
5. This photograph by Jean Larivière was no. 16 in the press file for the exhibition 'La photo publicitaire en France de Man Ray à Jean-Paul Goude' held at the Musée des Arts Décoratifs in Paris from November 2006 March 2007.
6. Belting's main proposition is that images in general screen us from the transience of the human body and death.

References
Belting, Hans. *Pour une anthro-pologie des images*. Paris: Gal-limard, 2004.
Chenoune, Farid (ed.). *Le cas du Sac: L'Histoire d'une utopie por-tative*. Paris: Le Passage, 2004.
Clemmer, Jean. *Nues. Paco Rab-anne. Entretiens avec Patrick Rambaud*. Paris: Pierre Belfond, 1969.
Crane, Diana. *Fashion and its social agendas: Class, gender, and identity in clothing*. Chicago: University of Chicago Press, 2001.
Crespelle, Jean-Paul. *La Folle Epoque*. Paris: Hachette, 1968.
Dagognet, François. *Eloge d'un méta-objet, Le cas du sac*. Paris: Musée de la mode et du textile, 2005.
Durand, Gilbert. *Les Structures anthropologiques de l'imaginaire*. Paris: Dunod, 1984 (first edition Paris: Bordas, 1960).
Monneyron, Frédérique. *La frivolité essentielle*. Paris: PUF, 2001.
Parrot, Nicole. *Le Stiff et le Cool: Une histoire de maille, de mode, et de liberté*. Paris: NIL Editions, 2002.
Purple Fashion Magazine. Fall-Winter 2006-7.
Rocamora, Agnes. 'La Femme des Foules: La passante, la mode et la ville'. Paper given at the CEAQ conference, University of Paris-Sorbonne, Paris, June 2005.
Vogue Italia, October 2006.

03.
Vivienne Westwood, spring/summer 2006 collection show

ODYSSEY IN FASHION 2001
ELECTRO-TEXTILES AND CARGO FASHION

Birgit Richard

01.
Philips, Lumalive technology
bodywarmer, 2006

CROSSING PAST AND FUTURE

The developments in young fashion today are marked by non-linearity, i.e. there are oppositions existing simultaneously. On the one hand, technology is making a further approach towards fashion in the form of 'wearable computing' and 'electro-textiles' while there is a tendency towards nostalgic recollection on the other. Retro-fashion opposes smart clothing in a conservative and preservative line, in one case in the form of bourgeois conformism in the Burberry Retro Look (Brit Chic), which is leading back to a tradition (e.g. Burberry and designers like Bernhard Willhelm, the creator of a kitchen and landscape collection) that expresses a desire for popular clothing and at the same time is free of technology. Also the second line of the retro look in the focus on punk during the eighties is contrary to the tendencies in up-to-date fashion and strengthens the aggressive (stud), the worn out and the shabby in its preference for things from the past. Here fashion has the function of an information system, recollecting the aesthetically suppressed. The fact that college fashion is returning to writing on basic garments (T-shirts and sweat shirts) is due to that function. A new aspect of that fashion is that there is no ambition to make any reference to brand names. This principle comes up in fashion on a regular basis as the symptom of a saturated market, and of elitist groups with a discriminating sense of brand perception who are striving to move from the perfect image of brand names to a seeming proletarian look: 'The rich can afford to look poor.'[1]

Basics printed in this manner are now also being produced by the famous fashion designers (initially by Helmut Lang) and correspond to the 'lomo effect' in photography: moving from digital perfection to machine-made, shabby-looking writing or apparent handwritten printing as presented in the collection by Louis Vuitton with graffiti by Stephen Sprouse.

Apart from basics, other fields in which there is an opposition to technology and its potential to produce an infinite number of variations is the sneaker market. Even here, there is a trend towards one main form (Puma Avanti or Nike Cortez, Adidas Superstar). Variations are produced by means of colour and material without changing the form, which implies an aversion to technology, unlike other high-tech models.

SMART FASHION AND INTELLIGENT TEXTILES

Technology determines the space of human everyday life, and not only by the existence of public and private rooms. It is also coming physically closer and closer to us. In the development of medial devices it occupies holes and gaps to become smart clothing, i.e. intelligent clothing elements. There is a difference between 'wearable computing/electronics' (Philips/Levis) and 'smart textiles'. The latter intelligent or microtech textiles can again be subdivided into technical textiles (special material coated in a special way to resist fire, to look firm, etc.), which have been on the market for quite some time, and electronic or reactive textiles (chemical, photochemical, medical) with a lot of new characteristics, from antibacterial and self-purifying properties to the ability to store energy (solar fibre). The transparent photovoltaic and washable fibre developed at the University of Stuttgart is a solar cell which is to be worn like clothes. It is made of plastic fibre, glass fibre and wire coated three times in amorphous silicon and its purpose is to produce energy.

The concept of 'wearable computing' implies that people can wear digital information and communication technology like clothes. 'Wearables', as understood by MIT and Neil Gershenfeld, are objects that considerably expand human abilities. Here, designers assume that the human being and his sensitivities are highly deficient and are in need of medial prostheses.

Wearable computers/electronic devices are either applications in themselves or they use existing niches for the integration of technology, whereas electronic textiles influence the design of the clothes and provide it with additional functions. Microtech textiles constitute a revolution in all clothing genres (workwear with special and protective functions, security, etc.) and at the same time create new ones (wellness/fitness, surveillance; Games and Fun). The functions of the new clothing are communication, location, surveillance, admission control, warning and climatic conditioning of the body. The second skin is going to be an intelligent one.

Intelligent fibre technologies are already in use. Their appliance has proved practicable in the special coating of workwear. Hardware for specimen 'wearables' like those produced in the scientific labs of universities such as MIT is far from being ready for the mass production of computer clothing suitable for daily use. A closer look at other clothing sections is therefore more promising.

Modern clothes seem to develop references and symbolic values: the integration of high-tech materials and trends called 'cargo', utility and futuristic looks that are mainly part of the youth scene, offer a pragmatic view of the future integration of technology. Analogous to the functional principles of clothing made for the special demands of cameramen or photographers, bags and pockets are included in the fashionable clothing of today that can accommodate these electronic 'gadgets'.

Object mobility began with technical-medial extensions like the Walkman and progressed from communicating, transmitting and receiving devices like the pager or WAP mobiles and watches such as Swatch the Beep and PDAs to online clothing. 'Wearable computing' turns media into clothing and clothing into media. The body becomes a transmitting and receiving surface. Technical preconditions for the acceptance and mass production of wearable media packets are miniaturisation, reduction in weight (especially concerning the field of energy supply) and networking abilities based on a common standard for data transfer. By standardising the individual BodyNets (PAN, or Personal Area Network) which emerge during this process, an invisible software uniform takes shape. The 'hardwear design' of electronic clothes is the only level to which fashionable variations can refer. New materials transform the material aspect of objects into soft pads or soft screens. The firm ElekTex weaves wires into polymer fibres, resulting in keyboards in jackets. There is also an effort being made to develop foil screens capable of integration. In addition, new materials water down the boundaries between hardware and software, haptically and optically.

As a prototypical example, the icd+ (Industrial Clothing Design Plus) collection - a co-production in 2000 of Levis and Philips - is the only complete product that has also been sold in a limited number. The two basic forms are the Agoon and the Courier jackets with an integrated MP3 player, a mobile phone and - according to the respective model - a headphone integrated into their hoods as well as a remote control.

The original concept of 'wearables' at MIT is defined solely on the basis of its function and does not have any intended aesthetic implications. Everything that is 'smart'[2] has no aesthetic form per se. There is an approach, however, that utilises the existing aesthetics of multifunctionality (from trekking), reintroducing loops for cable lead-ins. icd+ is linked to this multifunctional clothing. Conventional clothing elements like buttons will be developed to become input devices or microphones.

Even without the actual integration of high-tech elements, fashion styles in youth culture have visual expressions that imply smartness by including electronic 'gadgets' similar to the way the mobile phone became established in all social classes. What the low-tech and high-tech variations of wearable/portable technologies have in common is the possibility of wearing them as their basic principle.

WEARING AND BUCKLING ON

It isn't far-fetched to associate 'wearables' - the portable computers and the less burdensome objects worn as clothes - with the matter of transportation. Let us now investigate the development of containers and the different possibilities for wearing them. The shape of potential transport devices is closely linked to the different stages of human development. Babies and small children are carried around themselves and don't even have any containers of their own while being carried. The small male child first has pockets in his trousers as containers for all his personal bits and pieces, and later on he wears cargo trousers to carry any number of items. Small girls are given little bags to wear according to role expectations, and early on they get used to attaching things to their body. Their clothes have fewer bags because bags distract from their body shape. The older the children get the more carrier bags enter into their lives. In former days, there was the leather school satchel, similar to the knapsack for military use. Today there are school bags made of synthetic material (Scout) and rucksacks (Eastpak, 4you), sport bags for carrying short distances and the big rucksacks for travelling. The next step is that the bags become a private matter and an expression of independence. The bags are not controlled by the parents any longer; children pack their bags themselves.

There are different possibilities for carrying things and distributing the burden all over the body. Things can be carried on your back, in your hand, on your hips or on your shoulder. The bag is regarded as an accessory. Ingrid Loschek emphasises the trend-setting implications of accessories (the word comes from the Latin *accedere*: to

02.
Battery-heated jacket, 1968
03.
Nike, advertising campaign for
Nike+, 2007
04.
Philips and Levi's, ICD+ jacket,
Mooring model, 2000

05.
Hat with built-in radio, 1922
06.
Eleksen, *The Professional*,
messenger bag with built-in
iPod, 2007
07.
British Telecom, headwear with
integrated communication
technology

07.

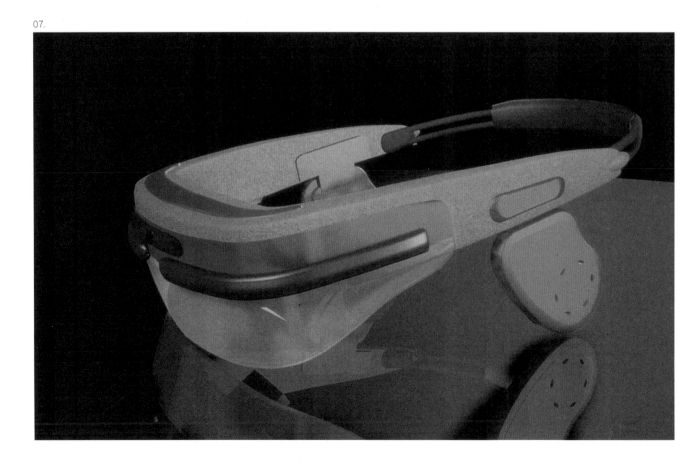

enter, to stand by, addition, equipments, attachments), which are even older than clothing itself and are by no means only casual. Originally the implications derive from the necessity of having collecting and transport containers with you while you are hunting and gathering food[3] and from the traditional use made by women for carrying burdens.

As there is no culture without some sort of container, the bag attached to a garment or draped round the body is supposed to be the oldest of accessories.[4] Shepherds and hunters use the *pera* (from the Greek *hippopera*, saddlebag), a bag made from leather that is put round one's shoulder.

Today there are subtle differences between the forms of containers intended for transport based on their respective function. Roughly these functions have to do with work, travel, sports, leisure and shopping in the city. There are the so-called dandy bags, the hip bags (from the eighties) or the small rucksacks (daypacks), the body bags to be tied crosswise (not to be confused with the bags used to pack up corpses in the US) and DJ bags (the DJ bag for the recordings), messenger, paperboy and cycle-courier bags. Typically, the most popular bag styles for teenagers are hung round one's shoulder or crosswise over the body. To wear the bag crosswise promises security (for bicycle couriers, for instance, supported by additional hip belts like those on Freitag bags). Diagonal binding also hints at military conventions. Cartridge belts are tied around the hips in a slanted position, crossing each other. The diagonal arrangement that is part of the military concept allows the wearer optimal access to weapons and ammunition. Young people prefer to wear things diagonally, not because they're more secure that way but because it opens up a new stylistic niche, which is to re-divide the body in a new way. In addition, slinging things crosswise round the body has infantile connotations: a kindergarten bag is draped diagonally around the body so the child cannot lose it. Crosswise slinging is much rarer in the grown-up stage; here the more vertical way of carrying things is preferred. Diagonal straps interrupt the lines of clothing ensembles, which are usually horizontally and vertically arranged.

A final important implication in the way something is worn is the 'attitude' of the young people, the way the bag is bound, its position in relation to the body, the moment of opening and closing it. Very often there is a redefinition of objects taking

place, as was evident in the comeback of the hip bag, which used to be the equipment of the middle-class tourist travelling to Ballermann on Majorca. The object with a negative implication is attached to the body in a new way. It is turned around backwards, thus contradicting the original function of carrying your belongings close to your body and within sight in front of you. The same goes for smaller rucksacks, the daypacks, derived from the big trekking rucksack. They are carried in such a low position that the intended ergonomic effect gained from being adjusted in proportion to the body no longer functions.

A redefinition of other forms of carrying and transport is evident in the adaptation of courier bags. Solid high-tech materials and signs of use give the pretence that the bag has already fulfilled its function. In addition, messenger and DJ bags by Freitag, Ortlieb or Aisbag have functionally motivated, often patented details such as adjustable clip clasps, Velcro fasteners that guarantee speedy access and security for the carried recordings, carrier packets or luggage. These fasteners have gained considerable importance as clothing elements and imply adaptation to function as a transport container or storage space. The clothes are equipped with Velcro fasteners, hooks, drawstring waists, zips, clip clasps and carabiners to attach objects to it. Other accessories that have changed function are money bags and keys worn around the neck. The latter has made a comeback as the lanyard key hanger.[5] Earlier, these were signs of being underage, which has negative implications: the money bag hung around the child's neck by the parents and the key dangling on a string is a visual sign of a latchkey child who is able to get into his family's flat on its own but whose possibilities of activity are limited because he is alone at home. These elements are transformed into stylistic signs of the autonomy of youth. The self-stigmatised 'latchkey child' wears the lanyard key hanger, which has a carabiner for holding the key and a band with a brand name on it for draping around the body or even hanging from the trouser pockets, whichever is preferred. Here the unintentional carelessness of not having got the key into the trouser pocket properly becomes a stylistic attitude.

The key chain wallet, a money bag on a chain, is a cult object used in different scenes: the Harley Davidson model moves from rock to the hardcore scene. The key chain wallet refers to the money bag that was once fastened to the belt and reminds us of the pocket watch hanging on a chain. Skateboarders prefer purses and keys fixed on chains and rucksacks as a functional solution, to keep their belongings from falling out of their pocket while doing jumps and grinds.

The youth scene uses and makes up new transport containers based on their activities and locomotion. Because young people very seldom occupy a place permanently, the 'street corner societies' consider the bag as an expression of mobility and flexibility, enabling you to carry everything important close to your body.

ELECTRIFIED CARGO CULT

The individual elements of everyday fashion testify to social changes in the transporting of personal objects. Originally, elements like shoulder bags and money belts mainly implied mobility and – above all – safety while travelling. First clothing was given a vaguely defined storage space. The so-called cargo fashion reutilises the former decorative bags, though at such an inflationary rate that they become ornaments again. In this connection another phenomenon is that small bags become independent and get detached from outer clothing like small money bags worn at the wrist or on the upper arm or legs. Cargo means transport and implies safe carriage as well as easy access to movable goods. In this connection you can speak of a futuristic cargo wardrobe that prepares men for worn technology. Bags are attached to every sort of clothing – shirts, trousers, skirts, shoes and boots – in order to hold potential electronic devices. To make this possible, objects have to shrink in size so they can be attached to the body. An example is the development of designs for telephones, whose miniature version moved beyond the normal standards of human scale, entering into the world of nano-sized quality.

It is not the miniature computer that is responsible for the integration of technology into clothing and thus for the concept of 'wearables', but the sharing out of function to a number of smaller devices. Levis and Philips also apply this procedure to the icd+ jacket, distilling the most important partial functions of everyday mobile applications such as playing music and phoning, though without having defined the market distinctively. The flexecutives of new markets don't necessarily listen to music, and the high-tech jacket is too expensive for young people.

In ordinary, non-electrified fashion there is the possibility of making technical upgrades by

means of functional 'utilities' and futuristic style. These terms come from haute couture or prêt-à-porter and are very much inspired by Prada's futuristic line. Here, waterproofed, hard-wearing high-tech materials and functional details come into play. The term 'utility' implies changeability of closure, such as the possibility of shortening long trousers by zips and changing them into shorts. The specific usefulness of certain fastener mechanisms or materials, which guarantee water-tightness in extreme situations, for example, becomes the aesthetic-formal expression of clothing. Outside the field of trekking, from which many elements derive, bags, zips, drawstring waists and Velcro become high-tech ornaments. Above all ornaments have an opening and closing function. These formal procedures become an artistic fastening practice that is connected to new noises, like the opening of a Velcro strip. Reducing the action of opening a garment is all too obvious and has to be seen as belonging to the field of infantile fastener variations. There are no bows to tie or buckles holes to find, but there is an easy way to fasten by means of a single movement of engaging or 'velcroing' or screwing up tightly, as in the case of republishing the Puma Disc.

The futuristic look and the cargo look reflect the changes taking place in the picture of the flexible human being. He is changing from the hunter and collector to becoming a postmodern nomad, a commuter and shopper, who is forcing the development of universal transport containers and at the same time bringing about a differentiation in bags for every situation. An important characteristic of changing bag use is the enforced mobility.

08.

08. 09.
Studio 5050, HugJackets, 2004

ODYSSEY IN FASHION 2001

Cycle couriers need bags that join with the body because of the particular transport conditions.

The human being appears as a homeless load bearer. The loads carried in saddlebags on horses and bicycles are now loaded onto the accelerated niche-man: the human being in general, and the man in particular, is turning into the self-serving pack mule again. Strictly speaking it was the woman who was the first pack mule. In early civilisations she gave men the opportunity to hunt while she carried the loads.[6]

Today, the flexible and communicating human being overtakes the machine-supported locomotive being in a state of raging standstill.[7] He only can carry modest burdens, but he is faster. Cycle couriers, for example, have mobile communication devices that use the niches set aside for automobile traffic. The cycle courier is the archetype of the techno-nomad who moves simultaneously in virtual and material places that intersect each other. To be more precise: he switches from the electronic to the urban sphere and travels through the necessary data streams with his body. The youth culture also takes on the picture of a flexibly communicating urban nomad who is characterised by the lack of predetermined fixa-

10.
Studio 5050, ClickSneaks, 2005

tion to a certain space. For those nomads, messenger and DJ bags represent a restless unbroken movement within the metropolis.

It is evident that 'wearable computing' is not going to have an influence on everyday life through the direct electrification of the body but through the symbolic references within current cargo fashion that offer the possibility of integrating electronic information and communication devices into the clothing. Even absolute low-tech phenomena can be symbolic signs: the retro-punk nomad wears his communicative messages in a way that is far from complex in the form of buttons attached to different pieces of clothes.

In the centre of the cargo cult is the mobile phone. In keeping with fashion it is capable of being integrated, changeable but at the same time focused on particular functions. The portable communication device worn close to the body is first of all hung from the belt as pure attachment and therefore is not integrated into the clothes. The mobile phone indicates the direction that 'wearable computing' will have to take in order to have mass effect.

The 'wearables' are meant to improve man by permanent net integration and by offering a new image of manhood that brings it more into line with cyborgs and robotics. Many of the projected fields of application, such as the surveillance function, allow the vision of a nomad to emerge that is flexible but permanently controlled and located. In this way the movement of the nomadic no longer appears directionless and unpredictable. The danger of a PAN (Personal Area Network) is that it will become integrated into bigger closed fixed net units that keep things under control (at work, for instance). 'Wearable computing' does not only sound like a heavy additional load, but it even impedes everyday life because the hardware has to be carried around.[8] However, the fashionable phenomenon described above includes possibilities of supplementing the clothes that only demand punctual integration. Wearing technology integrated into fashionable clothing is less associated with direct physical burdening and weight.

The evaluation of technology and its boundary with fashion are abolished at the very moment that technology is not determining the design and deforming the body but merely producing material to cut to size in a malleable fabric. This means of distribution makes intelligent textiles such as healing and communicating T-shirts made of solar fabric an almost imperceptible presence in our daily lives (like breathable fabrics, Gore-tex), as is already the case with the healthy ingredients in 'intelligent' food (e.g. yoghurt).

Young fashion has developed images for the mobile human techno-nomad, who learns technologies playfully without over-evaluating them. Here, there is an unwritten law dealing with mobile communication technologies that allows them to exist insofar as they are appropriate for the human body and as long as they develop the visual power of signs, which serves the expression of style. The aesthetics of style requires visible elements. In contrast to this, the developers at Philips and Levis have declared the computer, as an invisible processing garment, to be the aim of their efforts, and they want to integrate the computer into everyday life until it vanishes. It is interesting that both companies speak of computers but include mobile phones and MP3 player in their clothing.

Electrified fashion, whatever it might look like, will only be accepted if it meets the needs of particular techno-nomads. Since it is overtaxing for people to handle a phone and a car at the same time, intelligent clothing has to take human limitations into account and establish a balance between subjective and objective elements.

With the less complex cargo fashion the human being moves away from being 'metabolic transport' (Virilio) to being a data-loaded mule that attaches a mobile phone to himself like an attachment to an e-mail. Here, the human being is not outsmarted[9] by the intelligent world of objects; by integrating electronic communication devices into fashion he is showing a superior position because with such augmentation within the boundaries of human reality he is as capable of coping with the problems of mobile everyday life as a personalised and portable computer system is. With this, an e-subculture has newly emerged and has found its own ways to create images of the electrification of clothing within the boundaries of human limitations.

Notes
1. Angela Carter after A. McRobbie, *Postmodernism and Popular Culture* (London/New York: Routledge, 1995), p. 151.
2. See Morse 1995, 161, for smart food.
3. Ingrid Loschek, *Accessoires: Geschichte und Symbolik* (Munich: Bruckman, 1993) p. 6.
4. Ibid., p. 254.
5. For the terms of youth language see Birgit Richard, 'Computer/Mode/Musik', in: Trendbüro Hamburg (ed.), *Wörterbuch der Szenesprachen* (Mannheim: Duden, Langenscheidt, 2000).
6. For the connection with carrying and locomotion see Paul Virilio, *Fahren, fahren, fahren* (Berlin: Merwe Verlag, 1978), pp. 76ff.
7. Ibid., and Paul Virilio, *Rasender Stillstand* (Frankfurt: Fischer, 2002).
8. Steve Mann, see: <http://www.wearcam.org/wearhow/index.html>
9. See Ross's definition of 'smart': Andrew Ross, 'The New Smartness', in: Gretchen Bender and Timothy Druckrey (eds.), *Cultures on the Brink: Ideologies of Technology*. Seattle: Bay Press, 1995, 2nd edition, pp. 329-341.

References
Barfield, Woodrow and Thomas Caudell (ed.) *Fundamentals of Wearable Computers and Augmented Reality*. Mahwah, NJ: Lawrence Erlbaum Associates, 2000.
Gerken, Irene and Barbara Marken. 'Die neue Econony der Textiler', *Textilwirtschaft* 48, 30 (November 2000), p. 87.
Gershenfeld, Neil. *When Things Start to Think*. New York: Henry Holt Company, 1999
Loschek, Ingrid. *Accessoires: Geschichte und Symbolik*. Munich: Bruckman, 1993.
Lurie, Alison. *The Language of Clothes*. New York: Random House, 1981.
McRobbie, A. *Postmodernism and Popular Culture*. London/New York: Routledge, 1995, p. 151.
Morse, Margaret. 'What do Cyborgs Eat? Oral Logic in an Information Society', in: Gretchen Bender and Timothy Druckrey (eds.), *Cultures on the Brink: Ideologies of Technology*. Seattle: Bay Press, 1995. 2nd edition, pp. 329-341.
Richard, Birgit and Sven Drühl (eds.). 'Dauer-Simultaneität-Echtzeit', *Kunstforum International* 151 (July 2000).
Richard, Birgit. 'Computer/Mode/Musik', in: Trendbüro Hamburg (ed.), *Wörterbuch der Szenesprachen*. Mannheim: Duden, Langenscheidt, 2000.
Ross, Andrew. 'The New Smartness', in: Gretchen Bender and Timothy Druckrey (eds.), *Cultures on the Brink: Ideologies of Technology*. Seattle: Bay Press, 1995. 2nd edition, pp. 329-341.
Virilio, Paul. *Fahren, fahren, fahren*. Berlin: Merve, 1978, pp. 74ff.
Willis, Paul. *Jugendstile: Zur Ästhetik der gemeinsamen Kultur*. Hamburg/Berlin, 1991.

URBANHERMES
FASHION SIGNALING AND THE SOCIAL MOBILITY OF IMAGES

Judith Donath & Christine M. Liu

INTRODUCTION

Fashion is a signal of status and affiliation in a world of fluidly mutable social hierarchies. Social membership defines access to information, including information about new styles, new ways of dressing, thinking and being. When information flows slowly and social structures are relatively stable, fashion too changes slowly, over the course of years. Today, information flows at the global speed of the internet, social structures are highly mobile, and fashions change at an unprecedented rate. On the net, hit songs and news stories are the fashions of the online persona, the accessories of the blog and the homepage. On the street, styles of shoes, handbags, coats and pants change more rapidly than ever, but still far slower than their electronic counterparts, weighed down by their material incarnation.

The Urbanhermes project aims to bring the speed and intelligence of electronic fashion to the physical world by superimposing a connected and changeable medium onto everyday street worn garments. In doing so, we hope not only to unite the fashion worlds of online and urban but also to elucidate what fashion signals reveal about our technological culture.

Urbanhermes is a messenger bag designed to display and disseminate meaningful yet ephemeral images among people in the public realm. These images represent the daily zeitgeist; fashions emerge, grow and wane in popularity as knowledge diffuses. Wireless communication allows users to pass images from bag to bag, and proximity sensing adds awareness of others nearby who share similar tastes.

The goal of Urbanhermes is to enrich social interaction by bringing electronic fashion signals to the physical world, making it possible for people to express and observe richer, subtler and more ephemeral social patterns.

FASHION SIGNALLING

Most of what we want to know about each other is not directly observable. Is she trustworthy? Is he kind? Do you really like my cooking or are you just being polite? Instead, we rely on signals, which are the perceivable indicators of these hidden qualities of interest.[1]

Qualities can be almost anything: strength, honesty, suitability for employment, etc. We rely on signals when direct evaluation of the quality is too time-consuming, difficult or dangerous. A smile can be a frown of sadness, a wedding ring a signal of being married, and a big house a signal of wealth. Our language is full of signals, both the words we say and the way we say them. Saying 'Yes, I would like another helping of your tasty pasta' can be a signal of hunger or of politeness, and the accent with which it is said can signal country of origin and social class. Much of our communication, whether it is with words, gestures or displays of possessions, consists of signalling information about who we are and what we are thinking.

Signals have varying degrees of reliability. Some are quite reliable: upon seeing such a signal, one can be sure that the quality is present. Lifting a 200-pound weight is a reliable signal of strength; no matter how much a weaker person wishes to signal strength, without actually possessing that quality he or she will not be able to do so. Other signals are less reliable: those who wish to give the impression of having the quality without actually possessing it can imitate the signal. Most people who visit museums enjoy looking at art, but some who find little aesthetic pleasure in the experience go because they would like others to think they are the sort who does.

Signals are reliable when it is prohibitively expensive to signal dishonestly, but relatively cheap to do so honestly. Seemingly wasteful expenditure of a resource, such as energy, money or time, can reliably signal possession of abundant amounts of it. For example, displaying skill at something that took much time to master but that does not yield any practical outcome, such as growing a garden of bonsai trees, is a reliable signal that one has an abundance of leisure time.[2]

Fashion signals indicate affiliation and status in a fluidly changing social world.[3] The form of the signal changes while its meaning – the social position it indicates – remains the same. One must be able and willing to continuously learn about and adapt to new forms in order to keep signalling the same position. When information flows slowly and social structures are stable, fashion changes slowly. Today, information moves at unprecedented speed, social structures are highly malleable – and fashions are in rapid flux. Fashions signal information prowess: one knows what is next and is willing to adopt it. The difficulty in accessing the information, of sorting the good from the bad, is part of the cost that keeps the signal reliable.

Urbanhermes is a system for signalling one's access to information through a dynamic fashion object. Designing a usable, sustainable, and successful signalling system requires integrating critical social costs as well as the benefits that attract people to use it.

A SCENARIO

The day begins. Alana arises, makes coffee and begins browsing through her favourite news items, blog feeds and community postings on her computer. Her list includes relatively popular items as well as niche items. She reads a bit and wirelessly transmits three images to her bag: a new release's album cover from an experimental music blog, an image of a knitted Ferrari circulating around her crafting community and a photograph she took of Thom Yorke while attending a Radiohead concert the previous evening in the city. Downloading images to her bag is one of Alana's regular rituals, like figuring which jeans to wear, as she assembles her fresh images for the day. She sees it as having free reign in an enormous, ever-changing networked wardrobe and picking out what she will want to wear each morning. Alana displays the album cover on her bag as default, with the other two images stored invisibly within her accessory.

Alana heads out the door to work and waits for her ride at the train station. After a minute or so spent waiting, Alana's bag vibrates gently to notify her that someone in short-range is currently displaying an image that shares a common source with one of Alana's hidden images—the crafting image. Alana has the option to switch her display from the Radiohead photo to the Ferrari, but she first looks around to see if she can see who is displaying the related image. She soon recognises it, noticing a guy sitting a few seats away from her whose bag features another recent image from the same mailing list. She quickly assesses his character from other existing physical signals: his clothes, hair, face, posture. He seems like an interesting, artsy, innocuous stranger, so she changes her bag from the Radiohead photo to the knitted Ferrari. As they board the bus, her newly updated bag is visible to him. And to him, she is no longer a complete strange but a fellow member in the same crafting community.

Once she arrives at work, Alana switches her display back to the album cover. Grace, a curious co-worker, asks Alana about the image on her bag. As Alana describes the emerging artist, Grace is thrilled to learn about this fascinating musician.

Wishing to display it later at her reading club that evening (and impress a record label producer in attendance), Grace requests the image from Alana. Alana agrees and transmits the image from her bag to Grace's. However, since Grace's version is a copy, its quality degrades, being an artefact of second-degree from the source. Even so, Grace is pleased to have her own copy to display that day.

At lunch, Alana meets with her friend Hunter. As she says hello, she changes her display to the Radiohead photo since they went to the concert together. Since he had a fabulous time at the concert, Hunter recognises Alana's photo immediately. Hunter asks if he may acquire a copy of the image for his collection, since he didn't bring his camera but he'd like his bag to show that he was at the concert. She agrees and transmits the photo to his bag. He thanks her for the second-degree copy and dons it immediately.

Mid-afternoon, Hunter and Grace (who are unknown to each other) happen to be getting tea at the same cafe. Hunter wears the Thom Yorke photo while Grace has the album cover. Both of their bags vibrate privately, notifying each that someone in close proximity is displaying an image that shares a common social link with one of their own images. Specifically, both Hunter's and Grace's images have ties to a common intermediary, Alana. Grace doesn't recognise the Thom Yorke photo, but Hunter recognises the album cover from Alana's bag earlier that day, so Hunter realises that the woman in the cafe is somehow socially connected to Alana. Through the timeliness and meaningfulness of Grace's image, Hunter can infer more about Grace's place in their larger social milieu.

That evening, Alana attends a local live concert and espies another Urbanhermes bag in the crowd with an image of Matthew Barney's latest artistic work. Alana initiates transmission of a copy of this image to her bag, and this action creates an indelible link between her and this Barney-knowing stranger.

After the show, Alana logs onto the Urbanhermes website and reviews the trajectories of the images she was wearing today. She notices that Grace shared the emerging artist's album cover with the record label producer and the subsequent explosion in distribution after the producer posted the image to his blog. Alana received a friendly e-message from Jenn (the stranger at the concert) who wrote to anyone who has adopted her image to unearth possible fellow followers of Matthew Barney. As the images in Alana's collection are designed to expire after a certain brief lifespan, she is prepared to replenish her accessory with fresh images for the next day, or possibly the next hour.

The time she spends acquiring new displays signals her commitment to fashion; the content of the displays and the trajectory of their adoption are signals of her affiliations and her place in the social world.

THE PHYSICAL FORM

Although the form factor of Urbanhermes could potentially take many shapes (e.g. garment, jewellery, belt), we chose to implement this prototype as a simple, practical messenger bag. Unisex and minimal in design, it attempts to be accessible and attractive to people of all sexes, ages, backgrounds, etc. We did not want distractions of style or aesthetics to impede universal acceptance. Its use as an accessory gives the wearer freedom to take it up or remove it as desired (as opposed to a more integral article of clothing, such as pants, which cannot be removed unreservedly). This control also extends to the physicality of the bag, whether it is worn facing in or out, styled to contrast or complement the ensemble, or layered under or over various stratums of apparel.

The external bag is conventionally constructed, patterned and sewn from coloured felt. The felt was chosen as a suitable material because it is soft yet sturdy, playful yet universal, and because it establishes a simplicity that belies its more complex role as something more 'futuristic'. Established as a messenger bag, the form is generic to accommodate both male and female users, and its dimensions and proportions are appropriately balanced for most shapes and sizes. The flap of fabric overlapping the front part of the bag is designed to hold and secure the separate computational component, with its screen and buttons visible and accessible from the outside.

Additionally, an urban environment's prevalence of on-foot mobility gives way to nomadic inclinations. One carries a bag from one point to another, from home to work, from the cafe to the library, as a means of toting one's daily necessities on the body. The bag therefore becomes an extension of the on-the-go existence, a natural and functional adaptation that befits the mobile culture.

CONCLUSION

Urbanhermes enables communication through the display of rapidly evolving image vocabularies. As a technology it makes this cultural use available, but it is up to the users to embrace it and give it meaning. It is not the random uploading of images that creates fashion, the signals of affiliation and status, but the uploading of images that are both novel and meaningful to the community. We believe that the design of the system will foster its use, indicating access to dynamically changing information and thus establishing a basis for impression formation.

The boundaries between virtual and physical are dissolving. We walk through urban spaces connected to distant companions, mobile in our global communications. Urbanhermes brings the speed, the malleability and the traceability of virtual fashion signals to the physical street, a melding that we believe will allow people to disclose and perceive expressive qualities about themselves, which would not be possible by current material fashions.

Notes
1 Judith Donath, *Signals, truth and design* (Cambridge, MA: MIT Press, forthcoming). John Maynard Smith and David Harper, *Animal signals* (Oxford, UK: Oxford University Press, 2003).
2 Thorstein Veblen, *The theory of the leisure class* (New York: Macmillan, 1899).
3 Donath, *Signals, truth and design*.

BOURDIN'S WONDERLAND
THE RISE AND RISE OF ACCESSORY PHOTOGRAPHY

Nanda van den Berg

BOURDIN´S WONDERLAND

A random selection from any number of leading fashion magazines of recent years will show countless examples of fashion photography in which accessories play a principal role. This is not only because the focus is sometimes explicitly on a particular bag or shoe, as in the case of advertisements, but also because the accessory plays a role as a bearer of meaning in the larger context of the fashion editorial.

Fashion editorials are made by a photographer in collaboration with a stylist, also called a 'fashion director', who exercises more and more influence on the end result. One of the most talked-about stylists of recent years is Joe Zee. Zee has put together a large number of striking 'fashion stories' for the American fashion magazine *W*, one of them being 'Broken Dolls', photographed by Michael Thompson in 2001. The models, bedizened in heavy, smeared make-up, posed in a small room with chairs, cabinets, mirrors, chandeliers and other attributes. In an interview in *Tearsheet*, Zee said that the babydoll-like clothing they were asked to photograph had reminded him of Courtney Love. 'So the story came to birth through the idea of early '90's grunge. From there, we thought about how we could make it modern. For me, grunge was always an interpretation of Victorian times. [...] We reinterpreted it. There was a whole process that led to the final point. [...] Each page contains a perfectly chosen ring, brooch or anklet. Details are so important.'

The way Zee's editorials come about most closely resembles an opera production: a mix of disciplines that are dramatised as a kind of total theatre. Others have a different approach. One of them is photographer Juergen Teller, who in recent years shot the advertising campaigns for Marc Jacobs accessories. In this work he increasingly assigned the principal role to a single accessory in combination with a well-known personality. Most recently these were such notables as the artist Rachel Feinstein and the actresses Charlotte Rampling and Jennifer Jason Leigh. Teller chooses existing, nondescript settings such as an empty, brightly sunlit lot in a small American city or an area of dark woods in which the main character is surprised by a flash of light. The accessory is always photographed separately, but in the same context as the personality. It's a method that is snapshot-like and highly intriguing at the same time.

A third example that characterises the way accessories are being photographed today can be found in the work of Mert Alas and Marcus Pig-

02.

02.
Juergen Teller, advertising campaign for Marc Jacobs, 2006
03.
Alas & Piggott, advertising campaign for Louis Vuitton, 2006

gott, who produce hyper-artificial images for the advertising campaigns for the luxury brand Louis Vuitton (also designed by Marc Jacobs, by the way, but intended for a different public). In 2004, for example, they did a photo shoot in Dubai against the background of the desert, with hired top models posing on sand dunes. Model Karen Elson crept through the sand on her hands and knees wearing a glistening blue suit and holding a Vuitton bag with a white star on the handle that sparkles as if in a cartoon.

Vuitton's accessories themselves are laden with several layers of meaning. This was particularly evident in the most recent campaign of 2006/2007 in which the focus was directed specifically on the accessories. These include a 'hood' – track suit hoods, for example, but now made of mink – and a 'Stephen Sprouse leopard print stole', a design made by Sprouse in 2000 around the time that Marc Jacobs had asked him to apply graffiti to the logo of the more than 150-year-old luxury trademark (until then sacrosanct). The Stephen Sprouse graffiti bag caused a revolution because it reached a much larger public than the ordinary luxury LV buyer.[1] All these messages were reinforced by the digital treatment to which Alas and Piggott subject their photos, making the colours more intense, the surfaces gleam and the focus more compelling.

Even in 2003 Alas and Piggott made it known that the Charles Jourdan advertisements by Guy Bourdin from the seventies had been an important source of inspiration for them: 'The secret of a strong campaign is a great image and a great character'.[2] But the influence of Guy Bourdin is clearly evident in the work of the others as well: in the drama of the editorials directed by Zee, or the typical way of letting an object – a shoe or a bag – stand in for a missing subject, a method that Teller isn't afraid to use, as when he puts the Marc Jacobs bag alone in the middle of a dustbin in an American car park, without a human being in sight. The 'frightened rabbit in the headlights' effect that Teller's harsh flash creates in the portraits of personalities also has a great deal in common with the way Bourdin likes to portray his models: dazed, startled and caught red-handed.

Guy Bourdin, who was born in Paris in 1928 and died there in 1991, worked for more than thirty years for the French *Vogue* and for more than twenty years on his Charles Jourdan advertising campaigns. During that period he designed a visual language that not only formed a suitable vehicle for his own work but also could be used suc-

LOUIS VUITTON

CHARLES JOURDAN
PARIS

04.
J. Langlais, advertising campaign for
Charles Jourdan, October 1961
05.
Guy Bourdin, 'Prêtes à marcher',
February 1956
06.
Henry Clarke, 'Les fourrures jouent
sur deux tons', December 1957

cessfully by others, even decades later. This raises the question as to exactly where the expressive energy or the innovative potential of Bourdin's work can be found. Was he really a trail-blazer and source of inspiration, more than we may have been aware of thus far – and someone who deserves to be recognised as such? Was Guy Bourdin the founder of accessory photography as a separate branch of fashion photography?

FOCUS ON THE OBJECT

Bourdin's widely acclaimed Charles Jourdan advertisements had their start in 1964 when Guy Bourdin was introduced to Roland Jourdan, one of the two sons of the founder of the luxury shoe label, by Francine Crescent, editor-in-chief of the French *Vogue*.

For a long time advertisements for accessories had been drawn by artists. 'Shoes, like handbags, do not generally look good in advertisements, unless they are manipulated through artful lighting and digital means,' Riello and McNeil pointed out in *Shoes* by way of explanation. 'They are far too small, near to the ground and difficult to set in a stage-like way. By themselves they are, in many ways, too prosaic. It was perhaps for this reason that many shoe advertisements were drawn.'[3]

From 1960 to 1965 the Charles Jourdan advertisements in the French *Vogue* were drawn by J. Langlais. He set the shoe model 'Antinea' against the backdrop of a classical-looking Eastern beauty (*Vogue*, March 1960) and had 'Betshabée, Joconde and Mireille' floating in front of gold-brown garlands, plant motifs and bamboo instruments (*Vogue*, June/July). In 1961 Langlais began combining his drawings with photography. In one of the advertisements, for example, a tiny woman in a red dress and wearing the advertised model of shoe is sitting between gigantic rolls of paper featuring sketches of the same shoes (*Vogue*, October 1961). In 1966 the first advertisements appeared that were photographed entirely by 'Aldin'. Shoes drift in and out of the picture around the face of a delighted looking blond, with one shoe on her shoulder (*Vogue*, September 1966). That was the image of Charles Jourdan before the arrival of Bourdin – not essentially different from that of other brands of shoes from that period such as Bally, always prominent in *Vogue*.

Guy Bourdin had been working for the French *Vogue* since 1955, and it was the things that were notoriously difficult to photograph such as shoes and bags at which he aimed his camera in stories with titles like 'Prêtes à Marcher', 'Accessoires d'été' and 'Revue de details'.

Vogue in the fifties was surrounded by an aura of *luxe, calme et volupté*. The women on the pages swathed themselves in fur and jewels. They wore gloves, a hat with a veil or a Hermès scarf, and when they held a ladies' bag it was always one of stiff leather. When they travelled they brought along a set of Louis Vuitton suitcases that were carried for them. In fashion photos at that time suitcases were only shown in combination with travel.

Within this context, Bourdin photographed still lifes of objects in which a bag and a shoe would be combined with a glass, for example. To keep the static images interesting, he used repetitions of forms or alternated black-and-white or various colours in a rhythmic way. At a time when others approached the photography of things in a much more playful and less painstaking manner, Guy Bourdin's photographs were always careful to show all the details of the various objects, with an end result that remained exciting.

In August 1956 *Vogue* brought the special characteristics of its contributing photographers to its readers' attention by means of small photographs. In reference to William Klein *Vogue* wrote that he 'a mis son esprit et son ironie au service des modèles dits "de choc"'. They praised Henry Clarke's 'raffinement en son sens du luxe'. Sabine Weiss brought fashion 'ses dons de reporter'. There was one photographer, as could be deduced from the little photographs, who did not work with live models but with shoes, which he arranged with mathematical precision, then lit and photographed: 'Guy Bourdin,' *Vogue* wrote, 'opère avec la même patience qu'il apporte à dessiner tous les pétales d'un champ de marguerites. Poète, il est aussi humoriste: dans les chaussures tout confort il fait nicher des poussins.'

This sardonic-humorous tone only became clear in later years. In the fifties and early sixties of the last century Bourdin was still mainly combining shoes with blocks of wood, vegetables or pieces of quartz. The inorganic product, the shoe – shown in combination with organic material – becomes an almost alchemical apparition.[4] The meticulous staging is comparable to that of seventeenth-century still lifes, but that's where the similarity ends. For while the shoe itself may be an object full of meaning, the shining new shoes in these still lifes are only part of the composition by which Bourdin arrived at a pictorial solution.

05.

CLOUTÉE DE STRASS
une sandale en chevreau argent, au talon effilé comme le pied
d'une flûte à champagne. Elle brillera le soir. Capobianco.

INCRUSTÉ DE PIERRES BLEUES
un talon scintillant rehausse l'éclat délicat d'un escarpin du
soir en satin crème. Laure. Machine à écrire - Triumph - →

Faites pour danser

06.

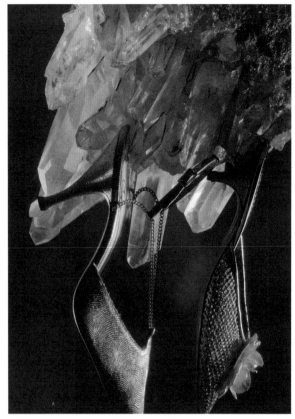

Before beginning his collaboration with Charles Jourdan, Guy Bourdin had already been photographing shoe advertisements in the fifties for brands such as Perugia and Mario Valentino. The shoes were photographed in spaces that were apparently context-free and weightless (perhaps Bourdin had been inspired by the experimental Bauhaus photography). He seems to have frequently been inspired by the arts. One deliberately blurred photograph of a model with a hat from 1955 is reminiscent of the methods of Surrealist photography, and a composition of a shoe, netting and golf balls from 1964 evokes associations with the collages of Kurt Schwitters.

An additional difficulty in photographing shoes and bags is that when it comes to interaction between the model and the bag – or model and shoe – there are few natural variants possible in the fashion pose. A bag is either carried or worn over the shoulder. In the fashion of the sixties the bag was noticeably absent for years. Shoes are simply worn on the feet.
So photographers looked for alternatives by stacking the shoes unnaturally on body parts (on the shoulders, in the hand, on the head), or by photographing the accessory as a separate object that could play a new role.

Photographer Sante Forlano had his model hold up a crescent-shaped sealskin bag while peeking through the handle (*Vogue*, October 1954). It's a rare variant that turned up again ten years later in an advertising supplement of 'Les couleurs Italiennes', in which the model looks sideways through the handle of the bag, which is balanced on its side on her shoulders. It wasn't until the sixties that the bag was photographed as an isolated object. In the early Gucci advertisements, for example, the bag is placed in the foreground against a familiar Italian background such as the Arno with the Dom of Florence.

Bourdin, however, developed his own dynamic for photographing objects. He suggested movement by drawing a hopscotch diagram on the ground or graphically indicating direction by means of arrows. Even in the sixties he photographed real movement by shooting the shoes of the season on a pair of strolling legs, or by having a pair of trouser legs flap wildly above the advertised slippers. A wind machine became a favourite piece of equipment.

The pose with the bag also underwent a metamorphosis in Bourdin's hands. In 'L'automne en 10 fourrures' (*Vogue*, August 1956) his main inspiration still seems to be painting. The model in her fur coat is clutching her Hermès bag to her breast in a pose with beautiful diagonal lines. But in later years the poses become more and more unconventional. For 'Hermès un nom de famille. Les huit Travaux d'Hermès' (*Vogue*, September 1972) Bourdin photographed a Hermès bag of crocodile leather – 'solide, beau, snob', according to *Vogue* – straight on, primly placed on the lap of a seated model who is shown with her head tilted and a vacant expression on her face. In 'Gros plan sur des cadeaux de marque' (*Vogue*, December/ January 1976-1977) the model is shown harshly lit against a tiled background, naked beneath a transparent plastic raincoat and holding up a gleaming leather bag from Bottega Veneta in front of her pubic hair.

None of his contemporaries were as successful in showing off accessories as Bourdin, and never in such an innovative way. Karen Radkai and Helmut Newton presented an overall picture in which the accessories were no more than an incidental detail without automatically attracting all the attention, as was always the case in Bourdin's photographs. Radkai portrayed women in every-day scenes, for example, in which shoes, bags and glasses had a practical function. Newton paid more attention to the story he wanted to convey or the mood he wanted to evoke than to the shoes the models happened to be wearing. Even in an erotically charged treatment such as a man taking off a woman's shoe, Newton's focus shifts to the woman's head, expression and breasts.

It even became popular in the fashion coverage of the seventies to photograph the accessory sepa-rately and feature it alone on the magazine page in a box next to the large main photo.

NEED FOR NARRATIVE

Bourdin's first campaign for Charles Jourdan was launched in 1967. These were formal studies of legs with shoes, such as the ones he had increas-ingly perfected in former years. The advertise-ments appeared with quite some regularity and Bourdin quickly introduced narrative elements. Because the subject was new shoe styles, meta-phorical usage was out of the question. On the other hand, satire and surrealistic effects were indeed a possibility.

For the campaign for the spring of 1968, real rep-licas of the shoes were made at gigantic scale. In one of the photographs, a huge, mustard yellow ladies' shoe is shown in a New York hotel corridor next to gleaming male shoes of normal size scat-tered around like dwarves. In another image from

07.
Guy Bourdin, 'Offrez lui des mules d'intérieur-mettez du rêve a ses pieds', December 1961
08.
Guy Bourdin, advertising campaign for Perugia, March 1960
09.
'Les couleurs Italiennes', May 1964
10.
Advertising campaign for Gucci, December 1964

11.
Guy Bourdin, 'L'automne en 10 fourrures', August 1956
12.
Guy Bourdin, 'Les huit travaux d'Hermès', September 1972
13.
Guy Bourdin, 'Gros plan sur des cadeaux de marque', December 1976

11.

12.

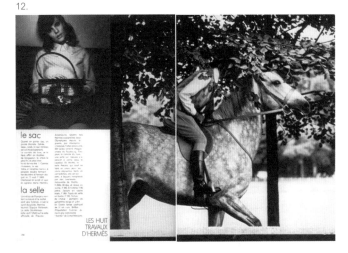

13.

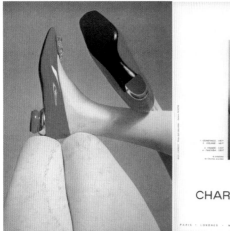

14

CHARLES JOURDAN

PARIS • LONDRES • MUNICH • MARSEILLE • LYON • DUESSELDORF

sachez CHAUSSER
vos robes

LA ROBE-T'AILLEUR

Le richelica. Mi-lézard,
mi-chevreau brun, il caractérise la mode aux em-
peignes lacées et montantes. Bally.

F 12 000.

that series a model has a giant shoe clamped under her arm as she runs away from two police-men in the shadow of the Brooklyn Bridge. A fol-low-up campaign featured tiny shoes among giant fingers next to beautiful faces.[5]

In 1966 Bourdin had photographed the artist Claes Oldenburg in New York for *Vogue*, and it is theoretically possible that Oldenburg's work had inspired him. On the other hand, the 'big shoe with a tiny woman' has been a recurring motif in the iconography of shoe reportage and advertising up to the present day.[6]

The influential stylist Katie Grand, who in past years has set the tone for top labels such as Prada, Bottega Veneta and Louis Vuitton, was editor-in-chief of the fashion magazine *Pop* when she had gigantic copies made of bags by Prada, Hermes, Gucci and Dior for a photo shoot in 2001. She admitted to having been inspired by an Old-enburg sculpture.[7] It was an effective way to express the gigantic commercial importance of these products. At a time when in principle every-thing can be manipulated with the computer, it is still an unusual method. It indicates an extraordi-nary passion on the part of the aforementioned photographer and stylist, who spared neither money nor trouble to impose their compelling vision on others. 'We destroyed a tree for each,' Gerard Tavenas, head of Jourdan's office in Paris, said about the production of the giant shoes in 1968. 'Mmm,' said Katie Grand with a shrug in 2001 in reference to her giant bags, 'I suppose it must have cost the fashion houses a fortune.' Nothing, however, could stand in the way of the ideas these people proposed: 'With Guy every-thing had to be just right,' recalls model Nicolle Meyer.[8]

Anthony Haden Guest claims that Bourdin was a big fan of Lewis Carroll, which must have served as the inspiration for his growing and shrinking shoes.[9] In any case, the adventures of *Alice in Wonderland* seem to have made quite an impact – consciously or unconsciously – on Bourdin's oeuvre. Guy Bourdin was an exceptionally super-stitious person with a great interest in the occult.[10] In those occult circles, the adventures of Alice are seen as a medium through which the philosophical principles of wisdom are revealed. The mere fact that the adventures of Alice (her name means 'truth', by the way) are passed from generation to generation via the ritual of love would confirm this idea. According to this explanation, one of those principles, that of 'the person who does not change', is illustrated by the fact that once Alice

14.
Guy Bourdin, advertising campaign for Charles Jourdan, February 1967
15.
Willy Ronis, 'Saches chausser vos robes', August 1959
16.
Sir John Tenniel, illustration from *Alice in Wonderland*, 1865

17.
Guy Bourdin, 'Les cadeaux sont un jeux d'enfants', December 1977
18.
Guy Bourdin, 'Les compensations de l'été', June-July 1975
19.
Guy Bourdin, advertising campaign for Charles Jourdan, October 1972

has grown large again and is almost bursting out of the rabbit's house, she does not realise that with such gigantic strength she ought to be able to rescue herself from the distressing situation in which she finds herself. In like manner every episode is supposed to stand for a separate principle.[11]

Whatever the explanation, much of Bourdin's iconography seems to have been inspired by Alice's adventures. The small, closet-like rooms that Bourdin seems to prefer as a working environment, stuffed with furniture and models scrambling over each other, bear a particular affinity to the story. 'If there was an enormous hotel, and it was a cupboard that stank and was two inches square, that's where he would take the picture,' British photographer Terence Donovan told Haden Guest.[12] The constant movement of running, jumping, waving and falling – and the attendant flying hair – the playing, laughing and swinging children, grubbing pigs and other animals, and the vacant, myopic gaze of many of the models who look as if they had just woken up in a marvellous world – these recurring motifs all underscore the connection with *Alice in Wonderland*. And the perspective from which Bourdin photographed the Jourdan advertisements in the late seventies – from the bottom up, so that the shoes become gigantic and the houses in the background seem small – was a reprise of the theme.

The makeup and the hair styles of the models always contribute to the special atmosphere of Bourdin's photographs. For years the makeup was the work of Heidi Morawetz and involved much more than the application of facial cosmetics. 'Il savait que j'avais fait les Arts appliqués,' she says in regard to her meeting with Bourdin in 1970. 'Il m'a dit: "Tu dois savoir te débrouiller avec la couleur".' She always made the lips 'très très rouges avec plein de gloss' and the eyes 'avec plein de halo, on collait les cils un à un.' The entire body was treated with colour and made as bloodless as the face: 'On apprenait la perfection, parce qu'il n'y avait pas de retouches sur ordinateurs.'[13] This was also why Bourdin asked Morawetz to use a colouring agent to make the seawater 'bluer'. For many years, the extreme, often teased hair complementing the whole was the work of the hip Parisian hair stylist 'Guillaume de Mod's Hair'.

GLORY DAYS

Guy Bourdin's manner of photographing had a great deal of influence on the work of his contem-

17.

18.

19.

20.
Sarah Moon, 'Robe, es-tu là?', May
1977
21.
Guy Bourdin, advertising campaign
for Charles Jourdan, September
1972
22.
Guy Bourdin, 'Les meneurs de la
mode', February 1973

20.

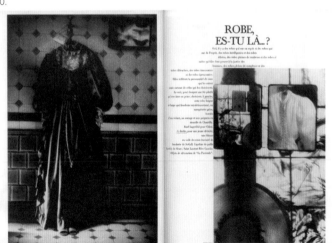

poraries, which became clear in the late seventies. Photographers such as Gianpaolo Barbieri and Tony Kent, who in previous years had engaged in unaffected fashion reporting, slowly began using more tension, narrative and unexpected perspectives in their work. The objects in the advertisements suddenly took on a meaning of their own. Brands such as Bottega Veneta and Christian Dior advertised only enlarged bags without any context or persons.

For the report 'Robe, es-tu là' (*Vogue*, May 1977), Sarah Moon imposed meaning on the objects (dresses, bags, shoes) without the intervention of any human presence. In 1977 Daniel Johanneau, one of *Vogue*'s regular accessory photographers at that time, photographed accessories in hotel rooms, where they supposedly have been left behind by hotel guests and remain to tell their stories, in the spirit of Sophie Calle's later art project *L'Hôtel* (1984).

Guy Bourdin was at the high point of his career during those years, and he photographed many disturbing tableaux, with subjects that, according to Haden Guest in his 1994 seminal article (the tenor of which was taken over by many others later on), seemed to hark back to a number of tragic and deadly events from Bourdin's private life, including the suicides of his wives.[14] Others have pointed to the fact that the seventies was an extremely uncertain and violent time, and naturally this was reflected in culture and fashion, and thus in fashion photography.[15]

Bourdin always worked on the Jourdan campaigns alongside his other fashion photography, and ideas and motifs recurred there with regularity. The photos often look like film sets, frequently photographed in hotel rooms and on hotel beds with maids playing a role, or voyeuristic tableaux with people looking in from the outside (through windows) or out at passers-by from the inside (shop windows). Painting nails and the putting on and taking off of shoes – sometimes by service personnel at the feet – is a favourite motif for photographing new shoe styles. Bourdin's colours are bright, saturated and painterly. The photographs are explicitly made for magazine spreads, with due regard for the perfect focus and symmetry. 'As always he had the layout of his photos in mind and used the double-page spread of the magazine as yet another intriguing device; the reader opened or closed my legs with the turn of a page', writes Bourdin's muse Nicolle Meyer.[16]

QUATUOR 290 F

CHARLES JOURDAN

22.

LES MENEURS DE LA MODE

Elle est partout, la mode tennis, toute blanche avec ses rayures, sa taille basse et ses jupes plissées Georges Rech - Synonyme. (Ci-dessus), cardigan et débardeur en tricot de laine, bordés tricolore. F 138 et F 99. Jupe plissée en crêpe blanc, Le Knip. F 290. Sandales Charles Jourdan. Collant Chesterfield. Bracelet Nicole Amiot-Houdard. Ballantyne. (A dr.), pull en double cachemire bordé tricolore. F 500. Jupe plissée en flanelle. Synonyme de Georges Rech. F 178. Sandales Walter Steiger pour Claude Carraz. Collant Exciting. Maquillage Moravetz pour Lancaster. Voir les adresses page 17.

En 73 : jupe plissée et style tennis

LES MAILLOTS
IMITENT
LES FAUVES

24.

Bourdin was an artist himself, and he always ana-lysed works of art in museums down to the finest detail. In the early sixties he exhibited his draw-ings as often as his photographs. In the end he decided to make 'art' *in* his photos, with Man Ray as his example.[17] His specific sense of humour played a big role in his photographic narratives, but the motifs he used often refer directly to examples from art. In her article on shoes and sandals in classical Greece, Sue Blundell points to the many meanings that shoes may have had at that time. Putting shoes on and taking them off – as depicted on steles and vases – could suggest the beginning of a journey, but it could also mark a symbolic passage between the public and the private or the sacred and the secular spheres, or it could symbolise a transition having to do with marriage or death. In paintings on vases, 'shoes or shoe-handling [could] help to intensify the erotic atmosphere of a scène. Discarded boots or shoes imply release from normal constraints [...] When attended by Eros, they are clearly dressing for love and if a male spectator is included in the scene, the action may appear seductive even if the sandal lacer is fully clothed.'[18] Blundell might have been describing many of Bourdin's photo-graphs with these words, with Eros disguised as a twentieth-century man in a suit.

The Greek bride put on new shoes when she was about to make the transition from unwed virgin to sexually active married woman. It is an 'invitation au voyage' that Bourdin depicted many times in his tableaux without showing where the journey is going. The treatment, however, contributed to the tension of the photographed story, in which the shoe as object imparts meaning to the whole.

CONCLUSION

In 1991 an impoverished Guy Bourdin died in Paris of cancer. His fruitful relationship with the French *Vogue* had ended when Francine Crescent left as editor-in-chief in 1986. In 1983 the other photographers had started doing fashion stories that were more and more interesting, indebted to Bourdin but with a vision all their own.

When we follow the work of the younger genera-tion of fashion photographers, we see that there has been a re-evaluation of Bourdin's work in recent years in the form of explicit indebtedness and in the form of references, visual citations and more hidden influences. The still lifes of Salva-tore Ferragamo's shoes in 'Crazy for shoe' in *Pop 2006*,[19] made by Toby McFarlan Pond, seem like a further elaboration of Bourdin's still lifes from the

23.
Guy Bourdin, 'Les maillots imitent les fauves', May 1984
24.
Vincent Peters, photo report with Gisele Bundchen, 2006
25.
Guy Bourdin, advertising campaign for Charles Jourdan with Nicolle Meyer, autumn 1977
26.
Dolce & Gabbana, advertising campaign 2006

25.

26.

DOLCE & GABBANA

27.

27.
Yves Saint Laurent, advertising
campaign 2006

28.
Yves Saint Laurent, advertising
campaign 2006

28.

fifties. Would Juergen Teller ever have thought of photographing a lost bag on a dustbin if Bourdin's tableaux for Charles Jourdin – where an abandoned shoe leaves everything to the imagination – had not preceded him? Whatever the case may be, Teller seems to have inherited Bourdin's irony – and this is what gives the images their mysterious quality, even though they look so simple.

Guy Bourdin brought fashion photography to a higher plane. With his army of assistants he tackled his projects like an opera director, working from a vision in which the standard ambience and hierarchy of what until then had been the standard style of fashion photography was completely swept aside. That is an accomplishment that is still rightly seen as an iconic contribution to the development of fashion photography. But the fact that Bourdin's work has always been regarded – and in recent years more than ever – as a source of photographic motifs that are constantly being repeated, has everything to do with the theatrical mix in his work: the narrative power, the suggested but implicit deeper meaning of his images, the intense use of colour and always his masterful focus on the products being sold. Right from his earliest beginnings in the fifties, Bourdin clearly began developing a visual language to express what he wanted to show. That language seemed to possess a universal power, not only for himself during that period but also today, half a century later. And in an area that is so volatile and dynamic as fashion and fashion photography, that in itself is quite remarkable.

Notes
1. Murray Healy, 'Marc on Sprouse', *Pop* (October 2006): 280-285.
2. *Time Style & Design* (Fall 2003): 'Fashion insiders' at www.time.com
3. Giorgio Riello and Peter McNeil, *Shoes: A History from Sandals to Sneakers* (Oxford and New York: Berg, 2006), p. 9.
4. Ibid. p. 402
5. Anthony Haden Guest, 'The Return of Guy Bourdin', *The New Yorker* (7 November 1994).
6. In 1959 Willy Ronis photographed a story for *Vogue* entled 'Sachez chausser vos robes', with a photomontage of miniature women beside the giant shoes that would best match their dresses. The Charles Jourdan advertisement has already been mentioned in which a miniature women is combined with giant sketches. In November 1968 the British *Vogue* featured tiny shoes being held by giant fingers like jewels, photographed by Horst Wickmann. And in November 1979 the shoe label Stéphane Kélian put an advertisement in the French *Vogue*, photographed by M. Pahin, in which a tiny women is pushing against a pair of giant shoes and wearing the same shoes in miniature size on her feet. All these are obviously photomontages.
7. See Angela Buttolph, 'My Prada Bag's Bigger than Yours', *Evening Standard* (London), 10 September 2001.
8. Nicolle Meyer, *Guy Bourdin: A Message for You* (New York: Steidldangin, 2006): II, p. 23
9. Haden Guest, note 5.
10. Meyer, note 8, p. 45 .
11. *Alice's Adventures in Wonderland* and *Through the Looking Glass* were explained in this way in 1928 by Dr Marc Edmund Jones, who founded the Sabian Assembly in 1923.
12. Haden Guest, note 5.
13. Marie-Dominique Lelièvre, 'Heidi Morawetz. Femme de couleurs', L'Express, 1 June 2006.
14. Haden-Guest, note 5.
15. For a lively and insightful portrait of the seventies see Peter Shapiro's *Turn the Beat Around: The Secret History of Disco* (London: Faber and Faber, 2005) and for a portrait of the Paris fashion scene see especially Alicia Drake, *The Beautiful Fall* (New York/London: Little, Brown and Co., 2006).
16. Meyer, note 8, p. 70.
17. Michel Guerrin, 'An Image by Guy Bourdin is Never Serene' in *Exhibit A: Guy Bourdin* (Boston, London: 2001).
18. Sue Blundell, 'Beneath their Shining Feet: Shoes and Sandals in Classical Greece', in Riello and McNeil, note 3, pp. 30-49, quote p. 46.
19. Alice Fisher, 'Crazy for Shoe', *Pop* (October 2006): 106-114.

ANIMAL ACCESSORIES

Arjen Mulder

01.

ORIGIN OF THE ACCESSORY

When walking on the beach, every one of us, at a certain moment, bends over somewhere along the shoreline and picks up a strikingly beautiful shell which is then looked at and put away in a pocket or bag. When, months later, you come across it again it's not easy to just throw it away, since you've had it for so long. You can put it on a shelf in the toilet or in a kitchen drawer, or you can decide to put it back in your pocket. It has become something. Someone might make it into a necklace, for which a suitable pearl plus a golden chain has to be bought. A little creature's shell thus becomes an accessory. Nor is it easy to come home after a walk in the woods without a pine-cone or horse chestnut in your jacket or trouser pocket. Mountain walks yield little stones and walks in the city knick-knacks purchased at a market or in a nice little shop. What is this urge?

Redmond O'Hanlon provides an answer to this question in his travel book *Congo Journey* (1996). At the end of the book the English writer relates how his Congolese travelling companion Manou has heard from a certain Doctor Lary that O'Hanlon has a room at home 'crammed with god-dam junk'. Doctor Lary had said, 'Old books, old pictures, that's okay, but, Manou, you wouldn't believe it, there's used-up pens and old boots in there, and goddam moth-eaten skins of foxes and bits of rabbit (they're furry things) and a stuffed stoat, like a civet, or a mongoose, and really horrible stuffed birds – you can't tell what they are – and birds' eggs, and bags of fur, and, worst of all, Manou, there's a burnt-up foot, the burnt foot of a friend of his and that, Manou, is in a coffee-jar!' To which Manou answered, 'Doctor Lary! I knew it! Our Redmond – he's a sorcerer! A sorcerer! He has a house for the spirits! That room, Doctor Lary, that's a fetish house!' O'Hanlon denies that his passion for collecting has anything to do with African superstitions, saying that it's purely a question of keepsakes, but he does add that these things bring him into contact with his true self, his 'deep self'. Exactly, says Manou, 'That's it! It's true! The objects! The ancestors! A fetish house!'

Picking up and carrying away something, whether it's a shell or an empty ballpoint pen, lifts the object out of the everyday sphere and places it in another, mythical sphere in which everything is charged, not so much with sense as with reality. The object acquires a symbolic charge that keeps its owner in contact with his or her 'deep self', with that which is real in himself or herself and not simply what is external or conditioned by cultural codes. Owner is perhaps not the right word; it is rather as though the object has chosen us to find and preserve it. We protect the object as long as the object protects us. Having elected us, the object places us outside the accidents of everyday life, in an order in which we acquire just as much an absolute value as the thing or the fetish, in the way that Manou alluded to. The German writer Ernst Jünger called the sphere in which chance is abolished and everything is laden with an indeterminate meaning 'Schicksalzeit', the time of destiny. In *An der Zeitmauer* (1959) he proposes that the human desire to be part of such a Schicksalzeit provides the explanation for the bizarre fact that in our ultra-industrial and rational world horoscopes continue to be published in newspapers day in day out. Not that we believe in them, but we do wish that they could be true and that not everything would happen just like that. So we also hope that the things around us are not dead and mute, but interested in our existence and linked to our destiny. This desire and hope occurs in us at an unconscious level, somewhere at the level of the instincts: our profound self, which, under layers of culture and civilisation, is as animistic as in prehistoric times.

The origin of the accessory is thus the little thing we find by chance and then hold on to. Cutting through a friendship bracelet after a year and throwing it away because it's become dirty just 'isn't done'. And if it gets torn in half by itself and you lose it, then it's highly inauspicious. There are some necklaces or earrings that you don't wear any more because you experienced something nasty when you had them on. For special occasions you take along particular accessories that have previously made their salutary influ-

01.
William Wegman, *Arm Envy*, 1989
02.
André Perugia, fish shoe with scales, 1931
03.
Stéphane Couvé Bonnaire, giraffe shoe with legs, 1996

02.

03.

ence felt. Accessories perhaps acquire their mythical charge because they are always worn on the body, just like amulets. What is important is that the objects are worn for a long time, day in day out. Buying a mobile phone and losing it within a week is not so terrible, but after a year it is, and not just because you've then lost all your phone numbers. Receiving a ring from someone and then losing it immediately – 'so it had to be'. But losing the same ring after ten years of marriage... Mourners often carry with them for years something that comes from the deceased, and the process of 'letting go' enters a new, crucial phase when that object is deliberately disposed of and rejected. A nagging, failed love affair can be cured by suddenly throwing that wrist watch he gave you into a river. Accessories are typical collectibles, as though they entice not only their finders but also each other. Collecting socks or waistcoats makes no sense at all, but there are countless examples of collections of shoes, watches, watchbands, hats, ties, electronic gadgets. Accessories are things that gain power over you, or that grant you power over your life because of a superstition that is uncontrollable and impossible to shake off. For whatever practical purpose accessories may have, they always tend to become 'part of your brains', as Redmond O'Hanlon puts it. This mythical value is crucial; what accessories cost makes no difference. You don't pay with money in the Schicksalzeit.

ACCESSORIES AND ANIMALS

The natural tendency of the accessory to become a fetish or amulet is enhanced when the object in question is of animal origin. It is then not a fetish,

but a totem. Totems are objects housing the spirit of a tribe and are therefore laden with taboos, for the spirit can bring both salvation and disaster. There are three ways in which a connection can be made between animals and accessories. First of all there are accessories for live animals. Secondly, live animals are kept as accessories. Thirdly, dead animals or parts of them are used as or incorporated into accessories. What these three quite different categories have in common is that they all express, in their own and sometimes contradictory way, a number of values and feelings that are located in or projected upon animals. Two of these are of concern to us here.

People tend by nature to think of elsewhere, of earlier or later, in any case not here. In order to survive, both mentally and physically, this drifting away into thoughts, daydreams, desires and fantasies needs to be suppressed, and from prehistoric times onwards the presence of animals in one's immediate vicinity was an appropriate means for this. Every animal is capable of providing us with an experience of 'immediate now-ness', the awareness that one is here and now and nowhere else. This happens when, during a walk in the woods, a wild deer suddenly steps onto the path in front of you, but the same effect also occurs with pets. A dog, cat or even the punk's rat and the cockroach of more recent fashion – animals that we often allow close to our bodies – opens our spirit to now-ness and the world in which real things happen. In other words, the world in which everything is not vagueness and chance, but fate, menace and luck. You can only enjoy, or be terrified, in the present. Everything that's nice is physical. A second ability of animals is known as metamor-

04.

04.
Felieke van der Leest, *Cockroaches in Metamorphosis*, brooches, 1999
05.
Alexander McQueen, autumn/winter 1999 collection show
06.
Hermès, page with accessories for dogs from the Hermès catalogue, late 1920s
07.
Jane Mansfield, actress, posing with a poodle, 1950s
08.
Jean Paul Gaultier, autumn/winter 2006 collection show

phosis. Primitive tribes – that is to say, groups of people without external media such as writing, telephone, photography, etc. – recount time and time again that they are able to feel in their body whether there's an animal walking around nearby. If a springbok, for example, is walking through long grass, they feel that as a tickle in their calves. The hunter leaps up and begins to peer around him to find out where the animal actually is. We cannot communicate verbally with our animals, but we can sense them very well – and they us. In tribal societies, it was the shamans who were able to transform themselves into the group's totem animal and then mate with the primordial mother of the bisons or other huntable prey, so that she would give birth to the herds that would populate the plains again in the spring. Cave paintings of animals are to be found at places where this mating ritual took place. Animal masks are part of this same metamorphosis. By changing himself into an animal, the shaman leads culture back to nature, with the aim of preserving that culture via nature (the animal prey). In order to keep a culture alive you have to abandon it now and then, otherwise you extinguish yourself and your culture degenerates into a collection of indifferent, hollow forms.

Let me elaborate on an example: the dog. Countless tribes all over the world recount that the primeval parents were a man and a dog. Biologically speaking, the dog belongs to the same species as the wolf (*Canis lupus*). Man has had an enormous hatred of the wolf ever since primeval times precisely because the wolf is a dog, but then wild, beyond culture, whereas the dog is a wolf who has defected to the side of man (something similar applies to the cat and the lion). The ancient Norse *Edda* describes a permanent war between a tribe that worships a dog and a tribe whose totem is a wolf. The werewolf is a man who, under the influence of the moon, goes through the process of civilisation in reverse sequence, becoming the ancestral wolf. The legend of Romulus and Remus, who are suckled by a wolf and then found a civilisation, belongs to this same mythical domain. The totemic value of the dog has never disappeared completely from our consciousness, however much the dog has been bred in order to be employed for very different human values: hunting dogs, lapdogs, fighting dogs, cuddly dogs, street dogs. Every dog remains capable of eating its owner should he die and there's nothing else to eat. Time and time again we hear of dogs biting babies or children in the street or in the woods ('He never does that sort of thing'). Sexual intercourse between humans and dogs continues

05.

06.

07.

08.

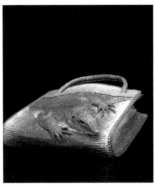

09.
Alligator skin beauty case, 1950s
10.
Lizard handbag from Indonesia,
1950s
11.
Vivienne Westwood, cat bag and
shoe, 2003
12.
Christophe Coppens, autumn/winter
2006/2007 collection
13.
Christophe Coppens, cape, haute
couture collection spring/summer
2005
14.
Idiots, *Ophelia*, 2005

11.

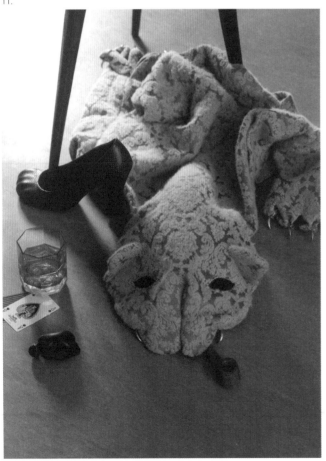

to be the most common form of bestiality. That dogs are dressed in cute outfits, and indeed elevated to kitsch and camp, does not make the animal in the dog any less an animal. As an animal they continue to shed hair, fart, lick your face, reveal a pink penis, bark and hump your visitor's outstretched leg (with all the now-ness thereof). On the other hand all owners look like their dog, often even in appearance (metamorphosis). No matter how sentimentally people often behave towards dogs, many a person would long have been reduced to mental pulp without a dog in the house.

An animal is never neutral material. Even animal remains barely recognisable as such, like the leather of a motor cycle jacket or the classic catgut on a violin, evoke an atmosphere that places the objects in question beyond everyday normality, either because they conjure up an association with violence or because, as in the case of catgut, they are connected with reveries as soon as they are made to resound. Added to this is the fact that the non-practical value of an accessory – what is generally called its beauty – is always more important than the usefulness of the thing, certainly if it's a fashionable accessory. A crocodile skin bag is first of all made of crocodile skin and then an object for putting your things in and carrying with you. The patterns and texture of crocodile skin are beautiful, spectacular even, but at the same time the awareness that the skin comes from a living animal that was once deadly ferocious makes the object more than just beautiful. It acquires a totemic value and the rough skin becomes the 'counter skin' to the delicate skin of the woman it finds itself next to. Everyone knows that crocodile skin is so beautiful because when alive its original bearer devoured cute antelopes and nice water fowl, skin and hair and all. Crocodile skin is hence a symbol of the bearer's comparable, hidden strengths; it is not a hunting trophy but rather a warning to those who might want to hunt the one who adorns herself with this animal skin: don't approach me naively or innocently, I hit back hard and I may attack. My teeth are sharp. Watch out.

CONCLUSION

A pearl as earring, the teeth of sharks and other creatures as beads on a chain, shells (the animal elements most used in accessories), red coral, dried sea horses, fish skin, ostrich feathers, the fur of the great-crested grebe (in the nineteenth century entire stuffed birds were incorporated into ladies' hats), the skin of snakes, lizards and

12.

13.

14.

15.

16.

15.
Matthew Barney, *Cremaster 3: The third degree*, 2002
16.
Idiots, *Corpse bride, vulture with victim*, 2006
17.
John Galliano, bird's nest wig, 1985

alligators, and then the foxes, the skin of exotic animals for handbags (if necessary in the politically correct form of a printed pattern), the skin of big game covering the case of the hunting rifle with which the same animals are shot dead – animals and animal parts refer to a realm that we are part of but which we have to forsake, time and time again, in order to become and remain human, and which we long to return to because, ultimately, nobody wants or is even able to remain just human always and forever. In order to be part of a culture you have to be able to step outside it now and then; to persevere in the order of chance you have to enter the Schicksalzeit now and then. These days it can be done through chemical or physical intoxication, stimulated by drugs, rhythms or speed. It can also be done behind a mask – and what is fashion if not a mask? Not being yourself for a while, that's what keeps our humanity bearable. Or, if necessary, making a part of yourself inhuman, subhuman with animal plumage, or transhuman like a robot or other cybernetic system.

This desire that crops up now and then to destroy everything in the hope that it comes to life again afterwards – to real life instead of a poor substitute for it – is what makes us human. The craving for self-renewal through autodestruction stems from the need to have to live as humans on earth, possessed of a consciousness that fundamentally needs no earth, no body and no humanity. At the same time, this desire for what is called a body without organs has to be repressed if we want to retain the earth, civilisation or, at a pinch, just our sense of good or bad taste. It is for this reason that new arguments are always invented for the use of animal elements in fashion, which are meant to give it a pretence of legitimacy. Queen Wilhelmina always wore a fox stole around her neck because this was supposed to ward off disease, or so she thought. This is not science, but magic. Minerals are supposed to have a harmonising effect. A rabbit foot brings luck and protects one from calamity. Let's say no more about the subject, it's clear enough. Animal accessories are not a form of strutting in someone else's feathers but of keeping manageable the general human aversion to one's own humanity, to biology and the cultural anthropology of our existence. That animal accessories live or have lived in a domain that our human consciousness cannot penetrate without losing its humanity gives them the numen, the sacred energy that enables them to draw us and keep us outside the human sphere for a while. That is what makes them so seductive.

17.

References
Baudot, François. *Fashion Dogs*. New York: Assouline, 2002.
Duerr, Hans Peter. *Sedna, oder die Liebe zum Leven*. Frankfurt am Main: Suhrkamp Verlag, 1984.
Freud, Sigmund. *Totem und Tabu*. Frankfurt am Main: S. Fischer Verlag, 1956.
Jünger, Ernst. *An die Zeitmauer*. Stuttgart: Ernst Klett Verlag, 1959.
Kretschmar, Freda. *Hundestammvater und Kerberos*. Vol. I, *Hundestammvater*. Stuttgart: Strecker und Schröder Verlag, 1938.
Mulder, Arjen. 'Waarheid van het lichaam', in: *Het twintigste-eeuwse lichaam*. Amsterdam: Uitgeverij 1001, 1996.
Mulder, Arjen. 'Uitverkorenheid', in: *Het fotografisch genoegen*. Amsterdam: Uitgeverij Van Gennep, 2000.
O'Hanlon, Redmond. *Congo*. Amsterdam: Atlas, 2006.

ICONS
ICONS
ICONS
ICONS
ICONS
ICONS
ICONS
ICONS
ICONS
ICONS
ICONS
ICONS
ICONS
ICONS
ICONS
ICONS
ICONS
ICONS
ICONS
ICONS
ICONS
ICONS
ICONS
ICONS
ICONS
ICONS

THE SHOE

Nanda van den Berg

When did the shoe become a genuine accessory? It happened at the beginning of the twentieth century, when, under the leadership of Paul Poiret, skirts became shorter and shoes became visible for the first time, on legs with daring coloured or flesh-coloured stockings.

It was also the time that talked-about shoe designers began to emerge. Among them was André Perugia, who was born in Nice in 1893 into a family of Italian shoemakers and had already opened a shop in Paris by the age of sixteen. The designer Paul Poiret discovered Perugia's special talent and there arose a fruitful collaboration. Perugia made shoes that were the perfect accessories to match Poiret's creations. In addition, Perugia had a growing 'belle clientèle' of his own for whom he made shoes to order and which consisted of aristocratic ladies, princesses and stars of the revue such as Josephine Baker and Mistinguette. His shoes were in fact personal portraits.

All the centuries before, one had not actually been able to see much of women's shoes. Women wore very long skirts, but under them were sometimes extreme examples of shoes, such as the Chopine, a platform shoe worn in Europe between the fourteenth and sixteenth centuries whose wooden or cork sole could be as much as fifty centimetres high. Knowledgeable people at the time could tell the precise status and identity of the wearer from the particular difference of height measured in centimetres. Wearing Chopines, however, had nothing to do with fashion or taste.[1] It was not really possible to walk on them without the help of a companion or a servant. For centuries, the woman was primarily immobile. Her paniers, petticoats, crinolines and corsets enhanced her decorative function but hindered her freedom of movement. Her shoes were covered with embroidered silk, since she was not in the habit of walking

01. **Manolo Blahnik's** *Donyale*,
Spring/Summer 2000
Shoe with 105-mm high heel, photographed by Eric Boman. Since the early seventies, when he set up his business in London, Manolo Blahnik has ruled over the domain of glamorous and imaginative shoes like a king. He is a true 'shoes couturier'. Blahnik has no assistants, designs all the shoes himself and each model of shoe is based on a specific inspiration. The height of the heel of this red *Donyale* might well refer to the impressive stature of *Donyale Luna*, the first black photo model to appear on the cover of Vogue.

02. **Gucci, stiletto with metal heel, autumn/winter 1997/1998 collection**
A sexually charged, almost dangerous shoe, depicted in a voyeuristic way by Mario Testino as though spotted by a surveillance camera. Part of the highly successful collections from the second half of the nineties with which the American designer Tom Ford freshened up the lulled image of the leather goods house founded in 1921. For this he used a hefty dose of sex. Despite the lack of any symbolic references to the house of Gucci, such as bamboo, green-red-green woven webbing, horse's bit or the initials GG, this best-selling shoe is immediately recognisable.

around outdoors in the mud. It was not until the mid-nineteenth century with the laying of paved streets – first in London and later in Paris – that weather-proof walking shoes for women came into fashion.

From the 1920s onwards, shoe designs started to show creativity and artistic originality. Another famous shoe designer who produced beautiful and comfortable shoes made-to-measure for Hollywood stars was Salvatore Ferragamo. In the late 1940s and the 1950s – the great years of haute couture – 'creative geniuses' in Paris worked closely with major talents in the field of shoe design, such as Roger Vivier (for Christian Dior) and Raymond Massaro (for Chanel). Combining the strengths of shoe designer and couturier was a tradition that would continue until well into the 1960s, as with the collaboration between Maud Frizon and Thierry Mugler for which Frizon made small, brightly coloured works of art in futuristic forms. Echoing Mugler's clothes, the shoes had a tight, pointed toe and a conical heel.

Shoes in the 1960s – influenced by the revolutionary tendencies of the time and the liberation from the strait-jacket of the old guard – were for a while very comfort-able, with a broad cap and a flat platform heel. But in the 1970s shoes became one of the most important acces-sories. Charles Jourdan's timeless and elegant designs, for example, achieved an ideal synthesis between beauty and wearability. Although women tended for a long time to wear low shoes during the day and only ven-tured onto high heels in the evening, shoes in the 1970s and 1980s were more prominent and more varied than the bag.

Shoes became a favourite object in the 1990s. Examples include the delicate, precious models by Jimmy Choo and Manolo Blahnik, immortalised as Carrie Bradshaw's 'Manolos' in the TV series *Sex and the City*. They were more jewels than shoes and were made of unusual mate-rials like feathers, lucite and paste stones, combined with improbably high stiletto heels. The price of the shoes corresponded to the heels, which apparently did not stop women from desiring them, buying them and cherishing them.

They were compensated for by 'designer trainers' or other types of hybrid shoes whose design was partly based on sports shoes and which offered casual com-fort, without the addition of beauty. With the advent of clothing designers who brought out lines of accessories a new ugliness set in. The intellectual designer Miuccia Prada, for example, devotes all her attention to the head and feet and for her second line Miu Miu she designed such extreme shoes that one is first amazed at their monstrosity and only secondly captivated by them.

A shoe is always more than just a shoe, which is some-thing that Prada understands. A shoe has a style, a meaning and a message, while beauty, practicality and a good fit are often side issues. The message recently being conveyed is rather violent, judging from the 'crazy coloured, heavy metal, super extra high, exuberantly excessive torture fetishes'[2] that have now appeared on the fashion scene.

Shoes are the mirror of the times, as is the case with all fashion. Experts say that the heavy models with enor-mously high wedges and platform soles shown on the catwalk by Balenciaga, Marc Jacobs, Chloë and Miuccia Prada in 2005 and 2006 reveal 'the tensions of combat-ive times'. These shoes display a similarity with blocks of concrete in which women's feet are imprisoned.[3] The lightness and mobility that shoes had offered women in the twentieth century is thus effectively denied them. In

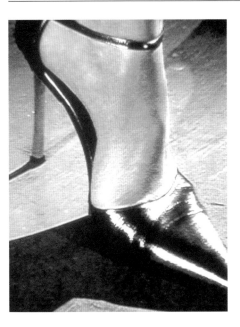

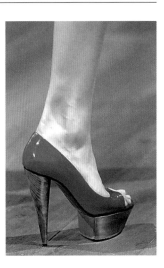

03. **Lanvin, pump, spring/summer 2006 collection**
Red patent leather platform shoe with open toe and conical, varnished stiletto heel. According to Lanvin designer Alber Elbaz, car parts inspired him to design shoes 'like var-nished cars – like a Cadillac!' The collection expresses speed, technology and modernity, an impression that is strengthened by the shoes.

the meantime their importance as accessories is growing and shoes are sometimes as exaggeratedly large as the enormous bags that fashionable women walk around with nowadays. It seems as though the shoe today would like to wrestle itself free from its secondary status as an accessory, the exuberance of designers only being tempered by the down-to-earth fact that shoes ultimately have to be worn on the feet. The true art of shoe designing seems to consist in shifting this functional boundary as far as possible and in such a way as to procure the maximum creative space for the design. Perhaps it is this very aspect that is turning the shoe into a fully-fledged part of the contemporary fashion world.

Notes
1. Andrea Vianello, 'The Venetian Chopine in the Renaissance', in: Giorgio Riello and Peter McNeil, *Shoes: A History from Sandals to Sneakers* (Oxford & New York: Berg, 2006), pp. 76-77.
2. *Purple* III, no. 5 (Spring/Summer 2006), p. 48.
3. Ginia Bellafante, 'I Am Woman, Hear Me Walk', *The New York Times*, 17 August 2006.

References
Blahnik, Manolo and Eric Boman. *Blahnik by Boman: A photographic conversation.* London: Thames and Hudson, 2005.
McDowell, Colin (with an introduction by Manolo Blahnik). *Shoes: Fashion and Fantasy.* London: Thames and Hudson, 1989.
Riello, Giorgio and Peter McNeil. *Shoes: A History from Sandals to Sneakers.* Oxford: Berg, 2006.

04. Chloé, platform shoes with wedges, autumn/winter 2006/2007 collection

In 1993 Naomi Campbell took a spectacular fall on Vivienne Westwood's extravagant platform shoes, and the same happened to the model Jessica Stam on these shoes during the Chloë fashion show. The control and concentration necessary to walk on these twelve-centimetre, tree-trunk-like wedges is comparable to a top sporting achievement.

06. Balenciaga, shoe, autumn/winter 2006/2007 collection

Calfskin platform shoe by Pierre Hardy for Balenciaga. Balenciaga designer Nicolás Ghesquière is known for his futuristic designs. He himself says that his collections are inspired by science-fiction films like Tarkovski's *Solaris* and Verhoeven's *Total Recall*. Models walk at his request in a robot-like way so that they look like 'dehumanised beings'. Since 2002 he has been working with the shoe designer Pierre Hardy: 'The almost prosthetic shoes that Pierre Hardy makes for me are part of that allure'.

05. Chanel, sneakers, without date

After becoming Chanel's chief designer in 1983, Karl Lagerfeld developed a magic formula in which he incorporated up-to-date elements. Items from the Chanel iconography – the logo, the combination of black and white, the quilting, the dark toecaps – were combined with the model of the sports shoe. In the context of fashion and without any connection with the practising of sport, sports shoes have for a number of years been the latest and most desired stars in the heaven of shoes.

07. Salvatore Ferragamo, platform sandal, 1938
Platform shoe made of cork covered with goatskin. In 1936, when steel was in short supply because of the economic sanctions against Mussolini, Ferragamo came up with the idea of using a piece of cork for constructing the sole and heel. Although the raised shoe that emerged from this idea was perhaps not so new within the centuries-old history of the shoe, Ferragamo's platform shoes were seen as the most spectacular shoes of the twentieth century. It was actually always Salvatore Ferragamo's aim to make comfort weigh as heavily as the design.

08. Chopines, Venice, ca. 1600
Pink and beige chopine. The chopine originally came from Turkey and was introduced into Europe during the Renaissance (1440-1500). It was mainly worn in Venice, but later in Spain, southern Germany, France and Switzerland as well.

09. Miu Miu, wedge shoe, spring/summer 2006 collection
Natural wood wedge sandals, 130 mm high, with thin patent leather straps over the toes and around the ankle and a gold buckle. Miu-Miu, founded in 1992, is Prada's second line. The brand's image is playful,

intellectual, sophisticated and also a little bit crazy. That these massive wedges were meant to be worn with see-through summer dresses shows, according to fashion editors, how Miuccia Prada deliberately breaks all the rules of clothing.

**10. Martin Margiela, tabi boot,
1990**
Based on the split-toe form of
Japanese 'Tabi' socks. Equipped
with a round heel the same
diameter as the average human
heel. The Tabi boots have always
featured in Margiela's collections since his first in 1989.

**11. Mule in the colours of the
French Revolution, France,
1789**
From the collection of the
shoe museum in Romans.
During the French Revolution,
shoemakers were also influenced by the spirit of the
times. It was wise to omit everything reminiscent of the
aristocracy and luxury. Fashions became simpler, but not
less elegant. Mules were
mainly worn at home. When
getting dressed to go out,
shoes with high heels were put
on as well.

**12. Pinet, silk boot, Paris,
1865-1870**
During the second half of the
nineteenth century the boot was
the dominant model of shoe in
France. Women wore silk or
velvet mules when indoors. Both
women's and men's boots were
richly decorated. The heel,
which had been low during the
reign of Louis Philippe in the
first half of the nineteenth
century, became higher again. It
was also at this time that shoes
were adapted to the specific
form of the right and left foot,
whereas before that they were
identical.

NANDA VAN DEN BERG

BAGS

José Teunissen

01. **Louis Vuitton, Steamer, 1901**
Louis Vuitton invented both the monogram logo and the first sturdy travel canvas. The combination of these two and streamlined designs created a unique bag aesthetic. The Steamer Bag was designed in 1901 and formed, together with the Keepall from 1924, the blueprint for almost all bags to follow. The Steamer was designed especially for travelling by ocean steamship. This is why the Steamer is a big bag with a tiny handle, which could be used to hang the bag on the hook at the back of a steamship cabin door. The proportions are said to have been inspired by a Mexican postal bag.

What is more important in fashion at the moment than having the right bag? Open any fashion magazine and you'll see all the fashion houses promoting their latest bag in their advertisements. For summer 2006 we come across Ralph Lauren's *Ricky* and *Aviator*, Burberry's *Margare bags* and Dior's *Gaucho bag*, the umpteenth variant on the highly popular saddle bag. For evening wear the same fashion house has introduced the *Dior Detective*, a bag strung with lace. Yves Saint Laurent comes up with the *bowsac*, a leather bag with an inwrought bow, and Chanel with *sac lingot d'or*, a gilded metal pocketbook with recognisable logo and numerals punched in. It's a random list to which hundreds of other bags could be added.

A few decades ago, fashion was still a matter of typical styles. In terms of silhouette, line, fabric and colour, seventies fashion was very different from that of the sixties or the fifties. The same went for bags. With Christian Dior's famous New Look in 1947 went an elegant pocketbook held in the hand by women wearing gloves. That was a radical change from the forties when women carried a shoulder bag with a somewhat military-looking suit. Paco Rabanne revived the shoulder bag in the sixties, but 'restyled' it with futuristic metal sequins so that it matched the taut modernist outfits from that time. Now that, for more than a decade already, fashion can no longer be pinned down to just a single recognisable style, and there are actually several styles in vogue at the same time, we see the same happening with the bag: instead of just one bag being fashionable there are a whole lot of them. It is striking how important the label is: nowhere is 'logomania' so present as in bag design. Every well-known fashion house or exclusive make of bag manages to update its image and look each season, even though the basis remains recognisably the same. Any label you care to mention - Dior, Chanel, Louis Vuitton, Yves Saint Laurent, Prada or Gucci - comes up with a few bags every season that are a recognisable variation on all their previous bags but are so new that women run to the shops so they can get hold of this 'it bag', which is usually produced in a limited edition.

Nowadays the bag is as self-evident an item in a woman's wardrobe as a pair of trousers, a shirt, a jacket and shoes. A bag is part of a woman's daily clothing needs, which is not the case for men. This is partly because there were originally, and still are, a lot fewer practical pockets in women's clothing than in men's. Another important factor is that women generally carry much more with them than men. For women, a bag is not only a place for keeping keys, handkerchief and money; it is at the same time a miniature boudoir in which make-up, mirrors and hairdressing items are stored, as well as an emergency supply of tampons, plasters and other things.

The bag only acquired this practical function in the 1920s when more and more women started to go to work and to lead a much more independent life. At that moment the bag became an essential item in the wardrobe, which was not the case before. The fashionable female elite who went out in the nineteenth and early twentieth centuries scarcely had to concern themselves with practical things. They had charge accounts in department stores or the man beside them paid. The servants were at home to open the door for them. Modern make-up had not yet been invented and what there was was considered vulgar. So there was little reason to go out with money, keys and other things in a bag. The small embroidered or beaded handbags and purses that were fashionable in these periods were meant for the knitting they took along to tea, or for opera glasses or a fan to use at dinner.

The origin of the handbag as we know it now lies in the rise of travel in the nineteenth century. With the advent of steam locomotives around 1850, already established firms like Hermès - known for its horse saddles and saddlebags - and Louis Vuitton - Napoleon III's cabin trunk maker - switched over to new 'luxury' baggage products. Besides cabin trunks and ordinary suitcases they developed special leather bags with a wooden or metal frame. These bags, which were kept on the person rather than being stowed away in racks, were called handbags so as to distinguish them from the rest of the baggage. With the advent of the automobile at the beginning of the twentieth century, Gucci and Prada launched a similar business in luxury baggage in Italy. Part of the charm of the handbag still lies in the fact that it is functional. In the thirties, Schiaparelli invented a bag with a lamp to enable the keyhole to be found in the evening. In the same decade Coco Chanel was the first to design handy pockets and mirrors in her bag so that various things

could be neatly stored in it. Nowadays every handbag has a special pocket for a mobile telephone.

Finally, every woman is aware that her bag has two opposing sides. The interior of the bag is intimate. She would rather not reveal the paraphernalia and personal valuables she harbours in it, but at the same time she emphatically wants to show its exterior. The bag's label, and particularly its 'special design', is effectively a statement. More than ever before it is the flamboyant sunglasses, the special design of the bag and the shoes that say what type of woman you are and whether you're in fashion. It can be in combination with an ordinary pair of jeans or a neutral black dress. Nowadays it's your bag that says who you are.

References
Chenoune, Farid. *Carried away: All about bags.* New York: Vendome Press, 2004.
Geoffroy-Schneiter, Berenice. *Bags.* New York, Paris: Editions Assouline, 2004.
Johnson, Anna. *Handbags: The power of the purse.* New York: Workman Publishing Co., 2002.
Steele, Valerie. *Bags: A lexicon of style.* London: Scriptum Editions, 1999.
Wilcox, Claire. *A century of bags: Icons of style in the 20th century.* London: Prospero, 1997.

02. Hermès, Plume, 1930
The Plume by Hermès was originally created to carry a horse blanket. However, Hermès altered the design into a practical bag: the Plume was the first bag which could serve as a bag for daily use as well as a weekend bag.

03. Hermès, Kelly bag, 1956
The first version ever of this bag was designed in 1892. The bag was designed to hold a saddle and was called the Haut à Courroies because of its tall shape and long straps. In 1930 the design was adapted for travel and in 1956 the bag became famous all over the world after Grace Kelly posed with it on the cover of Life magazine. Since that year the bag has been called the Kelly Bag. From beginning to end a Kelly Bag is made by one and the same craftsman in approximately eighteen hours. The Hermès artisan uses the famous double saddle stitch, piercing the leather on both sides.

04. Chanel, 2.55, 1955
The 2.55 Bag by Chanel is named after the month and year in which it was released: February 1955. The squared bag was quilted and had a chain strap. The initials CC were sewn on the inside of the bag. The bag was released in Coco Chanel's own favourite colours: beige, navy, black and brown, and in two different materials: leather and jersey. In the eighties Karl Lagerfeld turned the bag into a classic by fattening the chain, slapping a massive interlocking-C's logo on the front and releasing the bag on the market in all kinds of sizes.

05. Hermès, Birkin bag, 1984
The large Birkin Bag was designed by Hermès especially for actress and singer Jane Birkin after chairman Jean-Louis Dumas-Hermès had shared a flight on an airplane with her. After the launch the bag became increasingly popular, causing an incredibly long waiting list. The bag had become a phenomenon.

06. Prada, Pocone backpack, 1987
At the end of the eighties Miuccia Prada released a simple black nylon backpack, with her logo modestly sewn on the front. She thereby reinvented the products of her grandfather's old leather house and became a trendsetter in the field of luxury bags. The combination of Pocone nylon, normally used for parachutes, the casual connotation of a backpack combined with the classical heritage of Prada as a luxury luggage label made it an instant success.

07. Dior, Lady Dior, 2001
The house of Dior re-entered the market of luxury bags in the nineties. Their first luxury bag was the Lady Dior from 1995. The design can be recognised by the logo letters D, I, O and R dangling from the handle. In 1995 Lady Diana visited the city of Paris, where she was offered a Lady Dior by Madame Chirac in the Grand Palais. Diana was seen with the bag everywhere, thereby making the bag famous.

08. Kate Spade, Kate Spade Bag, 1996
Kate Spade was fashion editor for the magazine *Mademoiselle* before turning into a bag designer in 1993. She criticised the lack of classic, simple bags in lively colours and interesting materials on the market. Her 1996 tote was her first major success. The bag was made of classic and simple material: black nylon, silk stripes and tweed.

09. Fendi, Baguette, 1998
'I carry within myself a very strong visual historic and emotional memory which is tied to Fendi's history and to my personal life'. This quote of Silvia Venturini Fendi characterises the way in which the Fendi bags are created. She belongs to the third generation of Fendi-women directing the house. In 1992 she noticed the disparity between the house's bags and haute cou-

ture clothes. So in 1997 she released the Baguette: a bag that radiates luxury like tiny wearable jewellery. The Baguette is a soft, small bag with a short strap. It fits exactly under the arm against the chest and is carried like a French bread; hence the name. The bag was produced in shining colours made of luxurious materials and decorated with a big logo and two silver buckles on the strap.

Every new season the design of the Baguette is altered and part of every collection is a version that is released in limited numbers.

10. Stephen Sprouse for Louis Vuitton, graffiti bag, 2000
Louis Vuitton's logo has been sacred for a very long time: nothing was allowed to be altered. But in the year 2000 Marc Jacobs asked graffiti artist Stephen Sprouse to apply a graffiti version of name and logo on a selection of Louis Vuitton bags. Thus Marc Jacobs and Stephen Sprouse caused a run on Louis Vuitton bags.

11. Dior, Gaucho Bag, 2006

In the spring 2006 collection Dior launched the Gaucho Bag, based on the classic saddlebag form with a Western-inspired appeal. The bag has a vintage look thanks to the specially washed calf leather, the lambskin links and antiqued silver metal details. Every Gaucho Bag has a vintage Dior medallion from 1947 and a large key dangling on the front. The metal links and buckle on the shoulder strap are also vintage silver. The Gaucho Bag comes in various colours and sizes. The large model consists of folded over calf leather, like a real saddle, with each flap bearing a zipped bag compartment. With this bag Dior has created a present-day form based on the classic bag aesthetic. John Galliano is reported to have said about this bag, 'Every girl should wear one of these and go out looking for trouble'.

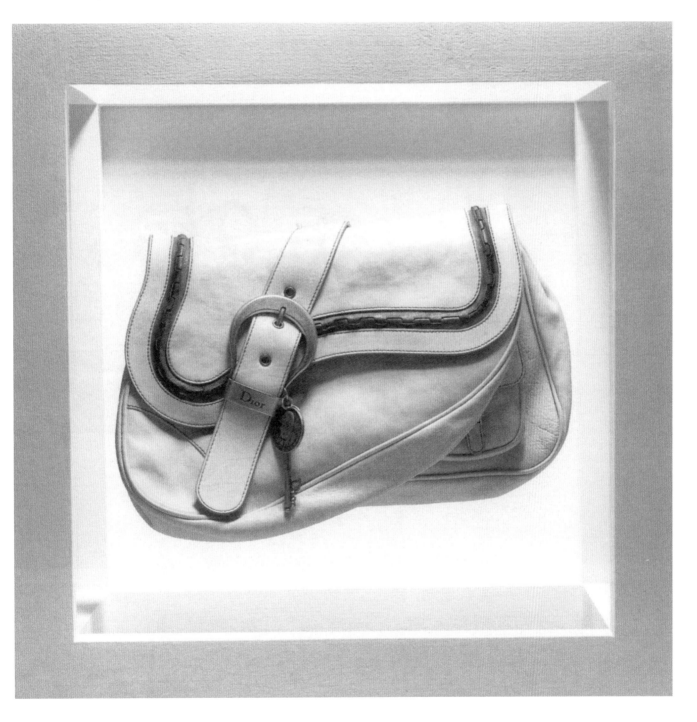

HATS

Karin Schacknat

PILLBOX
01. Jacqueline Kennedy with pillbox hat, early 1960s
The simple, closed and rounded form of the pillbox is part of the fashion of the early sixties. It has gone down in history as the hallmark of Jacqueline Kennedy. She wore a beige felt pillbox during the inauguration of John F. Kennedy as president of the United States, and when he was murdered she was wearing a pink model. For her the pillbox was the invention of the American fashion designer Halston. He got the idea from the pillbox Adrian had designed for Greta Garbo in the film *As You Desire Me* (1932).
In 1966 Bob Dylan's surrealistic song *Leopard-Skin Pill-Box Hat* hit the charts. This hat has since become a classic. You can find them on eBay, sometimes in a leopard skin print, or in bridal shops in white satin with tulle and artificial flowers.

Half a century ago, Christian Dior regarded the hat as the focal point of any fashion statement. While the fashion mechanism has undergone considerable change since then, the head is still at the top, which explains why headwear, as the 'crowning glory', is always so revealing. In fact, a hat sets the tenor for the overall picture, and it does so with an intensity that no shoe or handbag can match. The hat's position at the northernmost reaches of the human figure also places a special emphasis on the face, and thereby on the individuality of the wearer. Given the obsessive pampering of the individual in our society, we would have every right to expect a rich hat culture. But we would be disappointed. Today's street scene is dominated by bare heads. And the 'must have' accessories announced in the fashion press include very few hats.

It hasn't always been like this. In the nineteenth century, women from all strata of society wore hats when they went out. One's outfit was incomplete without a hat. The choice of the right hat was not easy back then, given the wide range of events that all required the appropriate headwear: morning, afternoon or evening, garden party or museum visit, birthday, funeral or charity bazaar. Books of etiquette declared which creations were suitable for which occasion.

The purchase of a hat usually began with a visit to a milliner. There a basic form was bought as well as material for the trimming. A selection could be made from numerous types of straw, silk, velvet, felt, ribbons, artificial flowers and feathers from every possible kind of bird. The actual decoration was up to you, but there were guidelines. Fashion magazines reported the latest ideas from Paris, and a gifted milliner had an eye for visual effects as well as for technical questions. Until far into the 1950s every major European city had a large number

TURBAN
02. Advertisement for turbans from the Sears Robuck catalogue, 1940-1941
03. Paulette (milliner), turban, 1950s
04. Prada, turban worn by models during spring/summer 2007 collection show
The original turbans have no permanent form. They're long pieces of cloth that are wound round the head in a certain way and then fastened. Turbans come from the Orient, where they were worn by the Osman sultans and desert nomads and are still worn by Indian Sikhs. This practical and elegant headwear keeps appearing in Western fashion. In Vermeer's 1665 painting *Girl with the pearl earring* the model is adorned in a turban. Paul Poiret became known for his turbans in the early twentieth century. During the forties, the famous Parisian hat designer Paulette rediscovered the turban. The turban was big fashion during the war years when practically nothing was available because of the textile shortage – a length of fabric at most. The American mail order company Sears Robuck sold ready-made turbans. In the autumn of 2006 the Capello hat shop in Nijmegen exhibited a collection of hats made by Dutch designers, with the turban as the starting point. And Prada made a smash on the catwalk with turbans in a wide range of colours for summer 2007.

of hat shops. In the thirties the amount of creativity in New York began equalling that of Paris on account of the many gifted women who arrived with the floods of new immigrants. These women turned to the traditional crafts because of their problems with the language.

In the Netherlands the hat enjoyed its last glory days after the Second World War. For the first time, the hundreds of milliners were faced with competition from male designers. Hat shows were held every season with considerable attention from the press.

Couturiers exercised a great deal of influence on hat fashion right from the start. Some relied on the imagination of their milliners, others did the designing themselves. Paul Poiret's trademark at the beginning of the twentieth century was a turban, an idea he got from his wife and favourite model, Denise. In the shows given by Elsa Schiaparelli, special attention was paid to hats. Her surrealistic creations made in the form of, say, an ink bottle, a lamb chop or a shoe have gone down in history. Jeanne Lanvin and Coco Chanel began as milliners, and the hat designs of both were admired because they revealed a new spirit of the times: simple and without the excessive romanticism of the Belle Epoque.

The grand master of balance and proportion, Cristobàl Balenciaga, designed all the hats in his collection himself. As a counterpoint to the volume of his clothing, his hats were often especially small or very large. He was a strict perfectionist and thought his customers should wear his outfits only with the hats intended for them; all other hats were out of the question because they disturbed the composition. At that time a total look was generally regarded as a sign of good taste, certainly when it came to couture. A Chanel dress demanded Chanel accessories.

These and other fashion formalities were all abandoned during the sixties. The young post-war generation experimented with new concepts of freedom and self-expression. One's own hair – first teased, then styled with a geometric cut, and finally grown extra long – had a higher fashion content than any hat could ever manage. Broad-brimmed floppy hats were worn in hippie circles by both men and women in around 1970. They bore the same nostalgic, non-conformist and anti-status message as John Lennon's round wire-rimmed glasses.

In recent decades we've also seen an informal assortment of headwear being worn in the street: large crocheted caps by Rastafarians and those in the ska scene, knitted caps by skinheads and hip-hoppers, and a range of hats with visors (the baseball model as well as the more voluminous types). Here and there you see the occasional cowboy hat. Hip young men sometimes wear classical fedoras, but pushed back on the head a bit, nonchalantly, like something casually picked up at a flea market.

Genuine ladies' hats are worn today at weddings and funerals. In the provinces they're still worn to church, and by the Salvation Army. In England there's the annual Ladies Day during the Ascot horse races, when ladies compete with each other with eccentric hat creations. It's true that hats are still being made for some haute couture collections, but they're often for the show alone and not for sale. In the Netherlands and elsewhere there are hat designers with an interesting oeuvre for lovers of the applied arts.

The hat as a general fashion attribute isn't what it used to be, but that may change. The revitalisation of the Balenciaga fashion house by Nicolás Ghesquière brought with it a certain *couture* look that included a

02.

03.

04.

helmet-like hat. Elsewhere there are *cloches* with down-turned brims in circulation. And Prada presented colourful turbans for its summer 2007 collections. All these are simple constructions that don't hamper movement in the urban hustle and bustle and contain no risk of overly emphatic elegance or, even worse, gentility.

References
Engelmeier, Regine and Peter W. Engelmeier. *Film und Mode: Mode im Film*. Munich: Prestel Verlag, 1990.
Finlayson, Iain. *Denim: An American Legend*. New York: Fireside, 1990.
Fraser, Kennedy. 'Hats', in: *The Fashionable Mind*. New York: Knopf, 1981.
Grijpma, Dieuwke. 'De hoedenma(a)k(st)ers: kiezen tussen kunst en commercie', in: *Kleren voor de elite*. Amsterdam: Uitgeverij Balans, 1999.
Hats. Amsterdam: The Pepin Press, 1998.
Kybalová, Ludmila. *Das großr Bilderlexikon der Mode*. Berlin, Munich: Bertelsmann Verlag, 1975.
Loschek, Ingrid. *Reclams Mode- und Kostümlexikon*. Stuttgart: Reclam, 1987.

Martin, Richard and Harold Koda. *Jocks and Nerds*. New York: Rizzoli, 1989.
McDowell, Colin. *Hats: Status, Style and Glamour*. New York: Rizzoli, York 1992.
Seeling, Charlotte. *Mode: De eeuw van de ontwerpers 1900-1999*. Cologne: Könemann, 1999. (Orig.: *Mode: Das Jahrhundert der Designer 1900-1999*)
The Fashion Book. New York: Phaidon, 1998.
Van de Schoor, Frank (ed.). *Boven Maaiveld: Hedendaagse Hoedenontwerpen*. Nijmegen: Cappello, 1999.

JOHN GALLIANO

BERET
05. John Galliano, baret worn by models during 2006 collection show
06. Faye Dunaway with baret in the film *Bonnie and Clyde*, 1967

Berets are flat, more or less limp hats that are usually round and have no visors. The use of the beret goes far back in history. As early as the sixteenth century it was the characteristic headwear of the humanists. Today berets are worn by soldiers, with various colours linked to specific functions: green for commando troops, red for airborne brigade, etc. The beret in a wide range of variations also has a lasting place in the world of fashion. Influences from the film world are the alpino cap worn by Lauren Bacall in the forties and especially the big beret – the so-called Basque cap – worn by Faye Dunaway in *Bonnie and Clyde* (1967), which unleashed an entire fashion trend during those years. John Galliano presented a large, soft beret in his 2006/07 autumn/winter collection

06.

CLOCHE

07. Fashion illustrations with cloche, ca. 1925
08. Furla, cloche, autumn/winter 2006/2007 collection

Cloche is the French word for bell, which indicates the shape of this ladies' hat: a tall, narrow crown, flaring at the lower edge in a narrow, turned-down brim, not to be confused with the brimless bowler. The cloche was fashionable in the 1920s, supposedly because it was more practical to wear during automobile rides (which were becoming more common) than the voluminous hats from the previous period with their wide brims and big feathers. The cloche has recently been making a comeback here and

CAP

09. Mao Zedong (1893-1976) in a cap
10. Chinese factory workers wearing caps, 1973
11. Chanel, advertising campaign for Coco Mademoiselle, 2005
12. Contemporary cap with a casual outfit, report from *WAD*, autumn 2006

'The guy in the cap' is another way of saying worker. The flat cap with a visor is the proletarian headgear par excellence. And it's not only part of their working attire. Workers and farmers have traditionally preferred to wear caps during their free time as well. Evidently it's an international custom, since communist leaders elsewhere in

the world – such as Lenin in Russia and Mao Zedong in China – liked to appear in public in caps, the sign of solidarity with the working class. The blue cap that was required dress for millions of Chinese created a sense of unity with an anti-elitist tone. In the fashion world caps have been featured in a variety of proportions, colours and materials. None of them is intended as a political statement. They're just meant to strike a light-hearted, 'rascally' note. Obviously the cap goes well with jeans (also originally workers' clothing). In the Chanel advertisement the cap is eroticised by being the only piece of clothing in evidence.

there, such as the model from Furla shown in the illustration (autumn/winter 2006/07), intended to be regarded as 'ladylike'.

08.

07.

09.

10.

12.

REAL PEOPLE
IN EVERY TIMEZONE

TIMEZON

11.

CHANEL

COCO
MADEMOISELLE

CHANEL
PARIS

FEDORA

13. Humphrey Bogart with
fedora, 1939
14. Brooklyn Industries,
advertising campaign, 2006

The classical Western men's hat
is made of felt and has a brim
that is flat at the front and
slightly raised at the back. Fedoras usually have a triangular
dent at the top of the crown and
two symmetrical dents on the
sides. This model has been
unchanged since the beginning
of the twentieth century. During
the sixties and seventies the
fedora – like all other formal
elements – fell into disuse, but it
has been revived in the new
millennium. The finest fedoras
were made by Borsalino, the
Italian hat manufacturer (since
1857), and were exported worldwide. A hat museum has been
set up in the former offices of
the company in Alessandria. In
the US the fedora was always an
essential part of civilised men's
attire. It was worn by presidents,
businessmen, mafiosi and detec-
tives, Humphrey Bogart, Bob
Dylan and Johnny Depp. Many
orthodox Jews wear black fedoras. A variation of the fedora, the

STETSON

15. Original Stetson label
16. Tim McGinnes with
Stetson, LS. Ranch, Monello,
Nevada (USA), 1985
17. Elvis Presley with Stetson
18. Christophe Coppens,
spring/summer 2007 collection

According to legend, in the year
1865 the American hat manufacturer John B. Stetson developed a practical and comfortable hat for the cowboys and
cowgirls of the West: a hat that
defied the sun and rain and was
waterproof enough to be used as
a bucket; a hat that held its
shape even after having been
perforated by a couple of bul-
lets. The shape would be derived
from the Spanish sombrero, with
a relatively high, somewhat narrow sloping crown and a broad,
stiff, somewhat curved brim. The
hat was made of high-quality
beaver felt and was henceforth
known as a Stetson, after its
inventor. That is to say, Stetson
is a trademark. The shapes and
colours of the 'cowboy hat' can
vary. According to another version of the story, Stetson was
originally a British invention.

pork pie hat, has appeared in the
ska music scene.

But even if that were true, this
legendary headwear became an
icon representing the myth of
the Wild West in film, advertisements, fashion and in the West
itself.

13.

14.

15.

16.

17.

18.

KARIN SCHACKNAT

BOATER

19. Gene Kelly with boater in the film *An American in Paris*, 1951
20. **Boaters as part of the school uniform, Harrow School, England, 1980s**
21. **Givenchy, boater, autumn/winter 1990/1991 collection**

In around 1800, England's Admiral Nelson introduced a straw summer hat for sailors. It was a round and somewhat stiff model with a flat crown that had a band running round it. Over time this 'boater's hat' became part of the summer uniforms worn by the pupils of various prestigious English public schools. But from the end of the nineteenth century until the 1930s it was a popular summer hat that was worn by the general population all over the Western hemisphere. It was supposed to be worn tilted to the side or the front, imparting a jaunty look. Coco Chanel claimed she had chosen the boater as one of her favourite hat types. Today you see this characteristic headwear worn as a man's hat mainly in nostalgic orchestras. In women's fashion the boater still makes an occasional appearance, such as here in the Givenchy collection for autumn/winter 1990/91.

20.

21.

19.

FLOPPY HATS

22. **Floppy hat, 1970s**
23. **Joseph, advertising campaign, 2006**

It can be made of felt, straw or cotton, with or without floral decorations or ribbons: the floppy hat has no authentic basic form and is not related to any designer or brand. It is simply a ball with a broad, limp edge that has many different expressive possibilities: mysteriously overshadowing the eyes, covering one eye so the other is left to ogle, framed open face, etc. In that sense it resembles the *respondent*, the hat worn by the musketeers in the first half of the seventeenth century. It, too, could correspond (French: *répondre*) to the mood of the day. But no matter what the mood, the flapping ostrich feathers on the hat gave its wearer plenty of allure. Among both the musketeers of old and the hippies of around 1970, this informal type of hat was at its best when worn with long hair. Floppy hats are suitable for communicating drama, romance or nostalgia, but they are not suitable for persons shorter than 1.70 metres.

23.

22.

HELMET-LIKE HATS

24. Audrey Hepburn met helmet in the film *How to steal a million*, 1966
25. André Courrèges, helmets, autumn/winter 1968/1969 collection
26. Rifat Ozbek, helmet, 1990s
27. Christian Dior, helmet worn by models during autumn/winter 2006/2007 collection show

Helmets were already being worn in a military context by the ancient Romans. Later helmets also served as part of workers clothing (as worn by miners, for instance) or in sports (such as equestrian sports) whenever special protection was required. In 1964, André Courrèges presented white helmet-like hats that were the finishing touch to his 'astronaut look'. But even without any reference to space travel, such headwear went well with the general fashion picture of the time (just like the pillbox) in which key words such as 'geometry' and a certain architectural hardness with rounded edges played a role (see Audrey Hepburn in *How to Steal a Million*, 1966). In around 1990, Rifat Ozbek came out with a helmet construction to go with his futuristic look. At the present moment – winter 2006/07 – the press everywhere is turning its attention to the helmet-like felt hat by Balenciaga, combined with clothing whose lines evoke something from the sixties. In his couture show for Dior (spring/summer 2007), John Galliano put knightly glamour on the catwalk that included helmets.

24.

25.

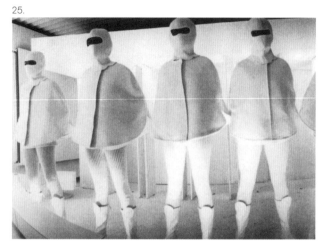

26.

27.

SCARVES AND SHAWLS

Georgette Koning

Scarves and shawls are a challenge. Just look at the innumerable ways in which these pieces of cloth have been worn through the ages. Scarves and shawls are draped like an item of clothing, gathered around the neck, knotted around the head as a fashionable head-dress and used to cover heads for religious or political reasons. There was even a time that shawls could cast a spell. In the mid-seventeenth century, Indian cashmere shawls played the main role in the seductive art of shawl draping practised by society ladies, of which Goethe was a famous victim. There have even been deadly scarves. A long scarf, all the rage in the 1920s, killed the dancer Isadora Duncan in 1927 when the ends became entangled in the spokes of a speeding Bugatti automobile. Nowadays scarves are no longer fashionable. Everyone possesses one or more, simply because it's nice to wear such a thing around your neck on chilly days and to cover your mouth when it's icy cold. But don't think we're waiting for the latest models from Marc Jacobs and Prada. A scarf is a non-fashionable accessory. That's how it is now. But who knows, maybe in ten year's time you really won't be able to go on the streets without the very latest model from that one brand that everyone has to have. In any case, this multifunctional accessory easily surpasses the actual meaning of the word accessory: something that matches.

The shawl or scarf is a length of fabric, that much is clear, although the boundaries are vague. Is the regal stole a scarf? Was the jacket-like shawl worn in Victorian times really a type of shawl? Did the boundary of the shawl become unclear in the mid-seventeenth century when women covered their low-cut neckline with the more scarf-like *fichu*? And when, a bit later, women folded this white overgrown handkerchief in two and inserted it into their square décolleté, can we still call it a scarf? Inventive draping led to the *fichu menteur*, a

01. Hermès, spring/summer 2007 collection show

02. Anthony van Dyck, *Portrait of Elizabeth, Lady Thimbleby, and her sister Dorothy Savage, Countess Andover*, ca. 1637
In the seventeenth century women draped scarves of gossamer-thin muslin as a frivolous accent along the tight neckline of a heavily décolleteé'd bosom. These loosely draped cloths contrasted sharply with the colour and material of the stiff silk dress.

02.

gauze-like piece of cloth decorated with embroidery or openwork patterns, which, towards the end of the eighteenth century, women folded and puffed up so as to suggest a full bosom. And that in an age when bare ankles were taboo. Let's just say that the shawl or scarf can be all these things. It illustrates how a piece of fabric keeps adapting itself to the dominant fashion and is automatically absorbed into new silhouettes or actually affects them. In the early 1920s, for example, a straight-falling silhouette became fashionable. In order to relieve this beanpole look, women knotted long scarves with fringes around their hips and sometimes, when it was party time, around their close-cropped heads.

The shawl of shawls is the cashmere shawl with its floral patterns. This shawl reached England in 1760 via trade with the East. Originally they were simply used as clothing, and in France they were cut to make petticoats. Only decades later, in the run up to the Empire period (1804-1814), did the cashmere shawl grow into a coveted object. Apparently the softly falling shawl just so happened to enhance the elongated neo-classical silhouette. The shawl's functions are surprisingly varied. Outwardly the high-priced, exotic shawl provides social prestige, but shawls are also indispensable as an elegant way of keeping warm. Most particularly, the shawl can be used as drapery. At actual shawl performances ladies would drape themselves in the Greek fashion, imitating the postures of ancient Greek statues.
Empress Joséphine, the fashion-conscious wife of Napoleon, at first disdained the cashmere shawls that her husband sent her during his exploratory journey to Egypt in 1798. In a letter to her son she wrote, 'The advantage is that they are light, but I doubt whether they will ever become fashionable.' A year later she

owned hundreds of them. The mania surrounding the cashmere shawl at that time is comparable to our mania for bags since the early 1990s.

In around 1800 in England, shawls were economically and technically important for the industrial revolution. The production of shawls with a pattern that was originally Indian flourished in the Scottish region of Paisley. In France, the shawl became artistically interesting as designers dared to deviate from the favoured Paisley pattern. It was then that the shawl began its advance as the first product of industrial applied art, even before hats and shoes. After 1870 there came an end to the long-standing Paisley shawl fashion. Many women had their shawls cut into *visites*, jackets that better matched the new trend of the *queue de Paris* or bustle, the padded back of a skirt that owed its form to an accumulation of fabric.

This did not mean the end of the shawl, but it never became as fashionable, status-raising, decorative and practical as it had been in the nineteenth century. Something else came in its place from the world of British sport: the scarf as a sign of group recognition. Think of the legions of football or rugby club supporters who can recognise each other from afar by the colours and design of their scarves. The same identifying function also applies to the Arab headcloth known as the 'Arafat' scarf or kaffiyeh. Left-wingers wear the black and white cotton cloth as part of their uniform, adding a new layer of meaning to the two that the scarf already always had.

References
Baseman, Andrew. *The Scarf*. New York: Steward, Tabori & Chang, 1989.
La Mode du Châle Cachemire en France. Paris: Musee de la Mode et du Costume, Paris, 1982.
Mackrell, Alice. *Shawls, Stoles and Scarves*. London: Batsford, 1986.

03. School of Golconda, Abdulla Qutb, *Shah of Golconda*, ca. 1670
In India, well-to-do men wore expensive cashmere scarves with finely woven foliate patterns that referred to their high social status. The *shál* (meaning an elongated shawl) reached England in 1760, where it was also initially only worn by men. Until the nineteenth century nothing was regarded as a scarf or shawl if it was not woven from cashmere wool. Indian cashmeres are woven from the soft belly hair of goats grazing on the high, cold slopes of the Himalayas.

04. Elisabeth Vigée Le Brun, *Marie Charlotte Louise Perrette Aglaé, comtesse de la Châtre*, 1789
At the end of the eighteenth century women wore handkerchief-like shawls known as fichus, which were sometimes knotted crosswise on the back. The bulging front sometimes reached to the chin and was treated with starch to keep its form.

05. François Gérard, *Madame Récamier*, 1802

If a society lady folded her cashmere shawl carefully she could expect the compliment that she was excellently draped. A cashmere shawl typically has a woven pattern in the form of droplets, which is a mix of Arabic and Hindu ideas. This buta pattern – known in the West as Paisley after the region in Scotland where it was woven between 1800 and 1850 – is a stylised cypress, the symbol in India for the tree of life. During the Directoire period of the French Revolution (1795-1799), the shawl changed into a stole. It acquired a single colour, such as pink, yellow or violet, was long and finished off with a pattern of rings.

06. Thomas Phillips, *Lord Byron*, 1813

After a sojourn in various Eastern countries, the poet and playwright Lord Byron was inspired by Orientalism – the Western interest in the Orient – and had himself portrayed in exotic clothing, including a turban. As a result of the Oriental play *Trois Sultanes* in Paris (1761), both the dressing gown and the turban became fashionable for men.

07. *Portrait of Beau Brummell*, 1805

A perfectly knotted scarf was indispensable for the outfit of a dandy like Beau Brummel. The scarf was usually treated with starch and reached up to the ears.

08. Champion & Gerard, 'Parfait châle breveté ou Trois chales en un', advertisement, 1847

In 1851 burnooses were shown at London's Great Exhibition, where novelties were on display. These large, semi-circular wraps decorated with paisley designs are similar to the cloaks that protect against sand and wind in desert regions. Victorian ladies wore the colourfully patterned shawls as a jacket over the enormous hoop skirts, which reached their biggest size in around 1850.

09. **Raoul Dufy, *La Jungle*, satin shawl, 1919**
Artists like Raoul Dufy and Sonia Delauny saw the shawl as a painter's canvas. Paul Poiret, the well-known couturier of the twenties, was among those who purchased Dufy's decorated shawls.
In the 1930s couturiers such as Worth, Patou, Chanel and Fath began using the shawl as a marketing tool and had their logos printed on them.

10. **Hermès carré *Sous les orangers*, 2002 collection**
11. **Hermès carré and tying model 110, 1998**
12. **Hermès carré and tying model 244, 1998**
13. **Hermès carré, 1972**
Hermès has been printing square silk scarves since 1937, initially with equestrian designs. The scarves are also worn as headbands or through the belt loops of a pair of jeans. The expensive Hermès carré is a typical French BCBG (Bon Chic Bon Genre) accessory.
The colourful silk scarves from the Italian Emilio Pucci were also especially popular with the fifties jet set. The bright colours of the Pucci scarf, such as turquoise and emerald, were inspired by underwater photographs of the Mediterranean.

11.

12.

13.

10.

14. Emily Hermans, spring/summer 2007 collection show
The Palestinian scarf (kaffiyeh) is worn in the West as a fashion accessory. The Belgian designer Raf Simons was one of the first to show the scarf on the catwalk. Since then, they regularly crop up in fashion collections. The Dutch designer Emily Hermans turned the fanciful check pattern into a knitting pattern and made skirts, rucksacks and sports shirts from it.

15. ... and beyond, hooded shawl designed for the movie *Marzipan* by Carolina Feix, 2005

16. Sandra Backlund, waistcoat, collection *Blank page*, autumn/winter 2005/2006
Voluminous knitted waistcoat as shawl by the Swedish designer Sandra Backlund who uses handicraft techniques like knitting in her experimental designs.

17. ... and beyond, foal shawl, collection 2005

18. Brigitte Bardot with Kirk Douglas at the entrance to the Hotel Carlton in Cannes during the 6th Festival de Cannes, April 1953

19. KIND, *Hot Legs*, cashmere scarf, winter 2005/2006 collection
KIND is a luxury knitwear label specialising in cashmere clothes and accessories. Some items in the Dutch label's winter collection were inspired by the work of the Surrealist fashion designer Elsa Schiaparelli.

GEORGETTE KONING

Gloves

Georgette Koning

You can be very imaginative when it comes to gloves, but the conceptual designs from 2006 by the Berlin designer duo Bless are certainly at the border of what can still be called a glove. They are knitted finger sleeves that only cover the first two bones of the finger, like the leftovers from a fingerless glove. These finger ornaments by Bless are more for decoration than for keeping the hands warm, especially as the cashmere 'fingers' are hanging from rings.

It's a long way from a basic accessory for keeping out the cold to the little work of art by Bless. But gloves have always been present in women's wardrobes in one form or another for the last four hundred years. The classic long glove made a comeback as a must-have fashion accessory in Prada's 2004 winter collection, where Prada used it as an extension of the 'new' three-quarter length sleeve. Two winter seasons later, gloves are everywhere to be seen on the catwalk: baggy with Louis Vuitton, wrinkled with Prada. Knitted ribbed gloves added the finishing touch to Burberry Prorsum's fashion image.

The ornamental aspect has always been an important function of gloves, but not the prime one. From classical antiquity until the year 1000 or so, gloves were usually bag-like mittens worn as protection against the weather or for certain types of work. The glove later acquired yet another function, that of bearing a symbolic message. From the tenth century onwards it was possible to tell someone's power and status from their gloves. The nobility and kings matched their impressive costumes with gloves decorated with precious jewels in order to display their power. A high-ranking person would own hundreds of pairs.

Religious leaders were also susceptible, it seems, to the fashion for fine gloves that spread from the Frankish region to Rome. It is purely from the aesthetic point of view, however, that bishops cover their hands with beautifully embroidered gloves, as they complement the decorated shoes and stockings with which they have long adorned themselves. It is always tempting to ascribe a symbolic meaning to something, and so the story about the purity of hands was later added.[1]

The church may well be an exception here, but the glove often has a symbolic charge, a fact we can deduce from the figures of speech that everyone can quote without difficulty. The basis for this was laid during the late Middle Ages, when the glove oozes symbolism. Transferring property by sending a glove was a custom at that time in various parts of the Christian world. Gloves were given to city fathers as a sign of their function, and knights received a pair on being knighted. Gloves also have a symbolic meaning in paintings. A good example of this is Rembrandt's Nightwatch (1639-1643) in which

01. Jean Paul Gaultier, gloves bag from the *Elégance Parisienne* collection, autumn/winter 1998/1999
In Jean Paul Gaultier's unusual use of supple leather, bag and gloves are combined to form a single entity.

the glove removed by Captain Frans Banning Cocq can be interpreted as a challenge (throwing down the gauntlet to someone), or a display of his willingness to fight.

From far back in history, gloves have always been an accessory for men. It was only from about 1500 on that they became an indispensable part of the woman's wardrobe. Gloves and marriage have long been associated with each other. To this day a bride's outfit is not complete without a pair of fine gloves. From the age of chivalry until the last century the glove could serve as the symbolic replacement for an absent person, enabling a marriage to be sealed by proxy. The Amsterdam Rijksmuseum possesses a portrait from about 1622 of the rich merchant's daughter Johanna Le Maire holding a pair of white leather gloves with lavishly embroidered gauntlets. Amazingly, the museum also has the gloves in its collection. These gloves were laid out after the engagement so that everyone could admire them. The more richly they were decorated the more esteem they earned and the greater were the gifts that could be counted on at the wedding.[2]

Although the function of the glove as a status symbol gradually became watered down after the seventeenth century, it continued to be an essential item amongst all the accessories in a women's wardrobe. Gloves are desirable as luxury articles, especially when sublimely perfumed, an idea that comes from fragrance-importing Italy. At the time when a kiss on the hand was customary, gloves impregnated with special perfumes stimulated the man's spirit and senses.

While the symbolism of gloves may well have slowly petered out, the erotic charge was – and still is – just as powerful. One of the ideals of beauty for the seventeenth century woman was snow-white arms and hands as vulnerable as porcelain. 'Revealing' these fairly erogenous zones to a man by pulling off the protective gloves agonisingly slowly was an intimate action comparable to the sophisticated peeling off of stockings. Yet there will certainly have been enough women who were ashamed of their less than exciting hands and were better off wearing beautiful gloves with slim, tapering fingers.

Gloves have been made and decorated throughout the centuries in innumerable models and with all manner of materials. The most remarkable are the sleeve-like, fingerless mittens that were worn by fashionable women during the mid-eighteenth-century Rococo period. They were excessively decorated and the floral motifs are repeated in the dress. They did not keep your hands warm, but besides being a highly decorative fashion detail they were particularly suited for wearing when doing needlework, a favourite pastime. It was a case of a nice way of combining usefulness with decoration.

A hundred years later gloves extended far above the elbow. They were pleasantly warm and perfectly matched the straight-hanging, puff-sleeved gowns. The new length lasted. Until today long gloves are compulsory when the prescribed dress code for a gala is 'white tie'. They are then supposed to be worn with a long, generously decolleté'd evening dress. It is the only remaining custom from a whole list of rules of etiquette for gloves that were prevalent until the 1960s. The exception to the rule is Queen Beatrix who, during a visit to the warm Antilles in 2006, 'wore' gloves that matched the colour of her ensemble, hat and shoes. She never had them on, but held them in her left hand or hung them on the strap of her shoulder bag.

The simplification of etiquette came about during the turbulent sixties, with the hat getting the short end of the stick. Even bishops adapted. Following the Second Vatican Council (1962-1965), gloves bit the dust (as did pontifical shoes and stockings). The Church wanted to get rid of all the hoo-ha, which nobody understood in any case.

Yet gloves will never disappear from the scene. In the winter they are simply essential. They are even becoming more and more innovative, since they are worn for winter sports like snowboarding, skiing and mountain biking. The new demands imposed on them means they are now electrically heated, windproof, water repellent and equipped with gel padding to make them shock absorbent.

With gloves almost as pure works of art, Bless is part of a splendid tradition. In the 1930s the Italian designer Elsa Schiaparelli made her best designs in close collaboration with surrealist artists such as Salvador Dalí and Jean Cocteau. They are designs with a broad wink or a joke, such as the black gloves with red leather nails sewn onto them. Schiaparelli was inspired by a photograph by Man Ray of hands that Picasso had blackened with shoe polish, except for the nails.

Gloves continue to be useful and decorative. As already mentioned, the symbolism of gloves has virtually disappeared. As far as that is concerned, all we are now familiar with is the lost glove. There's no sight sadder than that of a glove lying in the dirty wet snow – the lonely half of what shortly before was a happy pair. Nor is there anything more useless than such a lost glove, for what can you do with just the one? Yet there are people who take pity on them. Since the winter of 2006 a fence for lost gloves has been set up in Amsterdam's Vondel Park where, with a bit of luck, the other half can be found.

Notes
1. C. Staal, *De kleren van de kardinaal* (Zwolle: Waanders Uitgevers, 1992).
2. Boukje Detmar, 'Uitgelijnd', *Rijksmuseum KunstKrant* 28, 1 (Jan.-Feb. 2002): 16.

References
Blum, Dilys E. *Shocking! The Art and Fashion of Elsa Schiaparelli.* New Haven: Yale University Press, 2003.
Brooke, Iris. *English Costume of the Early Middle Ages.* Birmingham: Tindal Street Press Ltd., 1936.
Cummings, Valerie. *The Visual History of Costume Accessories.* London: B.T. Batsford Ltd., 1998.
Damase, Jacques (ed.). *Le Gant.* Franche le Reste: Archives pour l'histoire de la mode, 1984.
La mode et ses métiers. Paris: Musée de La Mode et du Costume, 1981.
Le Goff, J. and N. Truong. *De geschiedenis van het lichaam in de middeleeuwen.* Amsterdam: Bakker, Prometheus, 2004.

02. Daniel Mytens, *Portrait of Charles I*, 1631

Gloves were almost never worn before the eleventh century, but after that time they became a status symbol for members of the nobility. Models with beaker-shaped gauntlets were fashionable after 1600. The form of the cuffs can also be seen in the fashionable thigh boots, the folded rim of the hat and the voluminous cut of the impressive costumes from the period.

03. White gloves inscribed with the letters IHS in a heart of gold thread, belonging to the official Roman Catholic vestments, Haarlem, 1625-1649

We know from church inventories and books in which ceremonies are described that priests wore gloves from the tenth century onwards. Examples from that time, however, have not survived. Bishops' gloves, made of silk or leather, were embroidered with a cross or provided with an enamelled plate depicting Biblical scenes. They were put on ceremonially, that is to say they were presented on a gold tray and the pulling on was accompanied by a prayer.

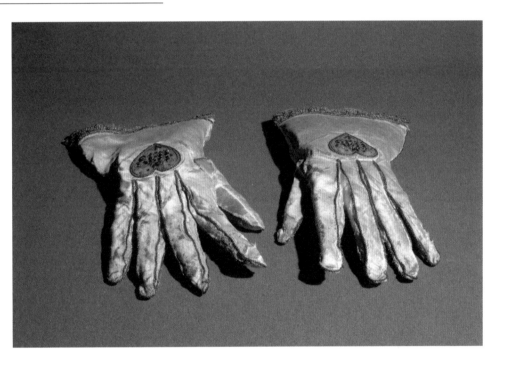

04. Nicolaes Eliasz. Pickenoy, *Portrait of Johanna Le Maire*, 1622-1625

Gloves as a symbolic wedding gift. The gauntlets are full of various embroidered symbols like peacocks and little pearl hearts pierced by arrows.

05. C.A. Coypel, *Charlotte Phillipine de Châtre de Cangé, Marquise de Lamure*, ca. 1745

Following the fashion, the Marquise de Lamure is wearing fingerless mittens (probably perfumed) with fur-trimmed edges. During severe winters men and women protected their chapped hands in muffs (pinafores). This practical and decorative muff is made of silk, velvet and fur.

06. Printed women's gloves from the Directoire period, ca. 1795-1805
White, short, patterned gloves with perforated scalloped edges. They are printed with abstract motifs derived from Greek antiquity and pictures of Greek amphorae or mythological scenes epitomising the extolling of Greek ideas in the eighteenth century.

07. Fashion plate from *Costumes Parisiens*, 1812
The glove industry flourished during the Empire period. Favourites included both long models and knitted or crochet net-like 'filets' - fingerless mittens. The fingers and thumb gained more freedom of movement thanks to the improved fit - a small part of the pattern offered room for the ball of the thumb.
The slightly baggy models made of non-stretchable materials like cotton or linen were affixed to the upper arm with a ribbon.

08. Elsa Schiaparelli, gloves, summer collection, 1939
Gloves as portable works of art. Mint-green, elbow-length models by Elsa Schiaparelli. The gold frills can be seen as a reference to the *mano cornuta* (the horned hand), the Italian gesture to ward off the evil eye or to indicate that a man has been cuckolded by his wife.

09. Willy Maywald, gloves by Jacques Fath, 1951
The 1950s saw considerable fantasy in the field of gloves. Elegant gloves were frequently worn. A well-to-do woman had a different pair for every outfit and for every occasion. The rules of etiquette required that gloves should also be worn indoors and during a dinner.

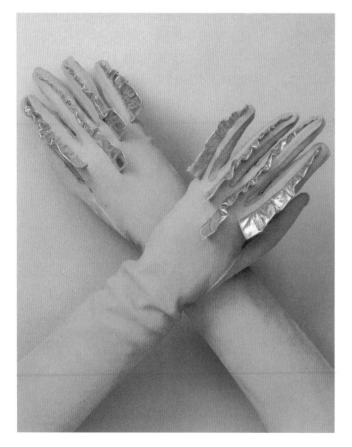

10. André Courrèges, 1964 collection
Short gloves, sometimes black and white, completely white or brightly coloured and provided with graphic motifs, were part of the Total Look in the 1960s. An extensive range of matching accessories - shoes, sunglasses, hat, handbag and panties - formed a whole.

11. Bless, gloves, 2006

'Gloves' by Bless as jewellery. The knitted cashmere finger warmers are attached to 'vintage' rings, making them look like a 'negative' version of fingerless mittens.

12. Thomasine Barnekow, gloves from the *Peau Précieuse* collection, 2006

Thomasine Barnekow, who graduated in 2006 from the Design Academy Eindhoven, incorporates jewellery into gloves. Only the designer knows the value of the hidden bracelets – are they made of worthless plastic foam or expensive precious metals?

13. Chanel, gloves, autumn/winter 2006/2007 collection

The return of long gloves at the beginning of the twenty-first century is due to the introduction of the cape and winter coats with three-quarter length sleeves. The designer – and fanatical wearer of gloves – Karl Lagerfeld devised for Chanel a combination of denim mittens under a classic, woollen Chanel suit. The tight gloves go perfectly with the slim-fitting jeans trend.

Glasses

Karin Schacknat

01.

02.

01. F.C. Gundlach, butterfly wing sunglasses, ca. 1952
02. Butterfly wing glasses in the shape of a bat, after 2000
 Butterfly wing frames came into fashion in America in the 1950s. The tips of the frame were often decorated and pointed upwards in a diagonal, which is why this model was also known as 'cat eye'. It remained popular until the 1960s, both for ordinary glasses as well as for sunglasses.
This 1952 photograph is by F.C. Gundlach from the series Fifties Fashion Photography. In more recent times it continues to make an appearance for the sake of contrasting postmodernist compositions. Here we see punk glasses advertised on eBay in the form of a bat with red lenses and red stones for the bat's eyes.

The very first glasses were made of beryl, a semi-precious stone, and were developed in the thirteenth century as a reading aid for priests and scholars; the majority of the rest of the population could not read or write. That changed in the sixteenth century with the invention of printing, after which more and more people came into contact with the printed word. The first opticians also treated shortsightedness, where the problem was not reading but good sight at a distance.

Beryl was replaced by ground glass; frames were initially made of wood, later of horn, metal, leather or bone. The chief problem was keeping the glasses in a stable position in front of the eyes. In the nineteenth century, after all sorts of laborious experiments, glasses appeared with clips for hooking behind the ears in the manner that we are now used to. In refined society it was regarded as impolite to wear glasses constantly. Attitudes became somewhat more relaxed after the French Revolution in 1789, but in the early nineteenth century it was still customary in large parts of Europe to remove the glasses in the presence of a superior or on greeting someone.

In the wake of nineteenth-century industrialisation more and more workshops arose (for metal working, for example) which required the use of special safety goggles. The same applies to the advent of the steam locomotive with open third-class carriages, and later the automobile. Diving goggles also came into use at that time, in a certain sense an early form of sports glasses. But they were not new – the first diving goggles had already been invented by Leonardo da Vinci around 1500.

The radical technological and cultural developments that took place during the last hundred years also had an effect on the production and use of glasses. After the First World War, following the American example, frames were made of celluloid. The international glasses industry shifted into gear. The first Ray-Ban pilot's glasses date from 1937. After the Second World War, the United States once again set the lead from both a technical and an aesthetic point of view. In the post-war reconstruction period the image of European fashion was determined by geometrical lines, Pop Art and a youthful counter-culture, and this also had an influence on the design of spectacle frames. The sixties saw models with a futuristic slant, followed by nostalgic round glasses in the Hippie era, large frames in the seventies and even larger ones in the nineties. There was no lack of original ideas.

In the meantime, the manufacturer's logo that had once been decently hidden on the inside was now becoming more visible – and more important. Designer glasses are a characteristic accessory of the last two decades. The most famous fashion houses also launched spectacle frames, with the design and logo being meant to support the respective image of the house.

At the opposite pole to today's glamour glasses are the ready-to-wear reading glasses that you can buy in any department store or chain of chemists for the price of a tin of dog food. The much-discussed aging of the population is one reason for the growing need for reading glasses; furthermore, there is a greater strain on our eyes nowadays because of computer screens, SMS displays or car navigation systems. According to a survey published in the *Volkskrant* newspaper, the number of people wearing reading glasses has increased by more than a million in the last ten years and people now generally own, in addition to prescription lenses, a whole series of disposable glasses for use with various everyday activities.

You don't wear glasses for pleasure, and certainly not out of vanity. Opticians have been recommending glasses as a chic and fashionable accessory since the twenties, a claim that is also made by advertisers, but in practice glasses do not make a face more attractive. People who wear glasses count at best as intelligent and well-read, particularly in the case of men. Would Harry Potter be so popular if he was a girl? Maybe, but only as long as puberty is still far away. According to the collective imagination, glasses do not go with eroticism. Glasses are nowhere to be seen on the catwalks, and romantic heroines (and heroes) in films always have perfect eyesight. In films, glasses typify the virginal librarian or the malicious office-clerk. A pair of glasses is always a prosthesis, and even though it may say Chanel or Gucci on the frame, glasses furnish as much sex appeal as a wooden leg – unless it's a pair of sunglasses.

The basic idea of sunglasses had already occurred to the Roman emperor Nero, who watched gladiator fights through an emerald so he would not be bothered by the bright sunlight in the arena. It will not have been by chance that he chose a green stone, since green, grey and brown lenses influence the perception of colour the least, while yellow increases the contrasts. There were regular experiments with coloured glasses over the course of the centuries, but it was not until the 1950s that sunglasses became hip and fashionable. Various celebrities were photographed wearing them. It was these images that set the tone, referring as they did to a life of luxury, including sojourns in sunny climes. Although the latter is no longer so special, sunglasses nowadays impart a much greater fashion awareness, not only when they come from a famous house of fashion but mainly because of the fact that they conceal the wearer's eyes, and particularly his or her gaze. This emanates a sense of mystery, as shown by the famous example of Greta Garbo who, in the twilight of her film career, eschewed publicity. Hiding behind dark glasses always suggests the possibility that something is being concealed, and in a metropolitan way it looks dishonest and anonymous.

There is also a certain power aspect in seeing without being seen. Anna Wintour, the notorious executive editor of the American edition of *Vogue*, usually appears in public wearing sunglasses. But, according to the gossip, this has less to do with making a display of power than with hiding her crow's feet.

References
Anziehungskräfte: Variété de la mode 1786-1986. Munich: Carl Hanser Verlag, 1986.
Brillen en Zonnebrillen. Amsterdam: The Pepin Press BV, 2005.
Marly, Pierre. *Spectacles and Spyglasses.* (Text J.C. Margolin and P. Biérent) Paris: Editions Hoëbeke, 1988.
Vervaeke, Leen. 'Leeshulp als accessoire: Voor elk moment en elke plek', *Volkskrant* supplement (*De Verleiding*), 25 November 2006.

03. Lorgnette, silver, ca. 1830

In the eighteenth and nineteenth centuries an elegant alternative to 'permanently' affixed spectacles was the lorgnette. The frame was attached at a right angle to a handle, which enabled the lorgnette to be politely removed in company, as etiquette demanded. This action could be communicative: raising the lorgnette to the eyes in a distinguished or critical way, then looking at the other appreciatively, mockingly, disdainfully or defiantly, and then lowering it again with an air of boredom.

In the same period the opera glass with a handle was also a particularly popular accessory. It consisted of a single lens, derived from the telescope, and it was used not only to get a better view of the performance but also to flirt with and spy on people's clothing and behaviour. Not for nothing was the opera glass also known as a 'spy glass'.

04. **Chinese glasses, tortoise shell, nineteenth century**
05. **Jean Lafont,** *Saigon* **frames, 1990s**

In ancient China wearers of glasses enjoyed a lot of prestige because of their supposed intelligence. The bigger the lenses, the greater the wearer's social standing. The lenses were not polished, though, and were therefore unsuitable as a reading aid. They were made of crystal or greyish tea stone which did make them sun-resistant. The first glasses were most likely introduced into China by missionaries in the seventeenth century. Here we see nineteenth-century tortoise-shell frames, and the Saigon model from the 1990s by the avant-garde French designer Jean Lafont.

04.

05.

06.

06. **Eskimo glasses, nineteenth century**
07. **Glasses with Venetian blind glass, Taiwan, 1960s**

The simplest way to protect the eyes from blinding sunlight is to half-close one's eyelids, although the delicate skin around the eyes is still exposed to wrinkle-producing UV light. The principle of narrowing the eyes can also be used in the construction of sunglasses. The photograph shows a nineteenth-century pair of Eskimo glasses made of bone with a strip of leather for attaching it to the head. The Taiwanese model from the 1960s is apparently inspired by the slats of a Venetian blind.

07.

08.
09.

08. Otto Dix, *Portrait of Sylvia von Harden*, 1926
09. Monocle, silver, nineteenth century

This painting by Otto Dix from 1926 shows the journalist Sylvia von Harden with a monocle. Dating from the early nineteenth century, the monocle was actually favoured by diplomats and officers. Here it is combined with other decisively unfeminine elements such as the hairstyle, the posture and the consumption of alcohol and cigarettes in public. Only very occasionally do we see monocles with an unmistakably feminine tone, as in this example from the nineteenth century with a setting of silver tendrils.

10. Lafont, sunglasses, 2006

The innovative Lafont brand has four shops in Paris, the oldest of which, in the Rue Vignon, dates from 1923. Here one can find old frames from all corners of the world as well as the firm's earliest creations. The other three shops sell new designs. The firm is currently owned by the husband and wife team of Laurence and Philippe Lafont, and it looks as though their son will also be working in the same line of business. They concentrate on innovative design, coupled with luxurious and high-quality production. They distance themselves from licences for fashion brands and mass-produced articles. The metal-edged Lafont frame has appeared in various designs and won several prizes.

11. Audrey Hepburn with sunglasses in the film *Breakfast at Tiffany's*, 1961

Audrey Hepburn with trend-setting large sunglasses in Blake Edward's film *Breakfast at Tiffany's* (1961). Tiffany's, the famous New York jeweller's, is not an obvious place to stand in front of dressed in a long evening dress while eating a take-away breakfast. But such a situation, with its sense of alienation, fits life in a big city that never sleeps. These components, arranged around the figure of Audrey Hepburn who represented the ideal of beauty at that time, resulted in a famous still that looks very much like a fashion photograph.

12. Pierre Marly, *Puzzle* frames, 1960s

In 1951, when the supply of attractive spectacles was still very limited, the optician Pierre Marly opened a shop in Paris. Right from the start he worked on producing spectacles that were not only of high-quality materials and construction but above all were fully-fledged fashion accessories, a total look consisting of stylistic building blocks that caused every sign of the wearer's visual impairment to be forgotten. Marly introduced an exclusive small collection every year and also designed individual frames for film stars and politicians. It became an avant-garde brand of the highest class. Besides the shops in Paris, Geneva and Tokyo, there is also the *Musée Pierre Marly – Lunettes et Lorgnettes de jadis* at 380 Rue Saint-Honoré in Paris. Here, over the course of four decades, everything has been assembled that has to do with glasses and optics.

The photograph shows Marly's *Puzzle* model from the 1960s.

13. Coco Chanel, 1937

Coco Chanel with glasses, photographed by Roger Schall in 1937. The house of Chanel supplies every conceivable fashion accessory, including spectacle frames. The grand lady herself (aged 54 in the photograph) often allowed herself to be photographed with a cigarette, but only seldom with glasses. But the fashion trade in all its details is just as hard on the eyes as reading. Jean Paul Gaultier also wears glasses, as is apparent on the website of the prominent French brand of spectacles Alain Mikli.

14. Chanel, advertising campaign, 2006

Glasses from a prominent fashion house (or actually the licence holder) are a favourite accessory among brand name fetishists. They are heavily advertised, and as a result spectacles and sunglasses make an important contribution to the fashion house's image. Part of the design involves ostentatiously placing the name or at least the logo of the relevant brand on the side of the frame next to the temples. Somewhat vulgar perhaps? At Chanel, Gucci or Dior they see no problem in this.

15. Chanel, advertising campaign, 2006

16. Gucci, advertising campaign, 2002

17. Dior, advertising campaign, 2005

PERFUME BOTTLES

Agnes Gomes-Koizumi

01. Jean Paul Gaultier, advertising campaign, 2005
The glass corseted figure released in the eighties continues to be released in limited edition tins. This feminine form is typical of the figural category of bottles, which includes glass sculptured forms such as flowers and geometric forms.

Once reserved for the few and wealthy, perfume has evolved in consumer society from a sixteenth-century luxury good to a twenty-first-century toiletry item. No longer kept under lock and key in specially crafted containers, perfumes are sold, marketed and developed with the bottle in mind.

Much like spice containers in the Victorian era, perfume bottles were handcrafted, ornate and very small. Until the dawn of the twentieth century and the subsequent rise in mass-production, perfume was sold apart from the bottle. Since the onset of mass-production, bottle design has been closely connected to advertising and marketing in an effort to keep the merchandise moving. Bottle design over the past 50 years has mirrored societal changes in gender roles. The packaging reflects a rise in consumerism exemplified by bottle shape and the materials used in manufacture. As perfume became more commonplace, the bottles gracing silver cosmetic trays, bathroom cupboards or dressing rooms have become a true fashion accessory.

Like handbags or shoes, most women today have more than one perfume – to coordinate with a mood, or more often, to distinguish daytime wear vs. evening wear. Unlike other accessories, perfumes cannot be 'tried on' in the same way. A scent reacts to each person's skin chemistry, such that a scent that smells wonderful on one person may be acrid on another. So how do most people purchase such a personal and unnecessary item? Advertisers have spent a lot of money on campaigns to encourage impulse purchases. By analysing the bottle design and ad campaigns we begin to understand how bottle form is imbued with 'sellable' lifestyle characteristics that may be classified as either masculine, feminine or neutral.

After the end of the First World War the perfume industry began to flourish, due in part to an increase in advertising and an acceptance of women in the work force. For the first time, women were earning their own disposable income. Also at this time, advertising campaigns began to debunk the myth that 'nice girls don't wear rouge'. Perfumes were lumped into the cosmetic category and became an integral component of their profits. This change in public thinking towards cosmetics coincided with these aggressive cosmetic campaigns. It has become increasingly common for an ad to present a scenario or group of people without providing any product information. This lifestyle advertisement is particularly common with perfumes – which, being scents, are not verbally tangible.

A study of bottle design from the 1960s to the present illustrates the disposable quality of perfumes. Physical examples of these bottles are difficult to acquire because women often do not keep empty perfume bottles. They are by nature mass-produced and mass consumed. To create demand, perfumes have been marketed as emotional or evocative/mood enhancing items for personal use or gifts. Merchandisers have revealed that package design is particularly important in the case of gift giving. This has become especially important with the rise of the self-serve industry. A scent in particular, may be purchased entirely based upon the bottle design because the product itself lacks any hard information other than chemical ingredients.

There are three broad categories of bottles based on shape. For the purpose of classification, I define a 'classic' shape as referring to rectilinear forms (forms with straight lines and 90-degree angles). 'Classic' forms have historically been defined as characteristically masculine based upon the architectural convention of the mid-nineteenth century. 'Romantic' shapes are correspondingly defined as curvilinear in form. This is also based on the same architectural principals - round, spherical, vase shaped, heart shaped and oval (etc.) are all feminine forms. The third bottle category is 'figural.' These bottles are akin to mass-produced glass sculpture - birds, flowers, corsets, etc. Figural bottles may be imbued with either masculine or feminine characteristics depending on the subject matter and lines (curvilinear or rectilinear).

The gender associations in the bottles from the sixties relate masculinity to luxury, wealth and travel - as exemplified in the advertising campaigns. Femininity is associated with relationships and sensuality/sexuality. While these associations may be considered traditional, it should be noted that both the masculine and feminine attributes can be found in women's perfumes. Clearly there are indications of shifting gender roles, which position women more prominently in the masculine or work-related world. Examples of these types of bottles include *Chanel N°5* (masculine), *Tweed* (masculine), *Essence de Chantilly* (feminine) and *Tigress* (feminine).

Prior to 1973, few women wore perfume on a regular basis. The use of metal as a component in bottle manufacture markedly increased in the seventies. Similarly plastic components in bottle manufacture increased, indicating that perfumes were becoming less of a luxury item and more of a cosmetic or everyday accessory. The seventies also brought a change in feminine form bottles - cylindrical and rounded in direct contrast to the predominance of the rectilinear masculine forms of the sixties.

Bottles in 1985 magnify the trends of the seventies. Shapes are still predominately rounded and feminine in form. However, the once masculine rectilinear form is beginning to take on more gender-neutral iconography in advertising. There is an increase in the use of frosted glass.

The most notable development is the increase in the use of plastics in bottle design. Plastics in packaging are typically reserved for disposable items (hair products, detergents, cosmetics, etc.). An increase in visibly plastic bottles may indicate that perfumes are entirely disposable items, to be used every day. Since bottles were not meant to be kept and the product was to be frequently used, manufacturers could produce more liberal or daring designs. Figural forms increased as did geometric forms. Examples of figural forms include *Jean-Paul Gaultier, Sculptura* by Jovan. *Exclamation* by Revlon is a good example of the whimsical geometric forms of the eighties.

Designer fragrances grew markedly in the nineties and prices dropped dramatically. Expensive and inexpensive perfumes were sold increasingly in drugstores - alongside toiletries and other disposable items. Both bottle forms resembled toiletries (e.g. the *Vanilla Musk* bottle is similar in form to a nail polish bottle, *Polo Sport* is similar in form to a shampoo bottle). Metal crown tops continue to be popular and the advertising iconography associates metal with wealth, similar to the masculine forms discussed earlier.

Fashion houses mostly used classic, masculine, rectilinear bottle forms. Examples of these types of perfumes include *Boss Elements, Gio, Coco*.

Perfume bottles over the last 40 years illustrate changing gender identities through bottle form and the materials used. By studying the iconography of bottle form and design we can learn to 'read' the society we live in. In doing so, we can see that by moving into the realm of cosmetics, perfumes have become disposable, everyday items - true accessories, like shoes or handbags.

References
Barile, Elizabeth and Catherine Laroze. *The Book of Perfume*. Paris: Flammarion, 1995.
Gomes, Agnes R. 'Perfume Bottles: A study of contemporary material culture'. Museum Studies Department, University of Toronto: http://www.chass.utoronto.ca/history/material_culture/gomes/.
Green, Annette and Linda Dyet. *Secrets of Aromatic Jewelry*. Paris: Flammarion, 1998.
Lefkowitz, Christie Mayer. *The Art of Perfume: Discovering and Collecting Perfume Bottles*. London: Thames & Hudson, 1994.
Perfume Bottle Quarterly. International Perfume Bottle Association.

02. Revlon, Charlie, advertising campaign, 1996

Released in 1973 by Revlon, Charlie was the first perfume that developed a lifestyle brand. The Charlie woman was 'modern and independent' or 'truly at ease with herself'. Note the rounded edges on the simple bottle.

03. Coty, Exclamation, advertising campaign, 1989

Found in most pharmacies during the nineties, Exclamation reflects the whimsical and disposable nature of perfumes. As prices dropped dramatically, the accessibility of perfumes increased. Even teens could afford to purchase this youthful fragrance by Coty. While made of glass, this bottle clearly indicates that perfumes have become disposable everyday items.

04. Coty, Vanilla Musk, 1994

Vanilla Musk was sold at pharmacies alongside traditional toiletry products. This popular brand by Coty was sold at 'everyday' prices. Note the similarity of bottle form to a typical bottle of nail polish.

05. Balenciaga, Le Dix, 1947

Launched by The Design House of Balenciaga in 1947, Le Dix has been marketed as a refined classic feminine fragrance. Accordingly the bottle has curvilinear lines. But you may notice that it is reminiscent of a Doric column in classic Greek architecture – which is considered masculine.

06. Cacharel, Anaïs Anaïs, advertising campaign, 2005

First produced by the French design house Cacharel in 1978, Anaïs Anaïs became a favourite of young girls around the world. Sold in an opaque white bottle with a floral motif, the bottle is feminine in form.

07. Chanel, N°5, advertising campaign 2006

Chanel N°5 was developed in 1921. Note the clean, classic lines of the bottle. This traditional form may be described as masculine when historical, architectural or material culture naming conventions are applied to it. Coco Chanel believed that perfume should be worn wherever a woman would like to be kissed.

08. Christian Dior, Poison, 1985

Poison perfume by Christian Dior was launched in 1985. The bottle form is feminine: rounded and curvilinear. Poison was paired with a strong marketing campaign directed towards 'seductive' women. Note the clear top and opaque dark, apple-like bottle.

09. Calvin Klein, CK one, advertising campaign, 2005

One of the first unisex perfumes, CK one has an interesting study. The bottle form has to be significantly masculine to entice a male consumer but not so masculine as to alienate women. The resulting bottle may be considered gender neutral. Note the similarity of this bottle to those masculine forms produced in the sixties. Also note the similarity to an alcohol flask or medicine bottle.

10. Ralph Lauren, Polo Ralph Lauren Blue, advertising campaign, 2005

Launched by Ralph Lauren in 1996, Polo Blue is housed in a cylindrical bottle with a metal crown top. Like CK one, the packaging is similar to an antique medicine bottle. With a strong lifestyle marketing campaign, Polo Blue continues to sell well among young people.

you're the one

Masks

Georgette Koning

Masks no longer exist as fashion accessories, strangely enough; for many people a mask would be ideal. Feel like being anonymous? Hidden behind a mask you're closed off from the outside world. A mask conceals wrinkles and protects you from the sun. For the heyday of the mask as a fashion attribute, however, we have to go back to the seventeenth and eighteenth centuries. In our time masks are only brought out once a year as carnival attributes, or more often, when made of latex or leather, to help stimulate sexual enjoyment.

Judging by the popularity of face-covering caps, sunglasses and 'hoodies' (hooded sweatshirts) as streetwear, it is surprising that masks have not yet made a comeback as a new fashion accessory. This may change, though, since designers like Vivienne Westwood and Walter van Beirendonck have recently been rediscovering the styling qualities of the mask. During the winter 2006/2007 shows, Commes des Garçons concealed the beautiful heads of the models behind hats and semi-masks. The Japanese labels Undercover and Junya Watanabe masked their models more extremely with black duct tape, tattered fishnet stockings and layers of fabric. Hermès and Viktor & Rolf did it more elegantly, with sophisticated net masks.

So many fashionable masked processions at the same time caused consternation among the international media. It was too strongly reminiscent of headscarves and other Muslim issues like the riots in the suburbs of Paris. The newspaper headlines talked about 'the muslimisation of fashion.'

But high fashion and politics rarely go together. 'Suddenly covering up has become just plain sexy', commented John Galliano, putting the fuss into perspective. For his Dior show, he made the models wear masks con-

01. **Viktor & Rolf, autumn/winter 2006-2007 collection show**
For their winter 2006/2007 collection, Viktor & Rolf adorned the heads of their models with net-like masks made of braided hair and metal. 'It was a reference to couture, to the mannerism of hats and veils. But we turned it into something surreal – we used the veil as though it was part of the hairstyle', they said in the Flemish magazine *Weekend Knack*, autumn 2006. During previous shows the fashion duo hid the models' heads in crash-helmets or painted them black. Since the faces were covered, people automatically looked more at the clothing, according to the designers.

02. **Wenceslaus Hollar**, *Winter*, **1643**
From the late sixteenth until well into the seventeenth century, well-to-do women wore black masks made of velvet, silk or paper when travelling and on other occasions. These masks offered protection from the weather and kept the skin pale. The social distinction between tanned labourers and ladies who did not have to work thus became quite apparent. Women also covered their heads for moral reasons. On the other hand, masked women were able to profit from the freedom offered by anonymity.

sisting of enormous glamorous paste-encrusted sunglasses. Are sunglasses the new masks? In their own way both sunglasses and masks grant anonymity. When people wear sunglasses you can't look them in the eyes. In that respect they work even better than a mask. By wearing attention-drawing sunglasses (how duplicitous), we try to come across as inconspicuous and unemotional. Celebrities and sunglasses have even become inseparable, whether or not the sun is shining and whether they're walking on the street or enjoying a cup of hot chocolate in a brasserie.

In France at the beginning of the seventeenth century, women profited from the freedom and privacy that the mask granted to them. 'Concealed by a black satin mask, they sometimes attended church or went to a ball or play, unrecognised by God and by their husbands.'[1] As the American sociologist Richard Sennett notes in his book *The Fall of Public Man*, at that time the street and public life in general were places where one could make contact with other people without exposing one's own personality.[2] In social contacts with strangers one is therefore figuratively and sometimes literally masked. One's personality is concealed, and because of this protection one feels freer than in one's intimate circle of friends and acquaintances. At the end of the eighteenth century, under the influence of the French philosopher Rousseau, the main thing that was demanded in all contacts was sincerity – one had to show on the outside what was felt within. In this period of Romanticism the mask was taboo and it disappeared from the fashion scene.

As befits a fashion article, the mask is more than just socially useful. Masks quickly became an indispensable expedient for vanity. In order to fulfil the ideal of beauty of those times, a lilywhite skin, fashionable women in the sixteenth and seventeenth centuries wore black velvet or silk masks when they were outdoors. In a satirical poem from 1636 the poet Pieter Cornelisz Hoofd – the PC Hoofdstraat, *the* fashion street of the Netherlands was named after him – spoke slightingly about what he regarded as the absurd custom of women of 'covering' their faces with velvet so as to keep their skin pale.

The great poet would have found it just as ridiculous that vain women at that time made masks from their own faces. A thick paste of make-up comprising plaster and toxic white lead created a layer so fragile that the 'skin' broke on displaying the least emotion. It reminds one of facelifts and paralysing botox injections that nowadays ensure a mask-like countenance and may even surpass sunglasses as a way of disguising and covering the face.

Masquerades, fashion and ideals of beauty do not always go together. In sixteenth-century Spain in particular, under the regime of the strict monarch Philip II, every self-respecting woman covered her head with a mask or veil for reasons of morality or decency. Women were already leading secluded lives, but masks put them in isolation. In other Western countries social mores were more relaxed and women wore masks mainly to keep their skin pale, as mentioned above, or as protection from the cold as we can see in the paintings of winter skating scenes by Pieter Breughel and Hendrick Averkamp.

In some parts of the world it is still customary to half conceal the face behind a nikab or fully under a burka as part of the Islamic tradition of hiding temptation. Until around ten years ago, veiled women were even more uncommon in the West than nuns. As a result of increasing immigration from Arab countries, they are no longer an exception in public places. The fact that Muslims can

03. Giandomenico Tiepolo, *Pulchinella in love*, 1797
There are two sources for the origin of the mask: theatre and religion. The masked art of the Commedia dell'arte – Italian companies that toured Europe with theatrical comedies – flourished from 1550 until 1650. Masks depicting human types, such as Pantalone the merchant and Colombina the clever servant girl, were popular during carnival festivities and masked balls.

04. H. Morland, *The fair nun unmasked*, ca. 1769
Masked balls were a pleasant and ambiguous court pastime in the seventeenth century. At that time women seldom wore masks in daily life, except when they did not want to be recognised. Etiquette required that women with a lower social status should remove their masks at home when in the presence of superiors.

tell from someone's eyes whether they like each other is difficult to imagine in Western culture. Most people associate covering the face with oppression and as an obstacle that prevents men from being seduced by women.

Ever since the aristocracy began giving sometimes wild parties it's been known that masquerades can evoke sensational feelings. At the court of Louis XV the mask symbolised impetuosity. Masks fell out of use, except during masked balls, in the early eighteenth century. Parasols suddenly turned out to offer better protection from climatic influences than masks, which really were quite uncomfortable. The impersonal yet somewhat frightening nature of masks meant that they fell out of fashion as accessories. It is precisely for these reasons that the current, albeit cautious, rise of the mask would seem to have a chance. Once again there's a lot to disguise.

Notes
1. Aileen Ribeiro, *Dress in Eighteenth Century Europe 1715-1789* (New Haven & London: Yale University Press, 2002).
2. Richard Sennett, *The Fall of Public Man* (New York: W.W. Norton & Co., 1974).

References
Ribeiro, Aileen. *Dress in Eighteenth-Century Europe, 1715-1789*. New Haven & London: Yale University Press, 2002.
Sennett, Richard. *The Fall of Public Man*. New York: W.W. Norton & Co., 1974
Vogelsang-Eastwood, G. *Sluiers ontsluierd*. Meeuwes, Uitgeverij Barjesteh, 1996.

05. **Willy Maywald, Veil by Jacques Fath, 1951.**
A sophisticated means of covering the face is the veil, which came into fashion in the fifties thanks to couturiers such as Christian Dior and Jacques Fath.

07. **Streetwear, knitted masks, 2006**
The American Rob Reger and Buzz Parker, inventors of the fantasy character Emily the Strange, popular among youth, wear face-concealing balaklavas which suit the sinister world of Emily, their pop culture phenomenon.

06. **Jean-Marc Nattier, *Madame de Céran*, 1754**
In order to make a mysterious and intriguing impression, women would wear the velvet, oval Moretta mask which concealed the entire face. The mask was held in place by a button clenched between the teeth. This mask originated in France and was meant for women visiting monasteries. It became a trend in Venice, the city of masks.

08. Hussein Chalayan,
*Between***, spring/summer 1998 collection**
Fashion's own criticism of face-covering veils found its repercussions in a collection by the Turkish Cypriot Hussein Chalayan. At the end of his show, models wore *chadars* of different lengths.

09. Romain Kremer, spring/ summer 2006 collection
The French designer Romain Kremer created a decorative form of mask by cutting away part of the fabric.

10. Peter Pilotto, mask, collection ... *carried away by a moonlight shadow* ... , 2004

12. **John Galliano for Dior, sunglasses set with Swarovski stones, autumn/winter 2006/2007 collection**
Sunglasses as masks. Like a mask, sunglasses – now also worn in the winter – offer ano-

nymity. Expensive designer glasses function at the same time as a status symbol.

13. **Walter van Beirendonck, *Aesthetic terrorists* collection, autumn/winter 2003/2004**
Walter van Beirendonck is fascinated by masks. Masks or references to them feature in

all his collections. The Belgian designer calls masks 'mysterious, challenging, fantastic, transgressive, universal, emotional, naive and hardcore' (interview in *LINK* no. 4, 2004).

14. Anticon, 2006 collection

By means of a simple intervention – putting a zip in the seam of a hood – the French label Anticon transformed a sweatshirt into a frightening disguise. Such concealment of the face is not tolerated. In 2005 the Bluewater shopping centre in England banned young people from wearing 'hoodies' (hooded sweatshirts). Because of their covered heads they cannot be recognised by security cameras and can thus cause a nuisance with impunity. The number of visitors to the shopping centre increased after hoodies were banned.

15.

15. Kate Moss and Pete Doherty during the masked ball marking the Möet Chandon Fashion Tribute 2006
16. Muses dressed in designs made by 'their' designer for the masked ball marking the Möet Chandon Fashion Tribute 2006, photographed by Nick Knight

Theme parties are popular in today's party culture, and that includes the masked ball. At the ball given by the British photographer Nick Knight, world-famous guests like Scarlett Johansson, Alexander McQueen and Kate Moss were not incognito but wore highly inventive yet revealing masks.

16.

THE DANGER OF HAIR

Anneke Smelik

Pelts of animals are made into fur as luxury products, which are used in many ways in fashion. Human hair, however, is a completely different matter. It is seldom incorporated in an accessory since it is actually rather gruesome when it is no longer on the head. We are more likely to encounter human hair in art than in fashion. We tend to regard loose hairs as nasty or dirty – think of the hairs caught in the drain of the wash basin. Human hair belongs to the category of bodily substances that become abject as soon as they are separated from the body. That is usually a question of bodily fluids such as snot, pus or urine, but hair or nail cuttings also evoke this experience of abjection: foul, distasteful and disgusting. This is because snippets of hair and nail clippings no longer belong to the living body, but have become dead material.

Human head hair occupies an intermediate position. It is actually only abject when it appears in places where it does not belong – in food, for example. But when hair is shorn off and made into a wig it is no longer nasty or dirty, since the beauty as well as the function of head hair are maintained. The wig is in fact the most well-known accessory made of hair. In our time wigs or hairpieces are used to replace one's own hair in the case of unwanted baldness, but we are also familiar of course with the era of gigantically high wigs, when the wig was an essential accessory fulfilling a role as part of the total 'look'. Dolce & Gabbana's 2006 winter collection makes a nod to the era of wigs, and Vivienne Westwood and John Galliano have also shown exaggerated wigs on the catwalk. The wittiest commentary, however, must be the wig made of fur that Bless (Desire Heiss and Ines Kaag) made in 1996 and which Martin Margiela has used in his shows.

01. **Bless**, *Fur Wig*, 1996
The fashion label Bless, created by the German duo Desire Heiss and Ines Kaag, negotiates the border between fashion and art. In 1996 they designed their first wig made of fur. The fashion designer Martin Margiela asked them to provide various wigs for his fashion show. The joke here is that, for humans, head hair and body hair are very different, while animals only have one sort of pelt which people then make into fur. By placing this fur on the head as hair, Bless shift the boundary between head and body hair and between human and animal hair.

02. **Meret Oppenheim**, *Object (Le déjeuner en fourrure)*, 1936
This surrealistic object, a fur-covered cup, saucer and spoon, makes a bizarre impossibility into a reality. The fur cheerfully deconstructs the breakfast service. This work of art also appeals to the imagination, as the fur eroticises an everyday object. The cup, saucer and spoon become something to stroke and fondle, or acquire somewhat more sinister meanings in their animality.

It takes some courage to do something different with cut off hair than the customary wig and to use it in accessories such as jewellery, bags, headdresses or in clothes. Because of its sometimes rather unpleasant associations, human hair is seldom used as a material in accessories. To start off with, a taboo against such improper use of hair had to be broken, which is what happened in the Surrealism of the 1920s and 1930s. This often involved putting hair where it does not belong, the classic example being Meret Oppenheim's *Le déjeuner en fourrure* (Fur-Covered Cup, Saucer and Spoon, 1936). In Salvador Dali's painting *Singularidades* (Singularities, 1937), all the figures and furniture are covered with human hair. And in the film *Un Chien Andalou* (1929) by Buñuel and Dali a woman's armpit hair disappears and then reappears on a man's mouth.

Another familiar Surrealist method was to equip women with a moustache and beard (here again it is a matter of hair being put where it does not belong), like the facial hair that Marcel Duchamp drew on a reproduction of the Mona Lisa in 1919, or the luxuriant moustache and beard with which Dali retouched Greta Garbo's face on the cover of a magazine in 1939. This fascination for 'women with beards' can also be found in the work of the photographer Zoe Leonard, as in *Pin-Up #1* (Jennifer Miller Does Marilyn Monroe, 1995).

Armpit hair and pubic hair often function in Surrealism as erotic elements. Body hair was generally not to be seen in old paintings, and pubic hair was not painted until the end of the nineteenth century. The taboo on armpit and pubic hair was only broken with the advent of Modernism . Depicting body hair is part and parcel of a Modernist style.[1] Depicting a nude with body hair turns the woman into a sensual and sexual being.

It is only in recent decades that body hair has once again become a taboo in popular culture. Body hair is now undesirable for both women and men. Moreover, the hair boundary is receding further. Under the influence of pornography, among other things, it is not only legs, armpits and chest hair (for men) that are shaved or waxed but also the pubic area, resulting in 'pubic hair fashion' with patterns such as the strip, triangle, heart or … a logo, as shown in Gucci's controversial ad campaign in 2003. The latest trend is 'Betty Beauty', a product designed to give the hair 'down below' a semi-permanent colour.

There are plenty of contemporary examples of a Surrealist approach to hair. In 1992 Robert Gober made a wax shoe with body hair 'growing' on the inside. The unnatural combination of wax and hair makes it a disturbing image, also because hair is found here in a place where it does not belong. Moreover, all sorts of dirty associations compete with each other, from stinking feet to abject body hair. More cheerful is the 'Finally Chesthair' T-shirt with a mat of chest hair designed by Walter van Beirendonck in 1996 (and currently on display in the Boijmans Van Beuningen Museum). Ann Huyben has done something similar by designing a T-shirt-like dress with a digital print of a naked body (male or female) for roller skaters, visibly showing a dark thatch of pubic hair, so that it looks as though he or she is skating through the city in the nude. In 1999 the aforementioned duo Bless made the 'Hairbrush', a brush with long, wavy hair, a useless object that plays on precisely those abject feelings that hair can evoke. The hairbrush seems to be a variant of Mimi Parent's *Mistress* (1996), a whip of golden tresses. These last two objects bring us close to the fetishistic element of hair.

---

03. Robert Gober, *Untitled (hairy shoe)*, 1992

This shoe made of wax, on the inside of which sparse hair is 'growing', gives the viewer a shudder. Here the same surrealist principle is applied as in Oppenheim's fur breakfast service, namely the juxtaposition of elements that do not go together. Shoe and hair are at odds with each other. Unlike Oppenheim's work, where the fur evokes pleasant associations of stroking, the isolated human hairs strike one as dirty and distasteful. The viewer thinks of sweaty feet and itching body hair, and tends to turn away in disgust rather than burst out laughing.

04. Cover of the magazine *Pour Vous*, 11 October 1939, with a photograph of Greta Garbo retouched by Salvador Dali

Hair where it does not belong: a woman with beard and moustache. The Surrealist Salvador Dali makes fun of the icon of feminine beauty, film star Greta Garbo, by 'retouching' her photograph with a growth of male hair.

Fetishism is a term from psychoanalysis. According to the strict interpretation by Freud, fetishism refers to a male disorder, namely the boy's defence mechanism against the fear of castration. To allay this fear he denies the woman's physical 'lack' by shifting his attention to other parts of the body. By turning parts of the woman's body into a fetish, the man experiences it as 'whole' and perfect again. In common use fetishism usually refers to a fixation on an object or part of the body that the fetishist finds pleasurable. Considering that thick tresses are often seen as a phallic object and that the whip is used in sado-masochistic games, we can understand the fetishistic attraction of Parent's whip of golden tresses. This also makes Daniëlle Smits's jewellery made of braided (fake) hair, or the braided headdress by 'Shoplifter' (Hrafnhildur Arnadóttir) less innocent than they appear at first sight. Hair simply remains a dangerous material that exists on the frontier between the living and the dead, the animal and the human, the beautiful and the abject, the physical and the sensual. Because of these disturbing properties hair will always be used more in art than in fashion.

Notes
1. Ann-Sophie Lehmann, 'Het andere haar', *Kunstschrift* 41, 2 (1997): 32-39.

References
Hollander, Anne. *Seeing through clothes*. Berkeley, California: California University Press, 1993 (orig. 1978).
Lehmann, Ann-Sophie. 'Het andere haar', *Kunstschrift* 41, 2 (1997): 32-39.
Mundy, Jennifer (ed.). *Surrealism: Desire Unbound*. London: Tate Publishing, 2001.
Nadeau, Chantal. *Fur Nation: From the Beaver to Brigitte Bardot*. London: Routledge, 2001.
Smelik, Anneke. 'Het haarloze ideaal: De virtualisering van het lichaam', *M9, Tijdschrift voor wetenschap, kunst & cultuur* 1, 1 (2005): 44-46.
Steele, Valerie. *Fetish: Fashion, Sex, and Power*. New York: Oxford University Press, 1995.

05. **Zoe Leonard,** *Pin-up #1 (Jennifer Miller Does Marilyn Monroe)*, 1995
Once again hair where it does not belong – in this case as a result of the disorder of 'hirsutism', which results in the growth of excessive body hair on a woman. The graceful pose of this female model with excessive body hair makes the viewer aware of expectations about gender roles. This piece by the British photographer Zoe Leonard is also a comment on the norm of hairlessness in today's visual culture.

06. **Silvia B.,** *Lily Lucinda*, 2001
The Dutch artist Silvia B. goes yet a step further by meticulously covering a model of a girl with artificial hair, glass eyes and fake nails, turning her into a charming and hairy creature. She is strokable and sympathetic, but also a bit gruesome. The completely hirsute girl is at odds with every contemporary norm of feminine beauty, where the ideal is to be as smooth as an egg shell.

07. **Ann Huyben, dress, no date**
This short, skin-coloured dress by the Flemish fashion designer Ann Huyben has a digital print clearly showing the dark thatch of armpit and pubic hair, making it look as though the wearer is roller skating naked through the city. The exaggeratedly full and dark body hair makes the viewer aware that nowadays armpit and pubic hair are more and more often removed from the body.

08. **Walter van Beirendonck,** *Finally chesthair*, **1996**
The Flemish fashion designer has designed a T-shirt with a mat of chesthair on the front so that every insecure man can feel masculine. At the same time the T-shirt is a playful criticism of the custom of male models to shave or wax their chests.

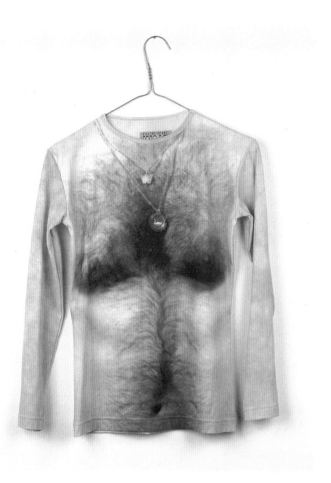

09. **Bless,** *Hairbrush*, **1999**
Like Oppenheim's surrealistic breakfast service and Gober's shoe, this hairbrush by the duo Bless is an impossible object. The hair is contained in the brush so it can no longer be used for brushing. It is funny, but also a bit creepy since it looks as though the hair has been violently brushed off the head.

THE DANGER OF HAIR

10. Mimi Parent, *Mistress*, 1996

The golden tresses negate the function of the whip but at the same time evoke associations with fetishism. Like the whip itself, long, wavy hair is often a fetish object. The tresses refer to attractive femininity, caress-ability and beauty, while the whip flirts with violence and dominance.

11. Daniëlle Smits, *Rapoenseltje*, 2003
12. *Rapoenseltje*, 2006

This jewellery made of fake women's hair looks innocent in itself, but naughtier suggestions also emerge. The thick, golden braid has both phallic and fet-ishistic qualities, thus acquiring sexual connotations. The neck-laces are also reminiscent of the lock of hair of a loved one, whether deceased or not, that people in the nineteenth century often wore in a locket around the neck. In these pieces of jewel-lery the hair is dead material that was once living and can thus serve as a keepsake. This gives them a macabre touch, which is further reinforced by the skull in the braids.

13. **Shoplifter (alias Hrafnhil-dur Arnardóttir) hair sculpture for Björk as part of the artwork for her album** *Medulla*, **2004**
These braided headdresses made of hair by the Icelandic artist Hrafnhildur Arnardóttir come the closest to traditional wigs. It looks as though the model's own hair has been used, so that the whole object has the appearance of a skilfully made up hairdo. But on closer inspec-tion fake hair has been braided and made into a headdress to be worn as an accessory.

FASHION JEWELLERY

Minke Vos

No one has had more influence on the development of the meaning and image of fashion jewellery than Coco Chanel. The starting point of this development can be indicated precisely: in 1924, as part of her collection, Chanel presented a pair of earrings featuring artificial pearls, one white and one black. These earrings were such a great success that other fashion houses began to focus on designing jewellery as well. Chanel suddenly endowed fake jewellery, which until then had been not regarded as chic, with a touch of class. All at once her 'cheaper' jewellery came within reach of a larger group of women, who could never have afforded real jewels before. Chanel thus helped make fashion more democratic.

In the nineteenth century wearing jewellery was still determined by rules that prescribed when, on what occasion and in what manner a particular piece of jewellery was supposed to be worn. Married women distinguished themselves from unmarried ones with the aid of jewellery. Wearing jewellery was connected more with social codes and status than with a particular style. Chanel was the first to break through these codes by introducing a new aesthetic with her 'total look', an important part of which involved jewellery. 'My jewellery never stands in isolation from the idea of women and their dress', Chanel said. By means of her jewellery she endowed the simplicity of her clothing designs with a luxurious appearance. Moreover she chose her materials for the effect they evoked; it made no difference to her whether the jewels were real or fake. Chanel attached importance to freedom in the choice of materials.

Chanel's jewellery designs were always rich and extravagant, evoking a supreme sense of luxury: bracelets, for example, were inlaid with precious stones. Chanel

01. **Versace, asymmetrical necklace, 1991**
Symbols derived from Italian history regularly appear in Versace's jewellery designs. What's more, his jewellery is often excessive, colourful and particularly large. In 1991 Ugo Correani designed an enormous rhinestone choker for Versace, which retains a solid look despite its asymmetrical form.

02. **Coco Chanel wearing pearls, early 1930s**
'I have said that black comprises everything. So does white. They possess absolute beauty.' In 1924 Coco Chanel caused great excitement by launching earrings with black and white artificial pearls. Chanel used artificial pearls not only for earrings but also for necklaces and chokers. Chanel's artificial pearl necklace became a classic, and in 1924 *Vogue* immediately devoted five fashion photographs and drawings to the first choker with artificial pearls. The pearls played a major role in Chanel's 'total look'. Coco Chanel herself wore them almost all the time, as can be seen in photographs of her.

played freely with motifs from classical antiquity and the Renaissance – the Byzantine cross, for example, appeared very often, usually in long, colourful strings of pearls. The camellia, a symbol of purity, was repeatedly used for brooches. What was special about Chanel's designs was that their extravagance always made them recognisable. We keep seeing the same type of long necklaces, familiar crosses and the umpteenth variation on the bracelet. Many of Chanel's designs have thus become icons: the jewellery retains the same form, but is always decorated differently.

This manner of designing was at odds with the Modernist way of designing jewellery that was developed in the 1930s, following Art Deco. The designs by Madeleine Vionnet are a good example of this. On the basis of a piece of draped cloth Vionnet designed dresses that possess an almost sculptural form. Her jewellery, simple in form, use of material and texture, and sober in the use of colour, formed a perfect match. Vionnet also used non-traditional materials such as glass.

With the launch of the New Look in 1947, Christian Dior capitalised on the postwar desire for a classic, extravagant femininity, expressed in clothes that emphasised both waist and bosom, and with wide skirts that created an almost nineteenth-century image of women. Dior also emphasised this femininity with long, large necklaces of jewels that covered and accentuated the neckline, thereby referring back to the style of the English Edwardian period and the late nineteenth century. Dior's jewellery was not particularly practical but was classically intended to adorn the woman. Dior, as well as Givenchy and Balenciaga, brought back a baroque style in the 1950s that emphasised class and luxuriousness. Chanel saw the New Look as an eyesore – she thought it put women back a hundred years.

In the 1960s, André Courrèges and Pierre Cardin introduced new forms and materials. Their designs were futuristic, geometrical and taut, matching the clothing designs of the Space Age. In the same period Yves Saint Laurent was combining not only 'real' jewels with 'fake' but also real jewels with completely different materials like leather, cord, wood and ceramics. Yves Saint Laurent's designs were also clearly influenced by primitive art. His jewellery collections were fanciful, original and innovative. They perfectly matched the spirit of the sixties, when young people and hippies bought their jewellery directly from India, Afghanistan or were influenced by traditional Dutch costume.

Christian Lacroix was one of the first couturiers in the 1980s to play with different styles in a postmodern manner. He combined the Byzantine cross with floral patterns in Rococo style, for example, and also merged all sorts of materials in his colourful jewellery. Opposed to Lacroix's exuberance was the monochrome jewellery introduced by Giorgio Armani in the same period. His designs were based on soft, natural materials like horsehair, fishing line and knotted string. Armani was using these materials to make a deliberate reference to other objects, as in his scarf necklaces.

The models who display the collections of the fashion houses on the catwalk nowadays wear the jewellery that goes with the latest collection. Stylistic elements from earlier periods recur in these designs. Balenciaga's bracelets from the summer 2007 collection are just as geometrical and rigid as a Pierre Cardin design from the 1960s. Fashion houses also continue to use their jewellery to create an aura of extravagance and luxury. The necklaces by Lanvin and Christian Lacroix are examples of this. Motifs and symbols that were once appropriated by a particular couturier and then became identified

03. **Chanel, bracelet with coloured jewels and stones, 1937**
Besides the pearl necklace and earrings, the broad, closed bracelet set with large coloured jewels and stones also became a Chanel classic. These inlaid bracelets, often made of imitation tortoise shell, referred to classical jewellery. The first versions of these bracelets were designed by Fulco di Verdura in the 1930s for Chanel. The most important motif used by Verdura and later by Chanel herself for these bracelets was the Maltese Cross. Innumerable variations based on this traditional eight-pointed cross were created in coloured stones. It was typical of Chanel that she often combined these conspicuous and rather bold bracelets with soft, delicate, even transparent evening dresses.

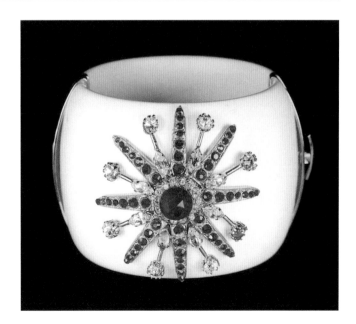

with the fashion house concerned continue to be seen in recent collections. Jewellery is supremely suitable as a recognisable symbol of a fashion house. Many of Dior's designs, for example, feature the lily-of-the-valley, while the symbol of Lacroix is, of course, the cross and that of Yves Saint Laurent is the peace dove. Karl Lagerfeld still uses classic Chanel elements in his contemporary collections for the fashion house. Vivienne Westwood regularly incorporates the symbol of the British monarchy, the crown, in her jewellery designs, whether or not in a subversive manner.

Jewellery is not always designed by the couturiers themselves. Many of them collaborate intensively with jewellery designers and makers. Ugo Correani, for example, designs jewellery for Versace. Roger Vivier has worked with Christian Dior and Loulou de la Falaise with Yves Saint Laurent. Fulco di Verdura and Paul Iribe designed for and with Chanel. Such designers are often a 'name' within the name of a fashion house. Diana Vreeland once wrote about Chanel: 'Chanel freed women. She gave them the momentum and the style.' Jewellery was an important part of this style, and so it continues to be. It is impossible to imagine that jewellery will ever disappear from the accessory collections of the fashion houses.

References
Mauriès, Patrick. *Jewellery by Chanel*. London: Thames & Hudson, 1993.
Milbank, Caroline Rennolds. *The Couture Accessory*. New York: Harry N. Abrams, 2002.
Snowman, Abraham Kenneth (ed.). *The Master Jewellers*. London: Thames and Hudson Ltd, 1990.

04. Givenchy, pearl necklace worn by Audrey Hepburn in the film *Breakfast at Tiffany's*, 1961

'There is not a woman alive who does not dream of looking like Audrey Hepburn,' said Hubert de Givenchy about his muse. The actress Audrey Hepburn and the couturier Hubert de Givenchy became lifelong friends when Hepburn came to look for clothes in Givenchy's atelier for the film *Sabrina*. From then on, Givenchy not only designed the clothes for virtually all of Hepburn's films, but also for her personal wardrobe. Together they created a classic and extremely elegant style. One of the highpoints of Givenchy's designs for Hepburn is the look for *Breakfast at Tiffany's* (1961), in which Hepburn wears Givenchy's chic-looking necklace of artificial pearls while looking longingly at the real jewels in the window of Tiffany & Co.

05. Christian Dior, brooch, 1951
06. Christian Dior, earrings, 1957

Christian Dior's pieces of fashion jewellery are classic, expensive and have a luxurious look. These earrings from 1957, for example, are completely encrusted with diamonds. The 2006 ad campaign for Dior jewellery shows that contemporary jewellery collections continue to have the same aura. Part of the Oval Collection from 1951 is a rhinestone bracelet in the form of Dior's monogram. Dior is referring here to the English Edwardian period, when diamond-encrusted monograms were in fashion. Following the use of the monogram for this brooch, the recognisable letters C and D regularly appeared on jewellery and eventually on the Lady Dior bag as well.

07. Pierre Cardin, necklace of metal and Lucite, late 1960s.
Various designers were influenced in the 1960s by new technological developments and the adventures of astronauts, whose exploits could be followed by everyone on TV. These influences led to futuristic designs featuring taut, geometrical forms. The use of new materials like plastic was also important. This necklace by Pierre Cardin is a piece of Space Age jewellery that not only has a taut form but also uses the new material Lucite, which was developed for test tubes.

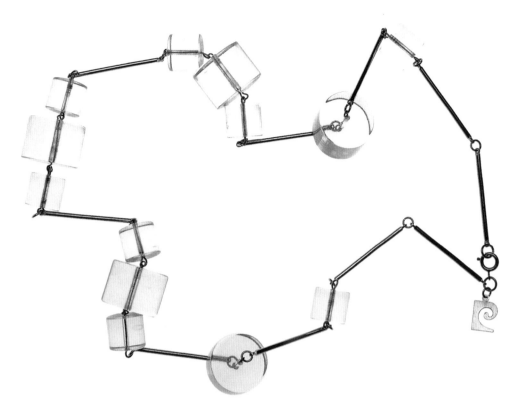

08. Yves Saint Laurent, drawing for heart-shaped pendant
09. Yves Saint Laurent, heart-shaped pendant, 1962
'What is more beautiful for a woman than to wear her passion in the form of a heart around her neck,' wrote Yves Saint Laurent on a design sketch for a heart-shaped pendant, which became a classic within his jewellery collection. The pendant was part of Yves Saint Laurent's very first collection and also featured in all his subsequent couture collections. During the shows the pendant was worn with Yves Saint Laurent's own favourite design from that year's collection, often the final piece – the wedding dress. Yves Saint Laurent's mother wore the heart-shaped pendant during the show of his very last couture collection in January 2002.

08.

09.

Quoi de plus beau
pour une femme
que
de nouer
autour
de
son cou
une passion
en guise
de
Coeur

Yves Saint Laurent

10. Christian Lacroix, cross pendant, 1989

11. Christian Lacroix, necklace, 1997

Christian Lacroix's fashion jewellery is characterised by a combination of various styles, materials and motifs, and is preeminently postmodern. A regularly recurring motif is the cross, as in this pendant on which coloured stones are applied to a gold-coloured background. The stones stand out against the background like faces on Byzantine mosaics. References to old stylistic periods can be seen in many of Lacroix's jewellery collections. For the Victorian-looking necklace with little tassels not only is new material used, but also vintage stones.

10.

11.

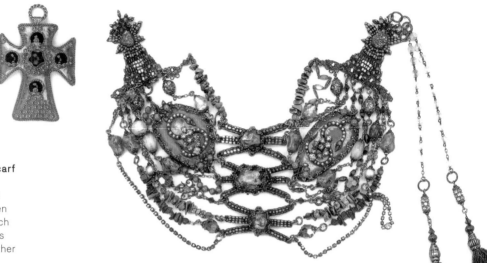

12. Giorgio Armani, mesh scarf necklace, 1994

Giorgio Armani's jewellery is mostly monochrome and often made of unusual material such as rope. His jewellery designs refer in a humorous way to other objects, as in this necklace made of mesh in the form of a scarf with tassels at the ends.

13. Karl Lagerfeld for Chanel, bracelet, 1990s

In 1983 Karl Lagerfeld took charge of the house of Chanel. His collections for Chanel used classic Chanel elements in a contemporary manner. The broad, closed bracelet set with stones made a return, based on Fulco di Verdura's designs for Chanel from the 1930s. Lagerfeld's bracelets are large and brightly coloured and are often made of plastic and glass. Lagerfeld's own jewellery collections and those for the fashion house of Chloe are often thematic in nature with an ironic, postmodern quality. One of his jewellery collections, for example, refers to the dressmaker's trade with spools hanging from necklaces and earrings in the form of pin-cushions.

14. Studio Job for Viktor & Rolf, Charm Chain, 2001
At the show of Viktor & Rolf's spring/summer 2002 collection the models wore the Charm Chain designed in 2001 by Job Smeets and Nynke Tynagel, who work under the name Studio Job. Hanging from the 90-centimetre solid aluminium chain are large charms, such as a crucifix, an anchor and a heart, symbolising faith, hope and love. The chain is a conspicuous accessory accompanying the completely white fashion collection by Viktor & Rolf.

CARNAVALESQUE

Karin Schacknat

01.

01.
Vivienne Westwood, *Storm in a tea-cup* collection, autumn/winter 1996/1997
02.
Olivier Theyskens, *Les Cyclopes*, autumn/winter 1998/1999 collection
03.
Elsa Schiaparelli, necklace from the *Pagan* collection, autumn/winter 1938

One of the most remarkable tendencies in fashion in recent decades can be described as 'the carnivalesque'. It makes you think of exuberant fancy dress parties like those customary in Catholic regions at the end of winter. In the context of contemporary fashion it is a notion that covers a rich variety of garments and accessories as well as their presentation. The element that connects all these images has no concrete form or stylistic characteristics. It is rather a question of atmosphere: recalcitrant, flamboyant, but also deceptive and with disturbing undertones referring to aggression, alienation, perversity, decay and death. Black humour à la Westwood, for instance, is as much a part of it as the macabre presentations of Olivier Theyskens' clothes in a charnel house.

Carnival comes from the Latin *carnem levare*, literally 'leaving meat aside', a reference to the time of fasting that begins on Ash Wednesday. In Mediterranean countries, it is related to the Dionysian rituals of ancient Greece and to the Roman Saturnalia which involved the abolition of class differences. The later Venetian carnival featured not only splendid costumes but also bloody rituals and butchery, with an orgiastic climax at midnight before the dawning of Ash Wednesday.

Intoxication, sex and death are Dionysian aspects. They disturb the peace, spread chaos and are completely opposed to reason, ingenuity and all social and technological systems that stem from them. Related stylistic elements with an emphasis on the morbid occur in certain nineteenth-century literary genres known as 'black Romanticism', as epitomised by Lord Byron who served as a model for the aristocratic vampire.

As a fashion principle, the carnivalesque style did not manifest itself in any form until the twentieth century. Some of Elsa Schiaparelli's surrealist inspired creations, like the beetle necklace or the dress with rips printed on it, are its forerunners. 'Doom & gloom' only really got going much later, when in 1971 the London label *Let It Rock* launched a torn shirt adorned with zips and pin-up photos, while chained together chicken bones formed the word *Rock* on a black shirt. These were the first creations of Vivienne Westwood before she started operating under her own name. Around 1976 there were suddenly bands like the Ramones from New York who performed in torn jeans, and the Sex Pistols from London who generated aggressive sounds supported by tattered clothes with safety pins, chains and spiky hair. It was the birth of Punk. The ornaments were an attack on the aesthetic standards of an abhorred bourgeois order. Notions like 'harmony' or 'success' were thrown overboard. 'Punk allowed one to be a flamboyant failure rather than a benign success', Malcolm McLaren said subsequently. There was no place for any ideology about improving the world; this eruption of

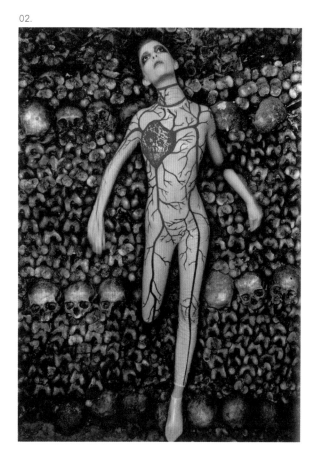

02.

03.

creativity emerged on the basis of denial. Black, the favourite colour of rebels of all times, was also rated the highest in the punk scene, followed by neon colours. Clothing was preferably torn, dirty and decorated with swastikas, skulls, razor blades and disruptive slogans like 'Destroy' or 'Anarchy'. Materials such as leather, latex, plastic and fishnet, combined with collars and armbands studded with rivets, were borrowed from the repertoire of pornography. There arose an urban anti-fashion that was supposed to look as unnatural as possible, thereby creating an identity of its own, rather than trying to be – as it was for the hippies before them – the natural expression of an already existing identity.

Punk is rich in accessories, especially ornaments. Stereotypes developed which even a whole generation later were commonly used as a way of declaring one's rejection of the social system. Punks like to see themselves as outsiders and outcasts, but their nihilism is actually a pose. Yet at punk's core there is something vital. The English sociologist Elisabeth Wilson sees in punk the fashion equivalent of Modernism in art, whereby objects are removed from their context and accepted aesthetic norms are attacked.

After the first punk wave, the early eighties saw the emergence of the Gothic style from London clubs like the Batcave. Clearly descended from nineteenth century black Romanticism, its adherents wore black velvet, lace and leather, tight corsets and long gloves. Hair could only be black, the face deathly white with eyes dramatically ringed in black. They looked like the Victorian un-dead, exuding dark secrets and a hint of doom.

Despite the great differences in atmosphere between punk and Gothic, many stylistic hybrid forms were created, the common denominators being black and the rejection of mass culture and its status symbols: competition, careerism and the state.

According to the American writer Greil Marcus, the punks and their adherents saw capitalism as their enemy, while, with its freedom of expression, it supplied the very conditions under which punk and related phenomena could function. In his quest for the history of negation in the twentieth century, Marcus establishes connections between Dada art and punk, and comes to the conclusion that there is a certain cyclical pattern in which citizens are given a fright by negatory movements despairing of civilisation and believing in anarchistically-tinged utopias of freedom.

Shock effects are more striking than positive notes. The free market economy of capitalism may well be reviled, but it does sometimes provide an ideal way of achieving a reputation. But, above all, what the shocking and sinister can do is transgress boundaries, which is why it

04.

05.

06.

07.

08.

can entail a certain avant-gardistic charge. Take for example Guy Bourdin's photographs for the French edition of *Vogue* in the seventies, where glamour is embedded in an ominous, often surrealistic context in which dream and nightmare lie close together. At about the same time the London couturier Zandra Rhodes launched her *Conceptual Chic and Punk* collection in which carefully placed holes in the clothes were held together with chains, safety pins and costume jewellery.

Since the nineties, stagings have become more gruesome and more numerous, and interpretations of the carnivalesque more extensive than ever. Sometimes these elaborate on the theme of punk and Gothic chic, albeit in a polished, aestheticising way. The most striking designer in this connection is Alexander McQueen, many of whose ideas are inspired by the past and by cruelty and violence, such as the bloody wars between England and Scotland referred to in his Highland Rape collection (autumn/winter 1995-96). His Dante collection (autumn/winter 1996-97) featured Victorian lace and Russian cavalry jackets worn by ghostly pale models. There were also direct references to death, such as a headdress with bones, a mask with a crucified Jesus where the nose should be, and a jacket with a photographic print of contemporary war combat. A skeleton sat among the VIPs in the front row next to the catwalk. McQueen's collections since 2000 have been presented less spectacularly. Among his popular accessories cherished by celebrities are chiffon scarves with prints of skulls or copulating skeletons.

Skulls and bones have been used over the years in Vivienne Westwood's scarves and jewellery, and in 2006 skulls with glittering stones in the eye-sockets suddenly appeared in Dior's jewellery collection.

The English fashion theorist Caroline Evans has conducted an extensive study into the sinister side of fashion at the end of the twentieth century, recognising in it symptoms of what is culturally hidden: trauma, loss, fear and death. The roots of this, she contends, lie in nineteenth-century urbanisation, technological developments and commercial relations, and the effects of these on people's sensitivities. The present is haunted by the ghosts of the past, comparable with Freud's return of the repressed, says Evans.

Elisabeth Wilson also emphasises the dissonances in the modern city as the key to what is summarised here under the term carnivalesque. She interprets the late nineteenth- and early twentieth-century Romantic movement as an early reaction to science and industrialisation.

The pattern of rationalism and urbanisation being answered with their irrational opposites has now taken

09.

10.

11.

04.
Vivienne Westwood, *Let it rock* collection, 1971
05.
Johnny Rotten, singer from the band The Sex Pistols, 1970s
06.
Sue Catwoman, woman from the English punk scene, 1976
07.
Punk band Bedorven Kip (Contaminated Chicken), Arnhem, ca. 2000
08.
Contemporary punk fashion report:

Kate Moss wearing a Giorgio Armani jacket, panties and fishnet stocking by Agent Provocateur and Vivienne Westwood shoes, *i-D magazine* April 2004
09.
Patrons of the Batcave Club, early 1980s
10.
Zandra Rhodes, photo for a *Conceptual Chic* poster, 1978
11.
Alexander McQueen, *Dante* collection, autumn/winter 1996/1997

on enormous proportions. An ideology of progress thrived in the wake of the Enlightenment and propelled the rapid advance of technologisation and digitisation. And with it, the carnivalesque blossomed. The emphasis was now on individuality, the creation of the self whereby extreme individualism coincided with extreme alienation.

Self-creation, alienation and the ultimate costume ball meet each other in the use of an accessory that was absent from fashion during the last three centuries: masks that cover the face, as in the collections by Undercover and Viktor & Rolf (autumn/winter 2006/07), and earlier with Rei Kawakubo (autumn/winter 1994/95) and Martin Margiela (autumn/winter 1995/96). In the Washington Post, Robin Givham ascribed to them a 'fundamental sadness (...) in the way they underscore a sense of universal loneliness.'

But masks also offer an anonymity that protects privacy, possibly a luxury in the near future when omnipresent cameras, implanted microchips and rigid identification controls represent a panoptic doom-scenario. On the other hand, our use of the internet has accustomed us to wearing masks in the form of pseudonyms or complete avatars.

A mask always contains a secret. And this aspect of secrecy and mystery takes us back to nineteenth- and twentieth-century representations of a favourite theme in horror movies and crime fiction.

Agatha Christie, Lord Byron, Johnny Rotten, Vivienne Westwood and Alexander McQueen: the genre of the carnivalesque has strong connections with England, followed more or less by other parts of northwest Europe and the United States. In France and Italy, for example, traces of it are hardly to be found, even though industri-alisation and urbanisation developed there at the same tempo. The ancient Anglo-Saxons knew nothing about carnival, but they did have Halloween. This was origi-nally the night of bewitchment in which a fissure in time opened the border to the Other World, so that all kinds of spirits could wander around on earth. People dressed up and masks were worn in order to prevent the doomed souls from taking possession of the living.

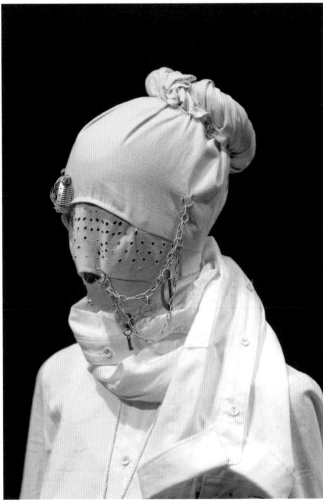

References

Anscombe, Isabelle. *Not Another Punk Book*. London: Aurum Press, 1978.

Attini, Antonio and Giovanna Pastega. *Venetian Colour: The Spirits of Carnival*. Vercelli: White Star Publishers, 2000.

Evans, Caroline. *Fashion at the Edge: Spectacle, Modernity and Deathliness*. New Haven and London: Yale University Press, 2003.

Givhan, Robin. 'Designers Give Women Their Wrapped Attention', *Washington Post*, 01-03-2006.

Groen, Janny. 'Greil Marcus: Ik weet bijna zeker dat Johnny Rotten nooit van Dada had gehoord', *de Volkskrant*, 29 July 1989.

Hennessy, Val. *In the Gutter*. Melbourne and New York: Quartet Books, 1978.

McLaren, Malcolm. 'Afterword', *Q*, Punk Special Edition, 2002.

Marcus, Greil. *Lipstick Traces: A Secret History of the Twentieth Century*, Cambridge, MA: Harvard University Press, 1990.

Polhemus, Ted. *Streetstyle*. London: Thames and Hudson, 1994.

Teunissen, José et al. (eds.). *The Power of Fashion: About Design and Meaning*. Arnhem: Terra Lannoo BV, ArtEZ Press, 2006.

Wilcox, Claire. *Radical Fashion*. London: Victoria and Albert Museum, 2001.

Wilcox, Claire. *Vivienne Westwood*. London: V & A Publications, 2004.

Wilson, Elisabeth. *Adorned in Dreams: Fashion and Modernity*. London: I.B. Tauris & Co. Ltd., 2003 (1985).

12.
 Alexander McQueen, *Dante* collection, autumn/winter 1996/1997
13.
Dior, ring, collection 2006
14.
Undercover, autumn/winter 2006/2007 collection show
15.
Cindy Sherman, *Untitled #304*, 1994
16.
Sarah Harmanee for Alexander McQueen, horns for fingers, autumn/winter 1997/1998 collection

15.

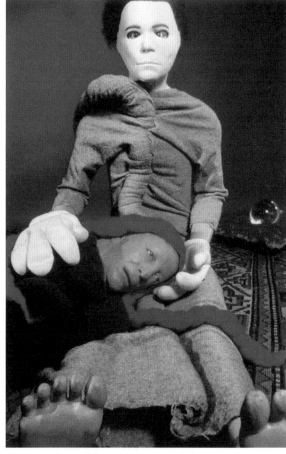

16.

SURREALISM

José Teunissen

01.

As the story goes, Meret Oppenheim and Dora Maar paid a visit to Pablo Picasso at the Flore, a Parisian café. Oppenheim showed him a fur-trimmed copper bracelet and said that was how she earned her money from the designer Elsa Schiaparelli. Picasso, commenting on the bracelet, said you could probably cover anything with fur. On her way home Oppenheim stopped in at a shop and bought a cup and saucer with a spoon. She covered them with fur in the same way and brought them to André Breton to be used as an object for the Surrealist exhibition at Galerie des Cahiers d'art. The rest is history. *Déjeuner en fourrure* (1936), or 'the fur-lined cup', became an immediate success. The Surrealist artist, a mere 23 years of age, became famous overnight. And *Déjeuner en fourrure* remains one of the best-known Surrealist works of art.

The beauty of this anecdote is that it illustrates the close ties that existed in the thirties between the fashion world and Surrealist art. An important driving force behind it was the Italian fashion designer Elsa Schiaparelli, who opened a sportswear shop in Paris during the late twenties which she expanded in 1930 to include couture and evening gowns. Right from the start Schiaparelli thought it was important for her designs to possess a sense of humour or to mislead the public. In 1928 she had her first success with a black jersey that had a ribbon knitted into it, giving it a refined trompe d'oeil effect. She elevated the magical quality and the design's double layer to her own style principle, which bore a striking relationship to the Surrealist school of art that was current at that time.

In 1924, André Breton laid down the most important principles of Surrealism in a Surrealist Manifesto. He described Surrealism as a school based on the expression of free associations such as those that come to us in dreams. According to Breton, the laws of logic, or our moral or aesthetic preoccupations, inhibit the way we associate and make connections. By having a Surrealistic experience you abandon the trodden path of associations in order to discover that your spirit and intellect are interwoven with your senses and reality in a different, 'realer' way.

One of the most successful ways by which the Surrealists managed to evoke these unexpected experiences was the principle of 'deplacement': an object was removed from its familiar environment and placed in an alien context, causing it spontaneously to evoke entirely different associations. This is the principle of Meret Oppenheim's aforementioned cup and saucer, which when taken from its daily surroundings and placed in an art context spontaneously becomes an intriguing object. But it also meant that Surrealist artists could produce 'art' by simply displaying it in the 'alien context' of something like fashion. A fine example of this is the

01.
Maison Martin Margiela, autumn/
winter 2006/2007 collection show
02.
Elsa Schiaparelli, newspaper bag,
1934
03.
Elsa Schiaparelli, shoe hat, 1937

03.

'poem' drawing of Jean Cocteau, which he designed especially for a Schiaparelli evening gown (1937) and had sewn onto the gown in beads by the Lesage embroidery house. Naturally, Salvador Dali, Meret Oppenheim and Jean Cocteau recognised a kindred spirit in Elsa Schiaparelli that bound them all together. But the fact that Schiaparelli offered these Surrealists the chance to express their ideas in the 'alien' world of fashion made it an inspiring field of activity for them. It led to legendary designs such as the famous shoe hat (1937) and the handbag with built-in lamp (1938), which Dali designed in collaboration with Schiaparelli. Another result was the fur shoe (1939) to which Meret Oppenheim was inspired.

What is striking about the Surrealistic fashion accessory is that it is based in the same way on existing forms – icons and everyday objects – that become 'alienated' by being applied in unchanged form. The black ladies' pump mentioned above, which Schiaparelli and Dali conscripted unchanged into the role of headwear, is an illustrative example.

But even in the forties and fifties, after Surrealism as a school had reached its zenith, these kinds of Surrealistic accessories remained in fashion. In the forties, for example, we see a revival of Surrealistic bags in the form of replicas of champagne buckets with ice cubes or a bouquet of flowers that could be carried as a handbag. Even during the sleek sixties, so strongly influenced by modernism, designers would occasionally play with a Surrealistic motif such as the eyelashes that Pierre Marly put on his modern plastic sunglasses. In the eighties the Italian brand Moschino even appropriated Surrealism as a design principle, which can be seen in a series of inventive bags such as the corset backpack (1985) and the 'pastry bag' (1995), which became very popular. Today we see Surrealism returning in the work of several designers. Stella McCartney designed a bag in the form of a life-sized embroidered guitar (2002) as an original alternative to today's bag rage. And last spring Martin Margiela created a splendid Surrealistic experience when he had his models walk around with picture frames about their necks for the 2006/2007 winter collection. Here, 'the frame', which had been placed in an alienating context, evoked wonderful associations. The picture frame functioned as a necklace, but at the same time the frame also outlined the model's upper body. The result was a living, walking painting. In this way, Margiela brought the principles of Surrealism to life once again as a series of new associations that sparked an entirely different visual experience.

The fact that the Surrealistic accessory usually plays with classical icons and existing, everyday shapes imparts something timeless to many of the Surrealistic

04.

05.

06.

07.

JOSÉ TEUNISSEN

bags, shoes and pieces of jewellery. These accessories do not betray themselves with an outdated or pronounced design, so they are more difficult to date than most other fashion accessories, which tend to reflect the spirit of the times. That resistance to time gives Surrealistic accessories a very special place in the world of fashion: they seldom become dated or out of fashion so they can always be worn.

And then there's one more striking feature. Normally, many accessories need glittering campaigns and carefully contrived photography to give them a magical aura. For the Surrealistic accessory this absolutely does not apply. It has its own magic, which means that it maintains its allure even in a bare display case or a dusty second-hand shop.

References
Baudoit, Francois. *Elsa Schiaparelli*. London: Thames & Hudson, 1997.
Mansén, Elizabeth. Fingertip Knowledge. (See internet: http://www.idehist.su.se/Forskning/mansenfingertips.pdf.)
Martin, Richard. *Fashion and Surrealism*. New York: Rizzoli, 1990.
Milbank, Caroline Reynolds. *The Couture Accessory*. New York: Harry N. Abrams, 2002.
Wood, Ghislaine (ed.). *Surreal Things: Surrealism and Design* (exhibition cat.). London: Victoria & Albert Museum, 2007.
Wood, Ghislaine. *The Surreal Body*. London: Victoria & Albert Museum, 2007.

08.

09.

10.
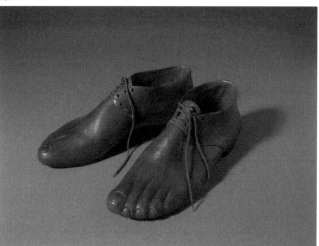

11.
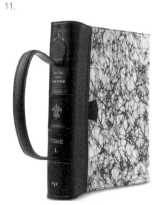

12.
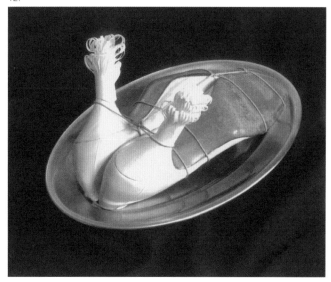

04.
Elsa Schiaparelli, boots, autumn/winter 1939 collection
05.
Anne Marie de France, champagne bag, 1940s
06.
Pierre Marly, glasses designed for Elton John, 1970s
07.
Stella McCartney, guitar bag, 2002
08.
Stephen Jones for John Galliano for Christian Dior, corset hat, autumn/winter 2000 collection
09.
René Magritte, *Le modèle rouge*, 1935
10.
Pierre Cardin, shoes with toes, 1986
11.
Jean Paul Gaultier, book bag, 1993
12.
Meret Oppenheim, *My governess*, 1936

MODERNISM

Els de Baan

580

The influential fashion website www.style.com incessantly recommends the latest must-haves from the world of fashion in its 'item of the week' section. Such a product regularly provides a slight shock of recognition. What's new about it? In what way is it modern? Isn't that a typical eighties bag? Tracy Reese's shiny patent leather belt (item of the first week of September 2006) is just such an untraceable and therefore illusive fashion accessory. The look of the material in combination with the austere design evokes memories of trends from the sixties and seventies. At that time this combination represented 'innovation', 'future' and 'modern'. The caption, however, does not refer to the past, but states expressly that this belt is now modern because it perfectly matches today's super-slender legs trend. In fashion, 'modern' is often a form of looking back, of re-interpreting, of literally re-modelling. It was not always thus.

In the mid-nineteenth century the unprecedented possibilities of mass production forced designers to adopt new attitudes. Two fundamental directions in terms of design could then be distinguished. On the one hand there were the traditionalists, whose ideas were associated with romantic concepts and historicising (neo-) styles, and who revered traditional handiwork. On the other hand, there were the reformers who were in search of a completely new aesthetic and welcomed modern manufacturing methods. It is in this latter direction that we find the roots of the Modernist movement that developed at the beginning of the twentieth century in virtually all the countries of Europe. Modernism is not a specific style of art, but rather a mentality. Artists and architects were seeking designs free of traditions and historical references. By adopting a rational approach to forms and analysing them objectively, by searching for rules and making use of technological achievements, they discounted personal emotions completely. Their view of the future was optimistic. These ideas found expression in international art styles such as Cubism, Futurism and Constructivism. In the Netherlands they were articulated and represented by the artists of the De Stijl movement. The famous motto 'Less is more' of the German-American architect Ludwig Mies van der Rohe connected seamlessly with Modernist thought. A minimum of form provides maximum expressiveness, as long as its proportions and materials are perfect.

Unnecessary decoration was abandoned and all energy was focused on a new aesthetic of pure, elementary forms and the display of clear structures. The key words were 'clarity, balance and harmony'. The Art Deco style, in particular, with its austere, geometrical and often symmetrical forms, brought forth fine samples of Modernist products. A great deal of attention was also devoted to functionality.

03.

01.
Paco Rabanne, dress, 1967
02.
Studio 5050, Day-for-Night dress
2006
03.
Tracy Reese, belt, 2006
04.
Gloves from the Gant Perrin label,
1925-1929
05.
Gloves from *Vogue UK*, May 1984

04.

05.

This new, modern language of form reflected 'modern life'. It was also expressed in a new ideal of feminine beauty in the 1920s with the advent of the 'boyish' look. For the first time in the history of fashion, women acted 'like men'. They smoked, drank, drove cars and cut their hair short. There was no room in this new feminine image for any accents that devoted specific attention to the bust, waist or hips. Here, too, taut angularity was the winning card. The woman's entire look, however, was imbued with luxury.

Fashion accessories became a perfect means for representing Modernist ideas and displaying a new sort of dynamism. In the twenties and thirties in particular this tendency manifested itself in jewellery, bags, scarves, shoes and related products. Although expensive materials had the upper hand, low-cost materials were also popular, with wood, bakelite, celluloid and unconventional mixtures of materials being used for ornaments like bracelets, necklaces and brooches.

Fashion accessories in the twenties and thirties contained references not only to luxury but also to the unadorned visual vocabulary of Constructivist art movements. This is easy to see in the apparently simple division of the surface in bags, shoes, scarves and other articles. The powder compact and cigarette case were essential elements in every lady's handbag. The flat surfaces were perfectly suited for displaying the new language of forms. Strictly defined, contrasting areas of colour and lines that were both playful and taut represented the new, progress-oriented spirit. This concept was implemented down to the smallest details, such as buttons, buckles and belts and in men's cuff links.

This same austerely designed simplicity was also evident later on in various articles and looks, as in the modest, two-tone pumps by Chanel (1957), Op Art-like chequered stockings (sixties), bags by Yves Saint-Laurent (seventies), Prada bags (late nineties) and today's products from the luxury Valextra label. Even the suddenly popular Ugg brand of shoe that turned sheepskin into functional, but not particularly elegant footwear, is presenting a line of bags for 2007 in which simplicity and clarity predominate. The coloured rectangular sections, tightly demarcated by seams, determine an image that immediately evokes associations with earlier Modernist expressions. Such objects are products of their time, it's true, but the casual viewer is regularly thrown off track. The current bags by Roger Vivier, for example, display characteristics from the thirties as far as the division of the surface is concerned, while the material and details are reminiscent of the eighties.

After the Second World War, Modernism retreated to the background as a form of artistic expression. The outlook for the future shifted from a futuristically-minded view

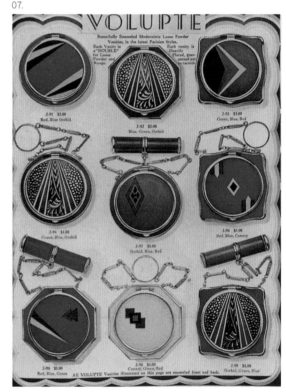

09.

10.

11.

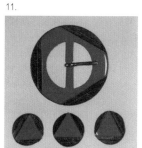

06.
Libiszewski, *Shopping for the ensemble, Vogue* illustration, 1930
07.
Advertisement for powder boxes from Volupté, 1931
08.
Karl Lagerfeld, shoes, 1990s
09.
Buckles from the collection of Cristiana de Reus, 1920-1930
10.
Christa Ehrlich, jewellery, 1929
11.
Wooden buttons, 1920-1930
12.
Aluminium handbag, France, 1930s
13.
Handbag with enamel decoration, France, 1920s
14.
Ugg, *Ultrarail* bag, 2007
15.
Roger Vivier, bag, spring/summer 2007 collection
16.
Miu Miu, shoulder bag with zips, no year

12.

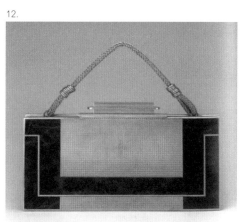

13.

14.

15.

16.

of progress to the practical consequences of postwar reconstruction. In the turbulent sixties the time was ripe for a new form of Modernism. Extreme simplicity triumphed with the emergence of Minimalist art. After the elegant, romantic style of fifties fashion, stylistic purity once again reigned supreme and this could also be seen in fashion accessories. Certain products, particularly jewellery, even seemed to be direct copies of items from the twenties and thirties. Although the materials used generally differed (plastic instead of prewar bakelite, for example), rings, bracelets and necklaces had a strong affinity with original Modernist designs.

In 1964, the newspapers were rejoicing at the real possibility of putting a man on the moon within the foreseeable future. These reports gave an enormous impulse to 'Space Age' fantasies. A new generation of fashion designers, including the French couturiers André Courrèges and Pierre Cardin, the Austrian-American designer Rudi Gernreich and the English Mary Quant, translated this into futuristic designs. Their straightforwardly designed garments had subdued, simple lines and clear, distinct areas of colour. There were no frills. Hats in the shape of helmets, glasses with slits and ankle-length boots by Courrèges and Cardin represented their view of what space travel would be like in the future. Jeanne Roos, the fashion journalist for *Het Parool* was there in August 1964 when Courrèges showed his first couture collection. The headline 'Clothes of the future gave an emotional shock' and the way she was affected by the 'abstract purity' of the clothes, which perfectly suited 'the demands of the era of space travel', concisely summed up the new fashion moment. Courrèges envisaged a woman with a specific attitude: 'She is active, moves fast, works, is usually young and modern enough to wear modern, intelligent clothes' (1967 interview). As regards her type as well as the lines of the clothes, this woman is reminiscent of the self-assured woman from the 1930s. The youthful sixties woman hurries forward with her eyes on the future; the slitted glasses, boots and helmet underscore this drive and at the same time make her look aloof, unapproachable and impersonal.

These sorts of distancing accessories regularly make their appearance in the fashion world. The helmet hat in Balenciaga's spring 2007 collection, for instance, manages to evoke an impersonal distinction. And the glasses by Prada and Paule Ka represent not only a revival of the futuristic sixties but also a contemporary view of the future in which technology likewise plays an important role.

Fashion accessories were also part of the 'total look' introduced in English fashions in the sixties. Simply designed clothes were complemented by attention-seeking make-up, simple accessories and asymmetrical

17.
Bracelet made of bakelite, late 1930s
18.
Lola Casademunt, bracelet, 2006
19.
Pierre Cardin, girl with glasses, 1960s
20.
Emmy van Leersum, collar with fastener and white dress, 1967
21.
Laura Biagiotti, collar, 1983

hairstyles, everything carefully coordinated. Although the accessories looked very functional this was not always so in practice. Ornaments were increasingly part of the total outfit, with the body serving simply as a clothes peg. This remarkable innovation was partly the work of the fashion designer Paco Rabanne who constructed garments from metal and plastic plates and rings so that the elements used as well as the final result looked like accessories. In the satirical cult film 'Qui êtes-vous Polly Maggoo', directed by William Klein in 1965-66, mannequins dressed in large metal objects parade across the stage. Such an object is at once a garment and an accessory. In no way at all do these abstract objects refer to an earlier tradition. In the Netherlands, designers such as Emmy van Leersum and Gijs Bakker produced these types of 'wearable objects' as genuine accessories, including austerely designed aluminium headdresses, shoulder collars, bracelets and necklaces. The accessory was an essential part of the total image and the wearable object only stood out when combined with a simple, undecorated garment. These products were suitable for both men and women, unisex also being a new phenomenon. Conventional views of functionality and wearability, far from being an issue, were actually called into question.

The technological designs in the 'One Hundred Eleven' series (spring/summer 2007) by the fashion designer-cum-philosopher Hussein Chalayan can be placed in the same line. The seemingly sober looking outfits appear at first to refer to Paco Rabanne's dresses constructed from plates. Hanging on the model like a large fashion accessory, they are gradually transformed into items of clothing from various stylistic periods. The 'objects' are neither functional nor wearable, but they do invite reflection.

21

The stylistic purity of forms continued to appeal to many designers in the seventies and eighties, although not as extremely as in the sixties. The interest in 'body-enveloping' accessories also continued. In 1975, the fashion designer Rudi Gernreich, who had become famous in the sixties, made fashionable-looking, simple black dresses and trouser suits connected with sculptural aluminium portable objects by Christopher Den Blaker. The functional aspect faded completely into the background.

Volume and large forms dominated fashion in the early eighties. Large, interchangeable collars were now regarded as a fashion accessory. The French designer Claude Montana and the Italian Laura Biagiotti designed bold shoulder collars consisting of clear basic forms such as rectangles and circles. Princess Diana was a leading ambassador in presenting such eye-catchers. Maria Blaisse used minimal basic geometric forms to make hats and caps that yielded a maximum effect (less is more). With just a single notch in a square or rectangular rubber plate she managed to create a three-dimensional accessory that invited the wearer to explore several ways of wearing it. These designs stood an excellent chance internationally, and she developed several hats for the Japanese designer Issey Miyake. Most attention went to the design; pure functionality was of less importance.

In the case of bags, however, functionality is decisive. A Modernist thirties lady's handbag neatly stored a powder compact, mirror, comb and other accessories in separate compartments. Today's modern person also likes to have everything within immediate reach, but she wants to keep her hands free as well. The bag, as well as waistcoats and belts provided with various pockets and compartments, are literally extensions of the body, embracing the body as it were. The traditional, highly functional rucksack and the postman's bag are continually undergoing transformations in order to function as a laptop bag, DJ bag or 'work' bag. An austere, minimalistic design conveys a chic look.

No matter how the image of fashion develops, simplicity and functionality, combined with luxuriousness and technological progress, will continue to be visible in fashion accessories, at least for the time being. Clothing fitted with the latest electronics, shoes loaded with technical gadgets and simply designed wristwatches ready for both deep sea diving and astronautical capers, make us feel that we can face the future without a care.

22.

23.

24.

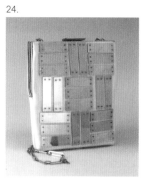

25.

References
Julier, Guy. *The Thames & Hudson Dictionary of Design Since 1900.* London: Thames & Hudson, 2004.
Kreidler, Richard. *Glanzstücke, Modeschmuck vom Jugendstil bis zur Gegenwart.* Munich: Prestel, 1992.
Lobenthal, Joel. *Radical Rags: Fashions of the Sixties.* New York: Abbeville Press, 1990.
Mulvach, Jane. 'Costume Jewelry', in: *Vogue History of 20th Century Fashion.* London: Viking Books, 1988.
Tolkien, Tracy and Henrietta Wilkinson. *A Collector's Guide to Costume Jewelry: Key Styles and How to Recognize Them.* Ontario: Firefly Books, 1997.
Unger, Marjan. *Het Nederlandse sieraad in de 20ste eeuw.* Bussum: Thot, 2004.

22.
Maria Blaisse, hat, 1985
23.
Lacloche Frères, bag with a watch in the clasp, 1930s
24.
Pierre Cardin, shoulder bag, 1960s
25.
Chanel, *Chanel 2005* bag, 1999
26.
Charles Jourdan, shoes, no year
27.
André Perugia, shoes, 1930
28.
United Nude, *Porn* shoe, 2003

26.

27.

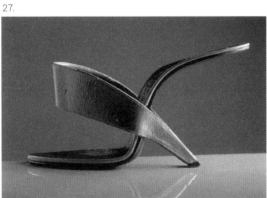

28.

POSTMODERNISM

Els de Baan

01.

One of the routes on which fashion will embark in the autumn of 2007 has been given the designation 'Abstract Modernism'. The cover of the leading trend forecasting magazine *International Textiles* features a colourful collage that aptly illustrates the mood of the winter to come. The lively colours and forms are a direct reference to 'Postmodernism', which flourished during the eighties under the leadership of the Italian designers from the Studio Alchymia and Memphis and of American architects. This artistic trend was a reaction to Modernism, with its sleek, rational and functional designs that determined the style of products and buildings. Modernist artists were opposed to historic references. The crop of designs produced by Postmodernists, however, embraced the past. But technique, mass culture, fantasy and kitsch also served as important and inexhaustible sources. Such breadth made this artistic trend both complex and difficult to define.

In 1988, the culture philosopher Jean-François Lyotard stated that art *and* man had become 'shattered'. Man, he said, has become alienated from himself and his own historic time because of new technologies, such as the computer. The all-pervasive mass media, the empty amusement culture with its bombardment of banal, visual violence, is inundating shattered man, and man is in danger of perishing within it. Art is besieging us with this 'dehumanisation' and with the meaninglessness of the present day. Traditional symbols, visual language and values are finished. Artists no longer aim for originality but for empty eclecticism, citations, spectacle, kitsch, irony, banality, playfulness and humour. They rummage about to their hearts' content in the inexhaustible reservoir of history, and with apparent carelessness they combine and assemble pieces collected from here and there, pieces that mean something different than what they actually are. At the same time they argue for a blending of high and low culture. Both the visual arts of the elite and expressions of populist mass culture serve as possible sources. What all this yields is a whirlpool of original images and forms. During the Modernist period the motto was 'Less is more'. For Postmodernism, the architect Robert Venturi replaced that motto with 'Less is bore'.

Surprisingly enough, the eclectic mishmash of 'visual languages' was not typical of the fashion of the eighties, the hey-day of Postmodernism. It was in the fashion accessories of that period, however, that the dehumanisation, the shattering and the emptiness were so strikingly expressed. At the same time, the historical citation, the playful combinations and the humour were also fully present. Postmodernist expression seems not to have found its repercussions in fashion until the very beginning of the twenty-first century, in a carefree mix-&-match style. This trend gazed back at the past, dabbled in exotic cultures and traditional accents, and

02.

03.

01.
Valentino, leopard wallet, 1991
02.
Hans Hollein, Austrian travel agency, Vienna, 1976-1978

03.
Charles Moore, Piazza d'Italia, New Orleans, 1976-1979
04.
Stanley Tigerman for Cleto Munari, cufflinks, 1986-1987

04.

embraced the promising technical innovations of the future. And that coincides with the sense of 'Abstract Modernism' that the forecasts were talking about.

In the case of many Postmodern products such as furniture and eating utensils, functionality was completely abandoned. There were bookcases in which no books would fit and cutlery that could not be used for eating. Form was placed above function.

Fashion accessories that were part of this art trend placed less emphasis on this principle, since many accessories are quite transportable – even when the wildest things were elevated to the level of fashion accessory. In the early eighties Karl Lagerfeld opted for a light-hearted, humoristic approach. He designed a necklace for Chloé made of a real shower head that was decorated with strass stones and fake pearls. The object exudes banality and irony and illustrates the ideas of one of the founders of Postmodernism, the designer Alessandro Mendini. Mendini was always making critical observations on the achievements of mass culture. According to him, objects (and this would include accessories) represent their own meaninglessness. They are caricatures of themselves. A design is built up of flashes, fragments of a visual system. He linked the large-scale production of objects with the notion of 'banality', which is why he called on designers to include 'kitsch' in their design process. Because with kitsch, the 'ugly', the designer can exaggerate conventions and allow the non-authentic to triumph. 'Kitsch is attractive and relaxing.' Artists and designers of furniture and consumer articles plunged into such kitsch translation with utter seriousness by and large. There was little to laugh about.

Fashion accessories were usually produced with a more playful, banal or ironic wink. In the world of haute couture, Karl Lagerfeld was regarded as one of the front runners. Besides his shower-head accessories he played with all sorts of banal products in the early eighties. An ordinary tool such as a monkey wrench was elevated to the level of luxurious broche, and a costumier's pin cushion was transformed into a decadent hat. They were like 'objets trouvés', found objects that accidentally fall into your hands. Such chance products have a long history in the story of art, beginning with the Dada movement and Marcel Duchamp from the period of the First World War. Meaningless products such as a bicycle wheel and a kitchen stool were brought together and a new work of art was born. The combining of familiar everyday things that are meaningless in themselves was also an important feature of Postmodern accessories. Assembling and combining according to the playful kitsch approach was expressed in countless shoe designs, for example. The series of wearable shoes that Gaza Bowen produced in 1983 with the comic name

05.

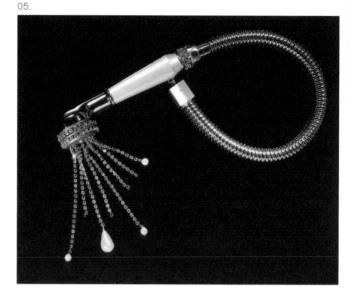

06.

07.

'Baby Needs a New Pair of Shoes' were put together out of 'objets trouvés'-like finds. A handful of dice served as the sole and heel, and the leather came from various 'accidental' bits that were playfully stitched together. With a mocking undertone she assembled trivial household components such as clothes pins, brushes and sponges into a feminist commentary on the traditional role of women. She presented such shoes as art objects.

Halfway through the nineties, various elements from the world of sports began top influence fashion. The concept of the sports shoe was combined with the basic pump, and various mixes of materials and colours yielded new, witty products. The high-heeled 'sports shoe' from NoBox (1996) was not only a parody of functionalism but may also have been poking fun at the prevailing compulsive attention for physical exercise *and* at the performance-oriented society in which a woman hurries to work dressed in the appropriate attire. Jan Jansen's 'Nike shoe' and the Miu Miu collection (1999) were also accessories put together with a knowing wink. In the latter, the functional anti-slip rubber sole, which normally is applied to sneakers, was playfully worked in as a decorative element in an elegant high-heeled sandal.

Fashion designer Martin Margiela chose an unorthodox approach to fashion and also frequently played with assembly techniques. His porcelain waistcoat (1989) was constructed of fragments of plates and saucers. The original porcelain products all had their own history and significance, but as broken bits they had become totally meaningless. By assembling them into an accessory they suddenly started telling a new story. Playful, contemptuous, kitsch or art? It's up to the observer to decide what meaning to attach to the picture.

The playful and unusual combinations of everyday elements, the new functions and the 'less is bore' ideology contrasted sharply with the practical, detached jewellery designed by Alessandro Mendini and Ettore Sottsass, the 'fathers' of Postmodernism. These design extremes reflect the breadth of the Postmodern mentality. The taut lines and unnamed, futuristic figures are completely meaningless, but they seem to conceal mysterious, intangible messages.

08.

09.

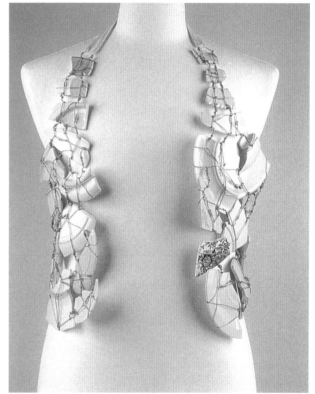

10.

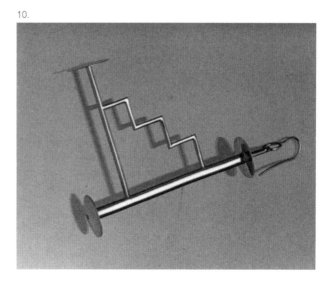

Mendini depicted his message of human degeneration in other ways as well. His shoes, hat and pistol from 1980 are less detached because of their playful airbrush-like colour areas. And this makes them seem innocent. But once again they are deliberately without content, which makes them meaningless. Such lively but at the same time trivial surface and line decorations appeared during the height of Postmodernism on all sorts of consumer products such as fabrics for interiors and clothing, writing pads, storage containers and clocks. Countless fashion accessories such as watches (the Swatch, for example), scarves, glasses, brooches and hair pins were also decorated with these indifferent and therefore apparently innocent patterns.

Citing the past was also an essential basic element of Postmodernism. This form of eclecticism was expressed in architecture and in interior design. The 'citationism' of architects and interior designers may refer to any period of art, but the classical periods were clearly their favourites. Greek pillars and pediments and Roman arches and mosaics were freely used as points of departure or applied as decorative ornaments.

Stripped of their original context, historical references also lent themselves perfectly to the design of fashion accessories. Postmodern watches and jewellery – such as the watches by architect Hans Hollein or the jewellery by Stanley Tigerman – consisted of classical elements. Ties and scarves were decorated with historic prints. The authentic meaning had lapsed and there was usually no new meaning either. This was expressed in another way in the series of scarves by architect Michael Graves. An industrial Italian fantasy landscape is covered with simple but non-existent architectural elements that refer to a history of an unknown past. The assembled image is ironic, alienating and empty, all at the same time.

The incorporation of historic fragments was also in use around the recent turn of the century. Artists, architects and fashion designers used the past in an eclectic way. Sometimes the intention was ironic or humorous, sometimes it was meant to emphasise emptiness and lack of content. For decades now, Vivienne Westwood has cited historic masterpieces in her fashion designs and accessories. She copies paintings directly onto a bag or hat. In so doing she tells a story. What story? That's for the beholder to figure out. In the 2006 bag collection from the Fendi couture house, Roman arches are combined with ornaments from the past. They're merely decorative and have nothing to say. Emptiness and stylelessness are trumps, and that suits Postmodernism down to the ground. But as with everything else connected with this trend, it's not a matter of just shaking things together at random. Every design is carefully considered, making the final result something quite refined.

11.

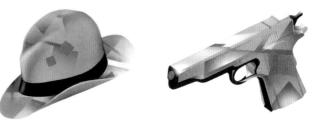

12.

13.

14.

References
Collins, Collins. *Post-Modern Design*. London: Rizzoli/ Academy Editions, 1989.
Hayward Gallery. *Addressing the Century: 100 Years of Art & Fashion*. London: Hayward Gallery, 1998.
Poletti, Raffaella (ed.). *Atelier Mendini: Een visuele utopie 1990-1994*. Venice: Fabbri Editori, 1994.
Radice, Barbara. *Memphis: Research, Experiences, Results, Failures and Successes of New Design*. London: Thames & Hudson, 1985.
Sato, Kazuko. *Alchemia: Never Ending Italian Design*. Tokyo: Rikuyo-sha Pub, 1985.

15.

11.
Alessandro Mendini, *Human life objects*: hat and pistol, 1980
12.
Hans Hollein for Cleto Munari, watch, 1987
13.
Hans Hollein, ring, 1986
14.
Vivienne Westwood, *Salon* collection, spring/summer 1992

15.
Tanner Krolle, advertising campaign with X-ray bag and pistol, no year
16.
Christian Lacroix, pirate hat, spring summer 1988 collection

16.

Els de Baan after completing the degree programme in Textile Arts and Crafts at Delft Teacher Training College, Els de Baan studied Art History at Leiden University. Since 1989 she has been working at the Willem de Kooning Academy as an instructor of Art and Fashion History and Criticism. Since 1990 she has also been teaching at the Royal Academy of Art in The Hague in her special field: fashion and textile history. She occasionally gives guest lectures in the Textile Restoration programme of the Netherlands Collection Institute and at the Design Academy in Eindhoven. Els de Baan works as a freelance fashion journalist for the newspaper *Trouw*, where her articles on current developments in the fashion world appear almost weekly.

Jan Brand is head of the ArtEZ Press and dAcapo-ArtEZ, the publishing house and General Studies Department of the ArtEZ Institute of the Arts, as well as editor and producer of many books on art, architecture and design. He also works with ArtEZ professor José Teunissen developing programmes and issuing publications for the Modelectoraat.
A selection of these publications are: *Architecture and Imagination* (Waanders Uitgevers, 1989), *The Words and the Images* (Centraal Museum Utrecht 1991), *Allocations, art in a natural and artificial environment* (Zoetermeer: Floriade Foundation 1992), *Gerrit Rietveld* (catalogue raisonné, Centraal Museum Utrecht 1992), *Sonsbeek 93* (Stichting Sonsbeek, Snoeck-Ducaju 1993), *Het Drinkglas* (Fort Asperen Foundation/Uitgeverij Waanders 1997), *The Ideal Woman* (Nijmegen/Amsterdam: Uitgeverij SUN 2004), *Global Fashion / Local Tradition* (Uitgeverij Terra Lannoo 2005), *The Power of Fashion* (Uitgeverij Terra Lannoo/ArtEZPress 2006).

Nanda van den Berg is an art historian, editor and publicist. She writes about fashion and fashion photography. Recent publications are 'Echter dan echt: Over hedendaagse mode-fotografie' in *De Gids,* no. 1

(2003) and 'Dooie poppen met jurken: Dilemma's rond een Nederlands modemuseum' in *Boekman,* no. 61 (2004). She was one of the authors who contributed to the book *Mode in Nederland*, which was published in 2006 (Warnsveld: Uitgeverij Terra Lannoo).

Judith Donath is an Associate Professor at the MIT Media Lab, where she directs the Sociable Media research group. Her work focuses on the social side of computing, synthesising knowledge from fields such as graphic design, urban studies and cognitive science to build innovative interfaces for online communities and virtual identities. She is known internationally for pioneering research in social visualisation, interface design and computer mediated interaction. She created several of the early social applications for the web, including the first postcard service ('The Electric Postcard'), the first interactive juried art show ('Portraits in Cyberspace') and an early large-scale web event ('A Day in the Life of Cyberspace'). Her work has been exhibited at the Institute for Contemporary Art in Boston and in several New York galleries; she was the director of 'Id/Entity', a collaborative exhibit of installations examining how science and technology are transforming portraiture. Her current research focuses on creating expressive visualisations of social interactions and on building experimental environments that mix real and virtual experiences. She has a book in progress about how we signal identity in both mediated and immediate situations. Professor Donath received her doctoral and master's degrees in Media Arts and Sciences from MIT, her bachelor's degree in History from Yale University, and has worked professionally as a designer and builder of educational software and experimental media.

Martine Elzingre has a Ph.D. in sociology. She is a permanent researcher at the CNRS France (Laboratoire: Cultures et sociétés en Europe, in Strasbourg, Université Marc Bloch). She is the author of various studies on dress codes and

design in contemporary fashion, such as *Femmes habillées: La mode de luxe: styles et images* (1996). A selection of some of her writings: *Femmes Habillées. La Mode de luxe: styles et images* (Paris: AUSTRAL, Essais, 1996, 173 pp.); 'Formes de socialité aujourd'hui. Plaisir et beauté. Femme et mode de luxe' in: *LeVêtemen* (direction Frédéric Monneyron, Colloque de Cerisy, Paris: L'Harmattan, 2001), 'Vêtements et mode de luxe féminine. Créateurs de mise en scène', in: *Vêtement et littérature* (direction Frédéric Monneyron, Perpignan: Presses Universitaires de Perpignan Collection Etudes, 2001), 'Accessoires. Le Sac à mains', in: *Access to accessory* (Haute Ecole des Arts Appliqués, Geneva University of Design, 2005).

Georgette Koning studied at the Rietveld Academy. Now she works as a freelance journalist, writing about fashion and design for *NRC Handelsblad, NRC Next*, for the biannual magazine *MORF* and the magazines *Elsevier, Dutch* and the German magazine *ZOO*. As editor of the fashion trade magazine *LINK* she conducts interview and writes articles about recent developments in the fashion industry. Between 1989 and 1997 she had her own bag labels, Pearls for Swans and Georgette Koning Bags, and she worked as accessory designer for the Monoprix department store, the brand Morgan and fashion designers such as Karl Lagerfeld, Thierry Mugler and Junko Shimada.

Christine M. Liu is a media consultant, freelance writer and designer in Boston, Massachusetts. She currently develops style content for publications including the *Boston Weekly Dig, 02138 Magazine* and *80108 Media*. She is a recent graduate of the Media Arts & Sciences master's program in Sociable Media at MIT, focusing on networked communities and fashion signalling. Christine also co-produced Seamless: Computational Couture, promoting independent designers in clothing reinvention.

Gilles Lipovetsky is professor 'agrégé' in philosophy, doctor

Honoris Causa at the University of Sherbrooke (Canada) and at the Nouvelle Université Bulgare (Sofia), Knight de la Légion d'Honneur and Membre du Conseil National des Programmes (Education Nationale) until 2005, Membre du Conseil d'Analyse de la Société auprès du Premier Ministre and expert consultant at APM (Association progrès du management). His research lies in the field of individualism, fashion, luxury, consumerism, *les transformations des régulations, des valeurs et des comportements dans les sociétés développées occidentales.*

He is the author of *The Empire of Fashion* (Princeton University Press, 1987), *Le Crépuscule du Devoir* (Gallimard, 1992), *La Troisième Femme* (Gallimard, 1997), *Le Luxe éternel* (Gallimard, 2003; collaboration with Elyette Roux), *Hypermodern Times* (Polity Press, 2004) and *Le Bonheur paradoxal. Essai sur la société d'hyperconsommation* (Gallimard, 2006). His publications are or will be published in eighteen languages.

Arjen Mulder (1955) is a biologist and essayist. In recent years he has published a series of books, including *Het twintigste-eeuwse lichaam* (1996), *Het fotografisch genoegen* (2000), *Over mediatheorie: taal, beeld, geluid en gedrag* (2002) and *De vrouw voor wie Cesare Pavese zelfmoord pleegde* (2004). In past years he has written for magazines such as *Theory, Culture & Society, Vrij Nederland, Metropolis M, Raster* and *De Gids.*

Professor **Birgit Richard** teaches New Media in Theory and Practice at Goethe University, Frankfurt. Her research activities centre on new media, image cultures, the aesthetics of present-day youth cultures (youth culture archive) and everyday media (clips, games). Her publications include *Todesbilder: Kunst, Subkultur, Medien* (ed.) (Munich, 1995), *Sheroes: Genderspiele im virtuellen Raum* (ed.; Bielefeld, 2004). *Coolhunters: Jugend zwischen Medien und Markt* (ed., with K. Neumann-Braun; Frankfurt am Main, 2005); *Schönheit der Uniformität: Körper, Kleidung, Med-*

ien (ed., with Gabriele Mentges; Frankfurt am Main 2005); *Riskante Bilder: Kunst, Literatur, Medien*, (ed., with Norbert Bolz, Cordula Meier et al.; Munich, 1996), *Icons: Localizer 1.3.* (ed., with Robert Klanten; Berlin, 1998), *Dauer-Simultaneität-Echtzeit* (with Sven Drühl; Kunstforum International, Volume 151, July 2000). Professor Richard is one of the curators of the exhibition 'Coolhunters: Jugendkulturen zwischen Medien und Mark'. Website: www.birgitrichard.de

Semiotician, communication consultant, curator and Professor of Applied Semiotics at the Celsa (Ecole des hautes études en sciences de l'information et de la Communication) of the University Paris-Sorbonne, **Luca Marchetti** heads the Mosign Centre of the Anomos Association. He is co-curator of FIRs – Fashion Italian Roots (Brussels, 2004). He also contributes to magazines such as *Vogue Italia, Casa Vogue, Form* and *View on Color* and is the coordinator of the *Face au présent* meetings at the Centre Georges Pompidou in Paris.

Karin Schacknat teaches theory in the Fashion Design department of the ArtEZ Academy of Arts and Design in Arnhem. She is also a freelance instructor in Fashion and Communication at the Fachhochschule Düsseldorf as well as a freelance publicist. After completing her studies in fashion design at the Arnhem Institute of the Arts (now ArtEZ), she studied Dutch language and film and performance arts at the Nijmegen Catholic University. She is the author of several books on fashion, dress behaviour and other cultural phenomena.

Anneke Smelik is professor of Visual Culture in the department of General Cultural Studies at Radbout University, Nijmegen. She studied dramaturgy and film studies at the University of Utrecht and received her doctorate from the University of Amsterdam in 1995 with a dissertation on women's films and film theory. Among her published works are *Effectief beeldvormen: Theorie, analyse en*

praktijk van beeldvormingsprocessen (Van Gorcum, Assen, 1999, with R. Buikema and M. Meijer) and *And The Mirror Cracked: Feminist Cinema and Film Theory* (London: Macmillan, 1998). Her research has to do with the virtualisation of the human-technological body in digital art and culture, and the relationship between cultural memory and new media. Website: www.annekesmelik.nl.

Since 2002 **José Teunissen** has been a professor of Fashion Design at the ArtEZ Institute of the Arts (ArtEZ Modelectoraat) in Arnhem. Between 1998 and 2006 she worked as Fashion and Costume curator at the Centraal Museum Utrecht. She also spent many years working as a journalist for magazines such as *Skrien* and *Versus* and for newspapers such as *Volkskrant* and *Trouw*, and she created the fashion programme Small, Medium, Large for the NPS. A few of the books she has published and/or edited: *Mode in beweging: Van modeprent naar modejournaal* (Amsterdam: NFM, 1992), *De nieuwe kleren: Over mode en ecologie* (Amsterdam, de Balie, 1993), *The Ideal Woman* (with Jan Brand) (Nijmegen, Amsterdam: Sun/Boom, 2004), *By Alexander van Slobbe* (catalogue of the Design Institute, 1994), *Dutch fashion talent: 50 interviews met jonge ontwerpers* (1996), *Marlies Dekkers* (catalogue accompanying the retrospective shown at the Rotterdamse Kunsthal, 1997), *Woman by* (catalogue *Woman by*, Centraal Museum Utrecht, 2003), *Global Fashion/Local Tradition* (Uitgeverij Terra Lannoo, 2004)**,** *The Power of Fashion* (Uitgeverij Terra Lannoo, 2006) and *Mode in Nederland* (Uitgeverij Terra Lannoo/ArtEZ Press, 2006).

Marjan Unger is an art historian and publicist. Since 1995 she has been head of the Free Design department of the Sandberg Institute, the post-graduate programme connected with the Gerrit Rietveld Academy in Amsterdam. Before this she worked as editor-in-chief of the design magazine *Bijvoorbeeld* and director of the Dutch Form Foundation. Her book *Nederlandse sieraden in de 20e eeuw*

is a standard work that was published in the summer of 2004 by Uitgeverij Thoth in Bussum.

Virginie Viallon holds a Ph.D. in the science of language and has lived in Germany for several years where she taught Romance languages at university. She is currently teaching communication and semiotics at the Université de la Mode in Lyon. Her area of research is the analysis of images from advertising and the media, images as signs bearing sense, symbols and culture. Another focus of her research is on the role of culture and the intercultural dimension of communication. Her published works include *Images et apprentissages* (Paris: Harmattan, 2002) and *Identität und Diversität* (Berlin: Avinus Verlag, 2005) as well as French language articles and *Le flacon de parfum, un nouvel accessoire?* (Access to accessory, Geneva: Haute école d'arts appliqués, 2005).

Minke Vos is art historian and editor of ArtEZ Press, publishing house of the ArtEZ Institute of the Arts in the Netherlands. She is also the image editor of such publications as *Global Fashion Local Tradition* (Terra Lannoo Publishers, 2005), *The Power of Fashion* (Terra Lannoo Publishers, 2006 / ArtEZ Press) and *De Appel. Performances, installations, video, projects 1975-1983* (De Appel, 2006). She was involved as an editor and author in different research projects and publications in the field of visual art, photography, fashion and design.

COLOPHON

Editors
Jan Brand
José Teunissen

Editorial coordinator
Catelijne de Muijnck

Photo editor
Minke Vos

Authors: main articles
Nanda van den Berg, Judith Donath, Martine Elzingre, Gilles Lipovetsky, Christine M. Liu, Luca Marchetti, Arjen Mulder, Birgit Richard, Karin Schacknat, José Teunissen, Marjan Unger, Virginie Viallon

Authors: icons
Nanda van den Berg, Agnes Gomes-Koizumi, Georgette Koning, Karin Schacknat, Anneke Smelik, José Teunissen, Minke Vos

Authors: styles
Els de Baan, Karin Schacknat, José Teunissen

Translators
Michael Gibbs Nl > Eng:
(Teunissen, Schacknat, Mulder, Van den Berg, Koning, Smelik, Vos, De Baan)
Nancy Forest-Flier Nl > Eng:
(Van den Berg/Bourdin, Unger, Schacknat/Hats, De Baan/Postmodernism, Teunissen/Surrealism)
Tony Bulger Fr > Eng:
(Viallon, Marchetti, Lipovetsky, Elzingre)

Final English editing
Nancy Forest-Flier

Design and typesetting
Roger Willems, Amsterdam in collaboration with Katrin Menne

Typeface
Mercury, Radim Pesko

Lithography
Pixel-It, Zutphen

Printing and binding
Printer Trento, Trento (Italy)

Cover
Viktor & Rolf, *Flowerbomb*, spring/summer 2005 collection show, detail

The chapters *Luxury and the sixth sense* and *Modern and postmodern luxury* have been taken from *Le Luxe eternel (De l'âge du sacré au temps des marques)*, by Gilles Lipovetsky & Elyette Roux © Editions Gallimard, Paris 2003.

© 2007
Uitgeverij Terra Lannoo BV
Post office box 614,
6800 AP Arnhem
info@terralannoo.nl
www.terralannoo.nl
Uitgeverij Terra is part of the Lannoo group, Belgium

ArtEZ-Press
Post office box 49,
6800 AA Arnhem
www.artez.nl
ArtEZ-Press is part of the ArtEZ Institute of the Arts

ISBN 978-90-5897-679-6
NUR 452

This publication has been made possible by generous financial support from the Mondriaan Foundation and The Netherlands Foundation for Visual Arts, Design and Architecture Amsterdam, the Prins Bernhard Cultuurfonds and the VSBfonds.

Mondriaan Stichting
(Mondrian Foundation)

Prins Bernhard
Cultuurfonds
geeft cultuur de kans

VSBfonds

PHOTO CREDITS

The publisher has made every effort to honour all rights concerning the illustrations as stipulated by law. Any persons who nevertheless believe they are entitled to certain rights can get in touch with the publisher.

Arends, Marije: p. 176: 11,12
Bata Shoe Museum, Toronto: p. 131: 8, p. 132: 12
Bennet, Dave M./Getty Images: p. 171: 16
Bergengren, Ola: p. 122: 11
Boman, Eric: p. 128: 1
Bonajo, Melanie: p. 150: 19
Bourdin, Guy: p. 148: 13
Brading, Martin: p. 125: 17
Burbridge, Richard: p. 47: 9
Clements, Geoffrey: p. 173: 3
Constas, Ion/Studio 5050: p. 94: 8, p. 95: 9, p. 196: 2
Courtney-Clarke, Margaret: p. 75: 14
Ellis, Sean: p. 191: 16
Elzingre, Martine: p. 78: 1, p. 81: 2, 3, 5, p. 82: 6, p. 83: 7, 8, p. 84: 1, 2, p. 87: 3
Expilly, Sandrine: p. 148: 10
Falk, Oscar: p. 149: 16
Faust, Mary Anne: p. 199: 11
Fisher, Angela: p. 74: 12, 13
French, John: p. 154: 10
Horst, Horst P.: p. 72: 7
Janssen, Ward: p. 149: 15
Jones, Kayt: p. 57: 20
Knight, Nick: p. 51: 7, p. 171: 15
Kobal Collection, The: p. 180: 4
Laaken, Ton van der: p. 188: 7
Lamsweerde, Inez van/Vinoodh Matadin: p. 177: 13
Leibovitz, Annie: p. 58: 23
Liu, Christine: p. 98, p. 101
Markus, Kurt: p. 142: 16
Maywald, Willy: p. 16: 10
McGrath, Norman: p. 205: 3
McInerney, Niall: p. 189: 11, p. 190: 12
Mené, Marc le: p. 148: 11, 12
Moore, Chris: p. 41: 5
Mudford, Grant: p. 189: 10
Museum Boijmans van Beuningen, Rotterdam: p. 175: 8
Museum Catharijneconvent, Utrecht: p. 153: 3
Papadopoulos, Despina/Studio 5050: p. 96: 10
Polhemus, Ted: p. 189: 9
Prolitteris, Zürich/SODART, Montreal: p. 195: 12
Ray, Man: p. 178: 2
Rijksmuseum Amsterdam: p. 153: 4
Roberts, Michael: p. 186: 1
Salzmann, Dan: p. 81: 4
Schall, Roger: p. 160: 13

Sherman, Cindy/Metro Pictures: p. 191: 15
Silvia B./Ronmandos Gallery, Rotterdam/Amsterdam: p. 174: 6
Stigter, Peter: cover, p. 10: 1, p. 11: 2, p. 35: 3, p. 38: 4, p. 121: 8, p. 139: 4, p. 144: 27, p. 145: 1, p. 149: 14, p. 155: 13, p. 166: 1, p. 183: 14 (3x), p. 190: 14, p. 192: 1
Stokhuijzen, A.C.: p. 69: 2
Stoops, Ronald: p. 170: 11, 13
Sunset Boulevard/Corbis Sygma: p. 121: 7
Surwillo, J.: p. 205: 2
Testino, Mario: p. 128: 2
Willems, Roger: p. 42, 43